MW00413709

Leadership @ Infosys

LEADERSHIP @
Infosys

Edited by
Matt Barney, PhD

Foreword by
N.R. Narayana Murthy
S. Gopalakrishnan
Epilogue by
T.V. Mohandas Pai

PORTFOLIO
PENGUIN

PORTFOLIO
Published by the Penguin Group
Penguin Books India Pvt. Ltd, 7th Floor, Infinity Tower C, DLF Cyber City,
Gurgaon 122 002, Haryana, India
Penguin Group (USA) Inc., 375 Hudson Street, New York, New York 10014, USA
Penguin Group (Canada), 90 Eglinton Avenue East, Suite 700, Toronto, Ontario,
M4P 2Y3, Canada
Penguin Books Ltd, 80 Strand, London WC2R 0RL, England
Penguin Ireland, 25 St Stephen's Green, Dublin 2, Ireland (a division of Penguin Books
Ltd)
Penguin Group (Australia), 707 Collins Street, Melbourne, Victoria 3008, Australia
Penguin Group (NZ), 67 Apollo Drive, Rosedale, Auckland 0632, New Zealand
Penguin Books (South Africa) (Pty) Ltd, Block D, Rosebank Office Park, 181 Jan Smuts
Avenue, Parktown North, Johannesburg 2193, South Africa

Penguin Books Ltd, Registered Offices: 80 Strand, London WC2R 0RL, England

First published in Portfolio by Penguin Books India 2010

Copyright © Infosys Technologies Ltd 2010

All rights reserved

10 9 8 7 6 5 4 3 2

ISBN 9780670084951

Typeset in Sabon MTby Eleven Arts, New Delhi 110035
Printed at Replika Press Pvt. Ltd, India

CONTENTS

FOREWORD

As two of the seven founders who have led Infosys since 1981, we can say that leading Infosys has been our life's work. In the beginning, we had dreams, shared values, complementary skills and the willingness to subordinate individual preferences for the greater good of the company. We have taken some measured risks along the way, and together we have achieved greater things than any one of us could have by ourselves.

We've continually transformed our company through the decades as a leadership team—and the pace of change has accelerated as well. Just eleven years ago, in 1999, Infosys had only 3,000 employees, whereas today we have over 122,000. Earlier we provided only technology, but today we are a full service business solutions company.

We haven't been perfect but we have successfully bounced back when we were in error, and have learned from our mistakes. The marketplace will continue to demand this sort of nimble adaptation to future challenges of us if we are to realize our vision of sustaining Infosys for the next 200 years. Effective leaders are essential if we are to continue to successfully adapt Infosys to the future competitive landscape.

We believe our values are one element that will sustain Infosys into the future. We've always led with our values. We decided right at the outset that we would not be a family-owned company. We have refused to do anything that would be less than honourable to our various stakeholders. And because of our unwavering commitment to Infosys as a single leadership team, Infosys has prospered. For us, leadership has always meant that the company's needs come first. We have always played the role the company needed us to play, and subordinated our personal preferences for the greater good.

From the beginning we strove for respect. In fact, the key phrase in our vision statement was to become a 'globally respected corporation'. This meant that we would earn the respect of all stakeholders—customers, employees, investors, governments and the society—every day, in every transaction. Respecting, and being respected, is more important to us than any amount of wealth—and more important to sustaining Infosys in the long run.

A second key value we subscribe to at Infosys is 'leadership by example'. This means that leaders must follow the same rules and policies as other employees, and that leaders must be completely committed to Infosys and work harder than others. This is what creates the moral authority to lead.

Third, a critical part of our approach is to inspire our people to go beyond what they might think to be possible. We have spared no expense in investing in our employees' development, including building the world's largest corporate university in Mysore. To make sure our learning investments pay off, we have role-modelled a culture of learning, development and renewal at all levels, including the mentoring we do with our seniormost leaders. Leadership development is a critical ingredient required to sustain our long-term growth and renewal objectives.

These are just a few examples of how we see leadership at Infosys. This book will throw light on many more. We respectfully hope that this book will be one resource that will fuel your development. By going into our history, the latest science and ideas from our effective leaders we hope to help employees, students, customers and other stakeholders take their leadership to the next level.

N.R. Narayana Murthy
Chairman and Chief Mentor, Infosys Technologies Ltd

S. (Kris) Gopalakrishnan
CEO, Infosys Technologies Ltd

INTRODUCTION

Matt Barney, PhD

Infosys's leadership standards have guided the company since its founding, even before they were explicitly documented. The standards—our dimensions of leadership and values—are central to the way we lead. Unfortunately, this stands in contrast to the leadership debacles the world has witnessed in the last twenty years. Global political leaders have been cited for crimes of deception, graft and moral turpitude. Multinational corporate leaders have been caught cooking the books—with billion-dollar Ponzi schemes—and made poor decisions about uncertainty and transparency. Inauthentic leadership has harmed employees, shareholders and national economies. Whether the root causes were impoverished skills or values, the consequences of ineffective leadership were dire for all stakeholders. For practitioner–scientists of leadership, our key question is: What can be done to mitigate these risks?

Leadership scientists and practitioners who respect uncertainty and care about the evidence have useful insights. One model in the current research on authentic leadership seeks to separate legitimate from counterfeit leadership. Authentic leaders are said to have a clear moral centre, be transparent in their intentions, and make fair and balanced decisions (Avolio, 2005). As practitioners, we at Infosys have strived toward our own form of genuine leadership well in advance of the current trend.

Leading at Infosys

Central to our authentic approach to leadership is our commitment to values. In the earliest days of Infosys, our founders were committed to honesty and integrity despite a business climate in India that was used to graft and corruption. Similarly, the founders envisioned Infosys as a company that would be respected by all stakeholders. As the firm matured, Infosys leaders codified our values into a mnemonic that helps everyone remember the various facets: C-LIFE, which stands for Customer Delight, Leadership by Example, Integrity and Transparency, Fairness, and Pursuit of Excellence. Table 1 below gives an overview of each value.

Table 1: C-LIFE Values

Customer Delight	A commitment to surpass our customers' expectations
Leadership by Example	A commitment to set standards and be an exemplar for the industry and our people
Integrity and Transparency	A commitment to be ethical, sincere and open in our dealings
Fairness	A commitment to be objective and transaction-oriented, thereby earning trust and respect
Pursuit of Excellence	A commitment to strive relentlessly to improve ourselves, our teams, our services and products so as to become the best

Consistent with these values, Infosys has had a longstanding tradition of leaders who grow other leaders to be better than themselves in several areas. Even the title Narayana Murthy chooses for himself, Chief Mentor, signifies his personal commitment to developing leaders throughout the company as the central job task for our seniormost leader.

Leadership Processes at Infosys

Our approach begins with the deep commitment and passion each individual leader must have to increasing levels of responsibility and performance. We select people into our accelerated leadership development programme for high potentials that we call Tiers, based on the probability that they can take on more senior positions in the next three to five years. Ultimately, our goal is to grow a cadre of leaders who can succeed our seniormost leadership positions. We have a selection procedure (detailed in the chapter 'Objectively Measuring Leaders') to select leaders with the track record, aptitude and commitment to take their skills to the next level. Once selected, each Tier leader is assigned both a mentor—a Tier leader or Board member senior to himself/herself—and an Infosys Leadership Institute counselor. Like a private banker, each Infosys Leadership Institute (ILI) counselor is responsible as the single point of contact for each Tier leader to ensure highly personalized development.

The counselors begin their relationship with Tier leaders by interpreting individualized feedback from our Leadership Journey Series of assessments (again detailed in the chapter 'Objectively Measuring Leaders') in order to plan personalized developmental action plans. Since we have the pleasure of working closely with extremely effective leaders who want to take their expertise to the next level, our approach is similar to the coach of an Olympic gold medalist who seeks to beat their own world record. Only a subset of the investments we can offer the leaders would be appropriate given their interests, needs and bandwidth. Our counselors help the leader interpret strengths and opportunities, and focus specific actions that will likely pay off the next year when we reassess them. In addition, counselors ensure that the context in which very senior leaders grow junior leaders is integrated holistically into organizational development efforts.

In this way, we strive to achieve both relevance and leverage the scientific rigour of leader development. Every senior leader and Tier leader is expected to both develop himself/herself and to mentor and nurture junior leaders. This environment of support, feedback and renewal is central to Infosys's approach to developing leaders. Importantly, meta-analytic research, the gold standard in science, echoes the importance of leaders creating a supportive climate for learning investments to pay off (Blume, Ford, Baldwin and Huang, 2010).

But what do we grow? We've codified the different behavioural aspects of effective leadership into nine dimensions that are covered in detail in subsequent chapters of this book. Three dimensions—change, adversity and transition leadership—are highly interrelated, so we have combined these into a single chapter. Also noteworthy is our dimension called content leadership that is vastly different in the different domains in which Infosys or any individual leader might work. For example, a Chief Financial Officer's job is qualitatively different from a Chief Legal Counsel's job, even though both may desire to be thought leaders in their respective professions. Table 2 outlines the Infosys leadership dimensions on which ILI's work is based.

Table 2: Infosys Leadership Dimensions

Dimension	Definition
Strategic Leadership	Unique positioning, differentiation
Change, Adversity and Transition Leadership	Anticipating and leading through resistance, managing crises and integrating new lines of business
Operational Leadership	Flawless execution
Talent Leadership	Individual and team performance
Relationship and Networking Leadership	Social capital asset management
Content Leadership	Triumphing as a thought leader
Entrepreneurial Leadership	Launching new businesses and innovative offerings

In 2010, we also have begun to use 'road maps' that guide specific recommended and evidence-based investments a leader can make in himself/herself. Each 'road map' is a portfolio of possible investments a leader can make in himself/herself or in their team, and is matched to their specific results from the Leadership Journey Series of assessments. Consistent with our values around integrity and excellence, we rigorously evaluate the degree to which each investment pays off for the leader and for the company, using advanced psychometric and research methods.

Vehicles

We make a distinction between a portfolio of leadership investment and the specific assets in a given portfolio. We call the portfolios 'road maps' for development—bundles of investments designed to pay off in a certain area and the specific methods of learning that are bundled together. Just as in finance, some asset classes are more appropriate than others for a given domain, so also in leadership development, certain vehicles are best suited to a particular portfolio. Vehicles are what we call the ILI standards for a specific kind of intervention that may target different content supporting each road map in a slightly different manner. We strive to leverage the best science available, including books, courses, experiences, seminars, workshops, conferences, organizational development interventions, stretch assignments, action learning programmes and job shadowing opportunities to grow each facet of Infosys's leadership model.

We have prioritized two vehicles at ILI. The first is learning from one's work, or 'experiential learning'. We hypothesize that the vast majority of the way leaders learn is on the job. Part of our counselors' role is to coach each individual leader around learning more from their current assignment, seeking out appropriate stretch assignments in their current role, and ultimately sketching out the next set of assignments required to realize ultimate career objectives. Whether it means shadowing—watching other successful leaders in action—or moving out of a leader's comfort zone, ILI has structured several approaches to help leaders extract more value from experiences.

Second, we have begun to leverage simulations as a flagship methodology. Just as pilots train in flight simulators, or nuclear power plant teams practice emergency procedures in the safety of a simulation, we are creating virtual reality environments for various leadership skills. Our first, launching in 2010, is focussed on increasing client relevance where leaders must initiate relationships with recently retired CEOs and solve a mock business problem in Second Life, with a virtual team. We are cautiously optimistic about the prospect for virtual reality learning and development, but cannot declare victory with this method until our research supports our suspicions that this will be an effective, inexpensive way to grow the most difficult leadership skills that have dire consequences for failure in the real world. But because we're working with global experts including Prof. Emeritus Robert Cialdini (Arizona State University), Prof. David Day (University of Western Australia) and Prof. Gregory Neidert (Arizona State University), we feel we have a very good chance of taking our leaders to the next level with the next-generation methods.

Avoiding Missteps of Earlier Business Books

Consistent with our values of fairness, transparency and excellence, our goal for this book is to support an evidence-based approach to leadership. We have tried hard to avoid the numerous scientific problems noted in other books that claim scientific rigour without embracing it fully. As scientist–practitioners, we acknowledge that our work is uncertain, and no model is perfect, including our own. Our approach at Infosys may not generalize to other companies with different cultures and different strategies. In particular, we are inspired to address directly the problems outlined in Phil Rosenzweig's important book *The Halo Effect* (2007). Rosenzweig detailed nine fatal problems with highly successful business books that we try to avoid in several ways:

i) *The halo effect:* The halo effect is the favourable bias people have when a company or individual has performed well in the past. People assume if the company performed well, everything it does must be great. The same halo bias may be true for the individual leader. We have gone to great trouble to use the most sophisticated methods available to empirically model and extract the halo effect from ratings in the leaders noted in this book. In particular, Linacre's (1994) Many Facet Rasch model was used to estimate and adjust for severity and leniency bias. Further the Rasch Measurement approach leverages advanced quality control procedures to be used to make sure the resultant information is fair, accurate and usefully precise. Only after these painstaking analyses did we conclude which Infosys leaders were effective in each area—a bit more effort than even Rosenzweig took when celebrating leaders such as Andy Grove.

ii) *Delusion of correlation and causality:* Throughout each chapter, we have tried hard to be careful about not making definitive claims of causation when our research methods are based on measures of association. It is entirely possible that the explanation given by our leaders for why they think they have been successful may be partially or even entirely inaccurate. But while this sort of analysis falls short of double-blind controlled experiments, we hope it uncovers hypotheses that are worthy of testing. Importantly, there is a large body of social psychological work by people such as Alfred Bandura (1997), suggesting that learning vicariously from the examples of others is a strong model for development, and does support causal inferences. We hope that some of our causal hypotheses pan out in future studies.

iii) *Delusion of single explanations:* There are alternative possible explanations for effective leadership, other than those we articulate here, or those our Tier leaders express. The study of industrial–organizational psychology is replete with models that account for some, but not all—or even most—of the variability in leadership. This book is no different in that regard. What is different is that we have gone out of our way to adjust for various biases, and leverage Bandura's social cognitive approach to vicarious learning. We hope some of these ideas are useful to others, both for research in testing, and for practicing leaders to consider trying. Your results could of course be different.

iv) *Delusion of connecting the winning dots:* This bias is the problem of not looking at the full range of leadership to understand the phenomena. In this book, we haven't looked at dismal or moderate leadership very much. We are certainly interested in all the factors that account for the full range of leadership results, and to that end our psychometrically selected leaders revealed mistakes they felt they made in the past to highlight why they felt they were rated so highly. But our primary purpose was different. We have selected the samples for our exemplary leadership from results, for the same reasons as Rosenzweig: 'for the way they made decisions, for how they managed their companies, the way they made risky strategic choices with eyes wide open and then pushed for great execution. That sort of approach is an example to managers everywhere' (159). Our primary goal with the book was to be an extension of our tradition of 'Leaders Teach' where senior leaders systematically teach junior leaders as a major part of their job. We are hoping that this book takes Leaders Teach to another level that helps a broader set of stakeholders than is possible with our internal courses.

v) *Delusion of rigorous research:* Unlike other business books that emphasize the effort and the volume of content that went into their research and results, we want to emphasize the quality. Admittedly, we haven't done double-blind controlled experiments, nor meta-analytically derived every hunch we're sharing. What we have done is taken over a year doing multiple pilot studies and refinements before we concluded on our psychometric instrumentation or leader results. Unusually for a company-specific book, we have used both actual empirical evidence and advanced quantitative modelling. We've gone to some trouble to build our instruments, especially the predictors of leadership behaviours based on meta-analytic studies that summarize all that is known to predict leadership aptitude and performance. As noted previously, we've used advanced computer-adaptive Rasch Measurement-based 360 degree instruments where we explicitly removed halo/severity bias, and controlled for measurement quality. Even so, we acknowledge that these may also have flaws, and so our results are tentative. We hope future research from ILI and others will provide more definitive conclusions.

vi) *Delusion of lasting success:* We are actively studying our Tier leaders over time and will refine both our methods and conclusions if future measurements refute our hypotheses. In the end, our institute's success is measured by ensuring a sufficient supply of successors to the Board, and whether we successfully identify and grow such candidates will be a matter of empirical record for future investigation.

vii) *Delusion of absolute performance:* Rosenzweig points out that various predictors of leader effectiveness are actually correlated, as evidenced by thousands of studies. Similarly, there is plenty of research to suggest that some work behaviours are appropriate at some times and not at others—and the business need may change. Our purpose with this book is to explore Infosys's leader behaviours in our current model and provide our best educated guesses about what's driving them; that too may change of course as our leaders' job requirements change.

viii) *Delusion of the wrong end of the stick:* With this delusion, Rosenzweig is worried about effective interpretation of findings. Did we identify leaders effectively, or did we stack the deck where a few high risk takers float to the top, when risk-optimizing leaders actually had a better strategy overall? In our case, we hope we avoided this by using multi-source, computer-adaptive data collection procedures, and the subsequent psychometric adjustments that improve the likelihood that we have accurately and precisely measured our leaders. The attributes and tactics they claim they've taken may or may not be what led to their being perceived as effective by those who participated in the multisource assessments. One could argue that a leader's reputation—how others view his or her behaviours—is also not a good way to operationally define. We accept this possibility, but our approach builds on socioanalytic theory that suggests reputation may be more important than internal views of one's self (Hogan, 1983). Further, it is also possible that some actions our leaders took that they didn't think to mention to us were really responsible for their success. Even so, we think it's useful to consider their insights for hypothesis generation.

ix) *Delusion of organizational physics:* Rosenzweig's final delusion deals with inappropriate claims of mechanistic certainty and causation. We explicitly would like to acknowledge that we embrace uncertainty—the models we present do have error, and we're not claiming any certainty about the degree to which our leaders' insights have necessarily caused their effectiveness. We can't run laboratory-style experiments, but we're authentic about doing our best to reduce uncertainty and gain more insight into causation. Even if we fail to gain certainty about what is causing effective leadership, we hope that our attempt provides useful hypotheses that may be tested in the future.

*

Each chapter in this book is organized around a common framework. We begin each with a definition of one Infosys leadership dimension, and an overview of the contemporary scientific literature. Next, we have used our own Leadership Journey assessments to identify leaders who are exceptionally proficient in a particular facet of leadership. Effective leaders have contributed a quote, an example, recommendation and acknowledgements of where they have stumbled in the past, as part of their own leadership journey.

The Infosys Leadership Institute hopes that this book serves as a useful resource both to Infosys leaders seeking to take their careers to the next level, and to our valued customers, suppliers, partners and future customers seeking their own journey toward ever better leadership.

Bibliography

Avolio, B.J., Gardner, W.L., Walumbwa, F.O., Luthans, F. and May, D. (2004). 'Unlocking the Mask: A Look at the Process by which Authentic Leaders Impact Follower Attitudes and Behaviors', *Leadership Quarterly*, 15, 801–23.

Avolio, B.J. (2005). *Leadership Development in Balance: Made/Born,* New Jersey: Erlbaum and Associates.

Avolio, B.J. and Gardner, W.L. (2005). 'Authentic Leadership Development: Getting to the Root of Positive Forms of Leadership', *Leadership Quarterly*, 16, 315–38.

Avolio, B.J. and Luthans, F. (2006). *High Impact Leader: Moments Matter in Authentic Leadership Development,* New York: McGraw-Hill.

Avolio, B.J. and Chan, A. (2008). 'The Dawning of a New Era for Genuine Leadership Development', G. Hodgkinson and K. Ford (eds.), *International Review of Industrial and Organizational Psychology*, 23.

Bandura, A. (1997). *Self-efficacy: The Exercise of Control,* New York: Freeman.

Blume, B.D., Ford, J.K., Baldwin, T.T. and Huang, J.L. (2010). 'Transfer of Training: A Meta-Analytic Review', *Journal of Management,* 36(1), 1065–1105.

Gardner, W.L., Avolio, B.J., Luthans, F., May, D.R. and Walumbwa, F.O. (2005). 'Can You See the Real Me? A Self-based Model of Authentic Leader and Follower Development', *Leadership Quarterly*, 16, 434–72.

Gardner, W.L., Avolio, B.J. and Walumbwa, F. (2006). *Authentic Leadership Theory and Practice: Origins, Effects and Development*, Amsterdam: Elsevier JAI Press.

Hogan, R. (1983). 'A Socioanalytic Theory of Personality', in M.M. Page (ed.), *1982 Nebraska Symposium on Motivation*, Lincoln: University of Nebraska Press, 55–89.

Linacre, J.M. (1994). *Many-Facet Rasch Measurement,* 2nd edn, Chicago: MESA Press.

Rosenzweig, Phil (2007). *The Halo Effect…and the Eight Other Business Delusions That Decieve Managers,* New York: Free Press.

CHAPTER 1

LEADERSHIP AT INFOSYS: PAST TO PRESENT

Sreekumar T.S.

'The primary purpose of corporate leadership is to create wealth legally and ethically. This translates to bringing a high level of satisfaction to five constituencies—customers, employees, investors, vendors and the society-at-large. The raison d'être of every corporate body is to ensure predictability, sustainability and profitability year after year.'

—*N.R. Narayana Murthy, Chairman and Chief Mentor,*
Infosys Technologies Ltd

Infosys Technologies Ltd was started in 1981 by seven co-founders with Rs 10,000 (about US$ 200) of capital. Today, it is a global leader in the 'next generation' of IT and consulting with revenues of over US$ 4 billion and a market capitalization of over US$ 33 billion (as of May 2010). Along the way, our leaders invented new business models, inspired a generation of entrepreneurs and helped redefine India's image in the world.

The founders of Infosys had ambitions of building a professional company that would command the admiration of others. 'We discussed the objectives of the company and decided that we wanted to become India's most respected company. Seeking respect was behind our founding Infosys. We deliberately defocussed on revenue and profits.

1

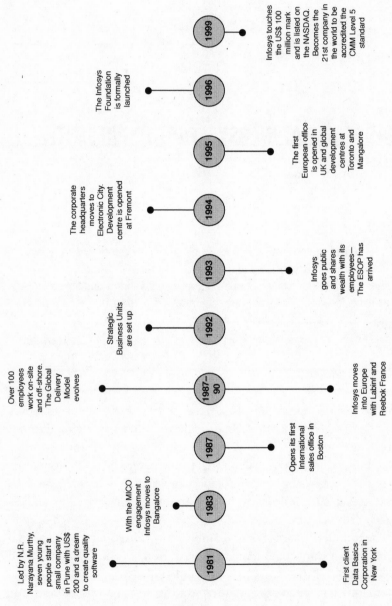

Infosys's historical milestones

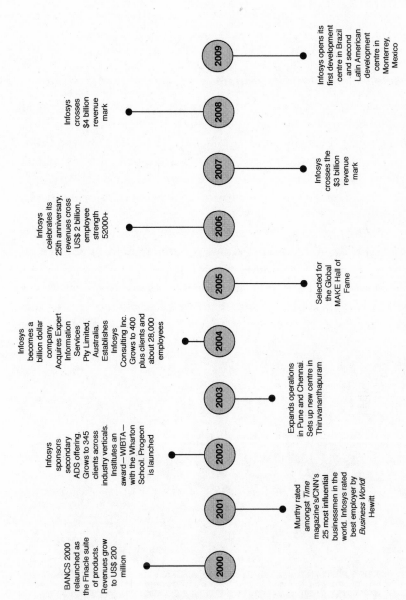

Infosys's historical milestones

2000
BANCS 2000 relaunched as the Finacle suite of products. Revenues grow to US$ 200 million

Murthy rated amongst *Time* magazine's/CNN's 25 most influential businessmen in the world. Infosys rated best employer by *Business World* Hewitt

2001

2002
Infosys sponsors secondary ADS offering. Grows to 345 clients across industry verticals. Institutes an award—WIBTA—with the Wharton School. Progeon is launched

2003
Expands operations in Pune and Chennai. Sets up new centre in Thiruvananthapuram

2004
Infosys becomes a billion dollar company. Acquires Expert Information Services Pty Limited, Australia. Establishes Infosys Consulting Inc. Grows to 400 plus clients and about 28,000 employees

2005
Selected for the Global MAKE Hall of Fame

2006
Infosys celebrates its 25th anniversary, revenues cross US$ 2 billion, employee strength 52000+

2007
Infosys crosses the $3 billion revenue mark

2008
Infosys crosses $4 billion revenue mark

2009
Infosys opens its first development centre in Brazil and second Latin American development centre in Monterrey, Mexico

Our goal was to do everything by the book. We realized that if we did the right thing, revenues and profits would come automatically,' says Mr Murthy.

Infosys's Early Years (1981–91)

Business in pre-liberalized India

The business environment in India at the time was difficult for all types of organizations, including Infosys's ambitious goals. India had a protectionist market for goods and services. Even worse, bribes were rampant, capital markets were undeveloped, and few people even used computers at all in the country. In spite of this tough environment, Infosys maintained a vision to become a global software powerhouse.

In the first two years, the leadership team made twenty to twenty-five visits to Delhi to obtain permission from the Indian government to import the first computer for Infosys (a Data General 32-bit MV8000), paying a 150 per cent import duty on the computer when it finally arrived. It took an entire year to get a telephone line and they had to request permission every time ten days in advance to get the

An old snapshot from the early days. Narayana Murthy is at the extreme left, Kris Gopalakrishnan is in the middle, and Raghavan and Shibulal on the right.

Reserve Bank of India's approval to travel outside of India. But most importantly for the leadership team and the values that they shared, Infosys never once took a short cut if it would involve side-stepping a legal and ethical way of getting the job done. They always put to one side the short-term gain that other business rivals might have taken, for the long-term advantage of clean hands, of a reputation unsullied and of a step nearer to their goal. 'Right from the start, we wanted not just to be successful but to be a trailblazer,' recalls K. Dinesh, Infosys co-founder.

Infosys explores hardware development

S. Gopalakrishnan (known as Kris) reveals how Infosys explored hardware development briefly in 1985, and why it quickly returned to its core business. 'We created a subsidiary, Infosys Digital Systems. We developed a product successfully and sold it in the Indian market—but realized very quickly that we had a limited appetite, limited capabilities and it was difficult to compete with global players with our limited resources at that point, so we quickly sold off that part of the business and got out of it.'

The Global Delivery Model

When Infosys redoubled efforts on direct marketing in the US, it encountered several prospective customers who felt India and the US were as different as 'night and day'. Literally, given the time difference, Infosys realized it had to have a value proposition that could excite customers, and hit upon a twenty-four-hour workday. At the time customers in the US went home from work and returned the next morning, a solution would be waiting for them. Infosys pioneered the concept and the Global Delivery Model (GDM), that is now used by many of Infosys's competitors, was born.

Srinath Batni's description of GDM is, 'Essentially it is where India is the hub with spokes at multiple locations around the world. Our delivery model has about 20–30 per cent of activities that happen near the client; the remaining 60–70 per cent happens from our development centres in India. It is very important to see how we distribute the activities not just between the spokes and the hub but also between multiple hubs and the spokes. My view is the future in GDM is going to be defined by multiple hubs located exactly where it makes sense . . . and with spokes all around the world.'

The KSA–Infosys Joint Venture

In 1987, Infosys entered into a joint venture with consulting firm Kurt Salmon Associates (KSA). KSA–Infosys was formed to leverage the power of KSA's management consultancy in the area of apparel and textiles, and the power of Infosys's technology consulting. 'At that time, this joint venture allowed us to build credibility in a market where we were relative newcomers and gave us access to a number of opportunities we would not have otherwise had,' recalls Kris, who was responsible for managing the relationship. The partnership ended amicably in 1994–95 and the decision was taken in line with Infosys's long-term growth objectives, with Infosys keen to have direct access to clients and branch out into other sectors.

Infosys gets its first direct customer

Digital Equipment Corporation (DEC), became Infosys's first direct US customer in 1987. DEC rented thousands of vehicles from various rental services. Infosys designed a vehicle handling system, which allowed DEC to efficiently handle the renting and management of these vehicles. The reputation Infosys had built with DEC and other customer referrals helped Infosys expand the client base in the US. Narayana Murthy recalls, 'While we were working in the apparel sector with Data Basics Corporation, many people saw us as hardworking, reasonably smart and committed. Once we decided not to renew our contract with Data Basics, we planned to move to other sectors like technology, banking etc. Several customers who had worked with us were happy to refer us to friends in these sectors.'

The context of doing business in India was exceptionally challenging at the time. Mr Murthy who was then the CEO, recalls, 'You know at that time India meant a poor country, with a very very staunch bureaucracy etc. So we had to have a very powerful model for our prospects and that is where our GDM, our 24x7 model and the fact that our people had done a wonderful job working hard, working smart and that we could leverage the power of referrals—I think all these things added up. Slowly we started chipping into the traditional mindset and opinion of India and we could create a new mindset that Indians are smart, Indians work hard, Indians can actually make us become more competitive.'

Near-death experience

Believing that Infosys, a small, unknown company with no brand equity, was as good as dead, founder Ashok Arora left to pursue opportunities on his own in the United States. Co-founder K. Dinesh reminisces, 'For hours, we went around the table lamenting how difficult doing business was and listing all the constraints limiting us. After about six hours of discussions, a view began to emerge that we should be prepared to sell the business for an offer of $1.5 million or more. Murthy had been silent throughout and spoke up now. "I am confident that the company will succeed eventually," he said. "If any of you want to leave, I will be happy to buy you out." There was total silence for a few moments. Then Nandan spoke up. "If you are staying on," he said, "then I am in it with you." One by one, every one of the other co-founders changed their viewpoint and agreed to stay on. As we pledged to redouble our efforts, Murthy made it very clear, "Let this be the last time we talk about selling the company under duress."'

On why he convinced Infosys's co-founders not to take the buyout offer, Narayana Murthy explains, 'We had already run this marathon for nine years. Somehow, I felt we were coming to the end of the tunnel. And because we had already made so many sacrifices, created such a cohesive group, slowly made inroads into the US market, because there was such a wonderful senior management team, I thought it would be a shame to lose everything for the small sum of a million dollars. Though I did not see it coming, the economic reforms of 1991 gave us an opportunity. We had gone through this long period, I thought God would be kind to us. It was a decision based purely on hope, rather than anything logical.'

As a result of this decision, there was renewed focus and energy all around redoubling the efforts to grow the business.

The Decade of Heady Growth (1991–2000)

The turning point—economic liberalization

Although in 1986, the Indian government, realizing that India had the potential to be a software export powerhouse, had formulated a computer software policy that loosened several restrictions and established new incentives, the Indian software industry had remained mired in extensive regulations and controls. In 1991, trying to overcome a balance-of-payments crisis, the government launched a programme of economic liberalization that relaxed several trade and exchange controls. Murthy refers to India's 1991 economic reforms as a 'seminal point' that dismantled the 'licence and permit raj'.

Co-founder Nandan Nilekani notes an important contrast between the 1980s and the 1990s. 'Customers started to appreciate Indian capabilities only in the 1990s. So if you see our growth pattern from the beginning, it took us about ten years to go from zero to $5 million and just ten more years to go from $5 million to $700 million. Clearly the growth rate in the second ten years was dramatically different. That is because two things happened: one, the environment changed, and second, our aspirations also changed. We said we must become world class, we must become a big company. We were to be international, to be global, to have a high value system, to have high ethics—all those things were there from day one, but it was in the early 1990s that we said, "We really need to get hold of ourselves and put in place the systems and processes and the technology, infrastructure, and all that is needed to achieve growth." That is where our mindset changed.'

Infosys spreads to Europe

Co-founder K. Dinesh recalls the need to diversify geographically. 'Until 1990, 100 per cent of Infosys's revenue was coming from the United States. We needed to review and explore our geographic risks on a long-term basis. Secondly, Europe offered a bigger pie. Keeping this in mind we decided to expand our operations to Europe.' Labinf Technologies was Infosys's first client in the region. Reebok (France) soon followed, with Infosys winning the contract to build a state-of-the-art information management system. The Infosys team deftly crossed language and cultural barriers and completed the Reebok project ahead of time, winning the admiration of the customer.

Infosys's Offshore Software Development Centre

Infosys became the first Indian software house to operate an Offshore Software Development Centre (OSDC) for General Electric in FY 1992–93. Constrained by US government visa restrictions from sending its professionals freely to the United States, Infosys management decided, in Dinesh's words, to 'convert a threat into an opportunity by investing in processes that would build client trust in their ability and thus enable Infosys to do more work "here" (in Bangalore) and less work "there"' (on-site). The OSDC concept soon became popular with Infosys's other customers too. The team completed the project ahead of time, establishing itself in the market.

NOTEWORTHY FACTS

- Infosys set up its formal Human Resources (HR) department in 1992, when the employee count was 250. The focus, from the beginning, was on evolving employee-friendly policies, while ensuring a high level of transparency.
- In 1992, Infosys set up its Quality department, at a time when quality as a conscious effort was still a fledgling thought in the software industry. It obtained the ISO 9001/TickIT certification in November 1993. Within a week of the certification, work began towards attaining Level 4 of the Capability Maturity Model (CMM) instituted by Carnegie Mellon's Software Engineering Institute.
- In 1992, Infosys opened its first international office in Boston. To leverage the relationship with its client Digital Equipment Corporation, which operated in the area, and to get new prospects, Infosys chose Boston, a centre for innovation and technology.

A milestone in offshoring—Infy gets a 64 kbps link

Although it was a sales office, Boston also doubled as the first network hub overseas. This enabled clients to connect effectively with Infosys's offshore network. In December 1992, the first 64kbps international private line for any company in India was established between Infosys's

US office in Boston and its headquarters in Bangalore. Co-founder S.D. Shibulal recalls, 'One of the early customers that Infosys acquired in the early '90s was GE. GE wanted connectivity to be established between our Bangalore office and their office in the US. They wanted a direct link from Bangalore to their office. We felt that if we had a link terminating in our office in Boston, we would be able to connect multiple clients with the same link. In 1992 we installed our first 64 kbps link between our Koramangala office and the Boston office. The total budget which was allocated by Mr Murthy for buying hardware, software and system integration was US$ 100,000 which was a huge amount at that point of time. We successfully installed the link, connected to GE and also implemented a voice line on the same link.'

Initial Public Offering

The liberalization of the Indian economy in 1991 dramatically improved Infosys's fortunes. Infosys's revenues almost doubled from US$ 5.01 million in FY 1992–93 to US$ 9.60 million in FY 1993–94.

The 1991 reforms allowed firms to open offices abroad, travel easily, and hire foreign consultants. The reforms also eased access to capital markets for private companies, making equity financing a viable option. Encouraged, Infosys made an initial public offer in February 1993 and was listed on stock exchanges in India in June 1993. Trading opened at Rs 145 per share, compared to the IPO price of Rs 95 per share. Infosys raised US$ 4.4 million in capital through this offer, and another US$ 7.7 million through a private placement of shares in 1994.

The letter to the shareholders in the first Infosys annual report (1992–93) was titled 'Driving Growth through India-based Software Development'. It shared the cornerstones of Infosys's strategy:

- Competing in the world market on quality and productivity, and not just cost
- Using an India-based software workshop for high margin and stable operations
- Becoming a solution provider in niche markets for high margins

NOTEWORTHY FACTS

- Underwriters had to bail out Infosys's first IPO from under-subscription.
- Rs 95 invested during the IPO was worth Rs 334,842 as of 31 March 2010.

Employee Stock Option Plan

Infosys was one of the first companies to democratize wealth in India. It made its 'creators of wealth' stakeholders of the company in 1994, when it launched its first Employee Stock Option Plan (ESOP). The move sparked a trend in the Indian IT industry. N.S. Raghavan, Infosys co-founder, says, 'The strategy was to create a very strong sense of belonging, a very strong sense of ownership among employees which when combined with high levels of job satisfaction (challenging job assignments) generated outstanding performance. It made them believe they are the true owners of the organization and they also share the wealth of the organization, which created high levels of motivation and commitment.'

Infosys shifts headquarters to new campus

Infosys moved its corporate headquarters to a five-acre facility at Bangalore's Electronic City in 1994. This was India's biggest single-location software centre, and had the country's largest computer network. With a gymnasium and sports area contributing to the campus-like atmosphere, the facility wasn't just state-of-the-art, it was also a fun workplace.

Infosys gears up for growth

In the mid '90s, Infosys set up Strategic Business Units to encourage autonomy of operation and generate the next generation of business leaders. Onsite-offshore communication grew increasingly seamless as the Global Delivery Model evolved. In 1995, the first video conference was held between Infosys's Boston and Bangalore offices. In keeping with its strategy of attracting professional talent by establishing Development Centres (DCs) at the most promising places in different parts of the globe, Infosys set up its first overseas DC at Fremont in 1994. By 1997, Infosys had multiple DCs across India, in cities like Mangalore, Pune, Chennai and Bhubaneswar. During this period, Infosys also opened sales offices across the US, followed by offices in the UK, Japan and Canada.

Disengagement with GE

In 1995, Infosys lost a major client. A negotiation for higher rates for Infosys services failed when General Electric, the source of 25 per cent of revenues (and 8 per cent of profits) for Infosys, refused the rate hike in favour of a more competitive offer from another company. Within forty-eight hours, Infosys disclosed to financial analysts that the two companies had 'parted as friends' and explained how the shortfall would be replaced. For Infosys, the incident became a lesson in pursuing risk-mitigating activities and the company decided that the revenue from any single client would be limited to a maximum of 10 per cent of total revenue.

In addition, it also established Infosys as a benchmark in the industry for fast disclosure and transparency, and boosted its share price. As K. Dinesh quips, 'When in doubt, disclose!'

Corporate governance

Board member T.V. Mohandas Pai recalls, 'In financial reporting our philosophy has been—disclose when in doubt. Ever since we started having annual reports after going public way back in 1994, this has been our philosophy. The next year we started looking at ways of enhancing shareholder information because our shareholders came from around the world. We started preparing financial statements under the guidelines of the US GAAP (Generally Accepted Accounting Principles) and the GAAP of six other countries. At the same time we provided additional shareholder information, all with the view that the shareholder is entitled to have as much information as necessary to come to whatever conclusions they want to come to and information should be disclosed fully as a matter of right. Disclose fully and disclose openly and become the trustee of the shareholders.'

Infosys's strong focus on corporate governance made it a trendsetter in India since its corporate governance practices went well beyond what was mandated by law. Disclosures were benchmarked against best practices in international corporate governance. Since its IPO, Infosys has chosen to include information that is relevant but not mandatory to stakeholders in its annual report, going beyond what is required by the law.

Infosys believes that sound corporate governance is critical to enhance and retain investor trust. According to T.V. Mohandas Pai, its corporate governance philosophy is based upon the principle that 'shareholders are owners of the corporation, the management is the trustee. Right from the time we went public, we based all our principles on this fundamental position.'

NOTEWORTHY FACTS

- In FY 1994–95, Infosys provided a comparison of the actual performance, vis-à-vis the projections made in the prospectus. The next year, the disclosure of such information became mandatory in India.
- Infosys was among the first Indian companies to voluntarily adopt US GAAP reporting in FY 1995–96.
- In FY 1998–99, Infosys became the first company in India to publish audited Indian financial statements on a quarterly basis. Announcements of quarterly results were made mandatory in India in FY 1999–2000.
- Infosys received the Best Annual Report Award from the Institute of Chartered Accountants of India for ten successive years since 1995.
- One of the early awards Infosys received for corporate governance was the first-ever National Award for Excellence in Corporate Governance, conferred by the Government of India in 1999.
- In 1998, Infosys was the first company to win a new award, Company of the Year Award, instituted as part of the Economic Times Awards for Corporate Excellence. Infosys's contribution towards corporate excellence, in enhancing shareholder value and pushing the frontiers of technology, was recognized by a readers' poll and CEOs' poll conducted by the national daily.
- Infosys topped the regional rankings for best corporate governance in *Asiamoney's* Corporate Governance Poll, 2005; it received the 2002 Golden Peacock Award for Excellence in Corporate Governance from the World Council for Corporate Governance, London; Standard and Poor's Corporate Governance Services assigned Infosys a strong CGS rating of 8.6.

Social responsibility: The Infosys Foundation

'The only hope for a stable society is for the corporations and the "haves" to realize their social responsibilities towards the less fortunate.'

—*Infosys Annual Report 1996–97*

Infosys established the Infosys Foundation in 1996. Since then, this not-for-profit trust has worked extensively in the areas of education, health, rural development and the arts. Its activities support the underprivileged and touch the lives of thousands across India.

Chief Mentor N.R. Narayana Murthy is clear as to why he felt the need to set up a foundation: 'The business of corporate philanthropy is entirely different from running a company. Shareholders need to be clear that the company's corporate citizenship initiatives are not diluting the way the company is run. The company's primary job is to satisfy customers and shareholders, while upholding the legal and ethical requirements of a business and focusing on innovation. By keeping the two functions separate, each one can enhance and not weaken the other.'

Nurturing young minds

Between 1997 and 1998, Infosys initiated social programmes for young audiences from two different sections of society. While the 'Rural Reach' programme introduced the computer to children in villages, the 'Catch Them Young' initiative identified promising high school students, trained and gave them their first glimpse of a professional IT environment. Both programmes continue today, spurred by the active involvement of Infoscions (what employees of Infosys call themselves).

Y2K as an opportunity

In the late 1990s, Infosys used the Year 2000 (Y2K) transition as an opportunity to build long-term relationships with clients. Kris Gopalakrishnan recalls:

Infosys looked at Y2K as an opportunity for us to establish GDM, to establish Infosys as a reliable trustworthy partner for their IT requirements and as well as to grow the business taking significant advantage of the Y2K opportunity. When Infosys was founded in 1981, those were the years mainframes were dominating. From that point of time we have seen the introduction of client server computing, network computing, the Y2K bug emerging as a major issue to be tackled, and a pervasive computing paradigm. All through this our focus on creating new solutions, enabling people through education and training, and making sure that we continue to focus on learnability of the people when we recruit, ensured the transition from one technology to another seamlessly, and we continue to be relevant to our clients and have the right solutions that meet the requirements.

Milan—connecting with customers

In the late 1990s, Infosys was among the first Indian IT companies to initiate an annual global meet for its customers. Called Milan, which means 'a meeting of minds' in Sanskrit, Infosys's annual client forum was recently renamed Confluence to better reflect its global reach. The meet, held in multiple regions, facilitates the sharing of best practices through interactive sessions, panel discussions and presentations by customers and thought leaders from the industry.

Globalization of Infosys—a strategic theme

In 1998, the theme of Infosys's Strategy and Action Planning event (STRAP) was 'Internationalization of Infosys'. Several strategic moves followed, geared to make Infosys a truly global player. Infosys expanded its footprint, opening offices and development centres across the globe. It adjusted leaders' roles to lay the groundwork for this growth. In 1999, Nandan Nilekani became Managing Director, President and Chief Operating Officer and Narayana Murthy Chairman and CEO, 'to focus on ensuring that the right steps are taken to take Infosys to the next millennium'.

In a nostalgic message published in the Infosys Annual Report 1998–99, Narayana Murthy introduced the new Managing Director of Infosys: 'Nandan became the new Managing Director, President and Chief Operating Officer on 11 February 1999. He looks after all day-to-day operations and reports to me. I continue as Chairman and Chief Executive Officer. I have known Nandan closely ever since he walked into my room as a twenty-three-year-old and charmed me into recruiting him as a software engineer when I was head of software at PCS, Bombay in 1979. My twenty-five-year-old hypothesis is that, in a rapidly changing industry like software, learnability, rather than knowledge base, is critical for sustained success. Nandan is a flourishing icon of this idea that has been independently accepted and practiced by other well-known companies.'

Infosys goes global

Nandan points out the trajectory of Infosys's global growth: 'In the late '90s we began to realize a very large global opportunity that lay ahead of us, that required us to act on several fronts. For example, we said we have to be a globally listed company in an international market like NASDAQ because our clients were Global 2000 firms and they would expect to work with a company listed there known for its international standards of public governance and shareholder transparency. Second, we wanted to be in charge of our own destiny— we needed to have our own sales offices in the US. We invested in various sales offices to establish direct relationships with clients so that they saw Infosys as their partners and their trusted advisor. Third, we wanted to make Infosys globally renowned. We went on a journey to build a global brand. Finally, we said we want Infosys to be a global employer and we embarked on a journey in building a global workforce. All these things together formed our journey to globalization.'

InStep—grooming international talent

Infosys started its campaign to attract bright international talent in 1999. The current programme, InStep, is an internship program for undergraduate, masters and PhD students from top academic institutions around the world; it is one of the largest institutionalized global internship programmes in India.

A small step for NASDAQ, a giant leap for Infosys

In March 1999, Infosys became the first India-registered company to be listed on NASDAQ. It raised US$ 70.38 million through the issue of 2.07 million ADSs, under the American Depositary Shares (ADS) programme. In an interview published later that year, Narayana Murthy told the NASDAQ *Amex* magazine, 'For us to advance our brand equity outside India, we needed to get listed on a global exchange such as NASDAQ.... It is a small step for NASDAQ, but a giant leap for Infosys and the Indian software industry.' 'This is where we felt we should rightfully belong,' said Narayana Murthy when Infosys was listed on NASDAQ, at the time an important step towards globalization.

NOTEWORTHY FACTS

- In July 2006, Infosys was included in the NASDAQ Global Select Market, a new market tier with the highest listing standards in the world. The standards for the NASDAQ Global Select Market—described by NASDAQ president and CEO Bob Greifeld as a 'blue chip market for blue chip companies'—will have financial and liquidity requirements that are higher than those of any other market.
- In 1999, Infosys made its debut at no. 6 on the *BusinessWorld*–Indica poll of India's most respected companies.
- In 1999, Infosys was voted India's most admired company in a survey conducted among 1,636 senior managers of the Indian industry by the *Economic Times,* the Indian business daily.
- In 1999, Infosys was named in *Forbes*'s list of the 300 best small companies after *Forbes* statisticians and reporters searched databases containing over 13,000 global companies to find 'the sharpest, fastest, supplest little firms on the planet'. The headline for Infosys's company profile read 'Big Bang in Bangalore'. The magazine reported, 'Infosys's history and culture are hardly typical of India. Indian business is full of lethargic dynasties . . . While well-capitalized, well-connected Indian software companies massaged the Indian bureaucracy, Infosys focused on its foreign customers.'

Infosys achieves CMM Level 5 status

In 1999, Infosys became the twenty-first company in the world, and the first in India, to be assessed at Level 5 of the Capability Maturity

Model (CMM) instituted by the Software Engineering Institute. Level 5–which indicates a very high level of process maturity–had been attained by only around 1.5 per cent of software companies in the world at the time. In 2000, Infosys took a step towards performance excellence when it began benchmarking its processes against the Malcolm Baldridge Framework.

When the Indian government removed regulatory constraints that had been limiting Indian entrepreneurial growth in 1991, the business climate changed and with it changed the fortunes of Infosys. From US$ 3 million in FY 1991–92, Infosys closed the decade with US$ 100 million in annual revenue in 1999.

NOTEWORTHY FACT

• The CMM Level 5 milestone was announced at the launch of the book *CMM in Practice: Process for Executing Software Projects at Infosys* by Dr Pankaj Jalote, a former Vice President (Quality) at Infosys. The book related specific characteristics of the CMM to real-life processes at Infosys.

The Current Decade (2000–10)

Core values—crystallizing C-LIFE

Narayana Murthy reflects on the one thing that carried the founders through challenges of the early days:

> It was a challenge to attract smart people to work with us; we had no name, no money, no brand recognition and no physical or financial assets. When we recruited in 1982, I managed to borrow some table space from a friend's company. Further, I approached another friend who had access to a large computer centre. He allowed us to use the computers during the night at an attractive rate. In fact, my wife had to pawn her jewellery to help pay our employees' salaries. But the best part was that in all these times of difficulty, we did not have to compromise on our value system.

Murthy elaborates further on what defines a value system:

It is the ability to accept deferred gratification, the ability to make sacrifices currently, the ability to work in a team based on an agreed protocol of do's and don'ts, subordinating individual egos and putting the interest of the organization ahead of individual interests, recognizing people competency and accepting the leadership of individuals in different areas. Right from the beginning my focus was on strategy and finance, Nandan was focussed on sales and marketing, Raghavan on people skills, Kris was focussed on technology skills, Shibulal, Dinesh and Ashok Arora were project managers par excellence. Whenever there was a debate on strategy or finance, people would listen to me; they would ask a lot of questions, but as long as I gave a certain rationale why certain things should be done in a certain way, people would accept it. Similarly in human resources, Raghavan's views were always accepted. This is very very important for a team to succeed: you have to subordinate your ego; and then of course we all had the ability to celebrate each of those successes. I think these were the essential tenets of our value system: sacrifice, deferred gratification, teamwork, always following the agreed protocols of behaviour, the ability to enjoy others' successes, subordination of ego, accepting the expertise of other people. Then of course deciding on every issue based on data and facts, to start every transaction at zero base and to say you can disagree with me as long as you are not disagreeable. And finally, leadership by example. The initial period was when all these attributes were required in plenty. For example, my salary was 15–16 times more than the salary of others like Nandan, Kris, Shibu or Raghavan. I realized if I want to call upon my colleagues to make sacrifices, then I have to first demonstrate that in my case. I took a 90 per cent cut in my salary and made sure that all others got a 20 per cent increase in salary. The result was they all realized there was a concern for other people from the leader of the team, the leader of the team led by example and therefore we could trust him.

In 1984, when Infosys imported the first computer to Bangalore, a customs official indirectly asked for a bribe. When Narayana Murthy pretended that he did not understand the request, the official refused to recognize a government certificate that entitled the company to a concessionary import duty of only Rs 100,000 compared to the regular duty of approximately Rs 1,000,000. The company ended up paying the higher duty, and had to go through a lengthy claims process lasting six years to recover the excess duty paid. Many such tests of ethical values continued. In 1996, the company refused to pay a bribe of Rs 400,000 for the purchase of the land on which its modern offices are located in Bangalore. It ended up paying Rs 4,000,000 extra for the land (40 per cent more than what other companies had paid in the same area). Such examples run throughout Infosys's history and are reflected in the company's interaction with various stakeholders.

Murthy's perspective on Infosys's values in the early days is:

> Our value system was like the British constitution—it was all unwritten but extremely well practiced. How do we stay together? We have unwritten rules. Everybody knows that if we want to work as a team we have to be transaction based. We start every transaction from a zero base. It is perfectly feasible for us to disagree on a transaction, but we start the next transaction without any bias. Only an argument that has merit wins; it has nothing to do with hierarchy.

Working in India while serving clients in the United States revealed the importance of establishing a foundation of values that were universal across cultures. Murthy believes that for any company, there are five 'context-invariant and time-invariant attributes' that lay the foundation for success:

> The first is openness—openness to new ideas in an environment of pluralism, and subordinating individual egos to accept better ideas from others. The second is meritocracy—making sure that the best idea is selected in everything that we do; making sure that all discussions are based on data, facts and logic, and not on emotions or past precedent. As I like to say, 'In God we

trust; everyone else must come with data.' Third is speed. We have to do things faster today than yesterday, last month, last quarter, and last year. Fourth is imagination. Are we bringing better ideas and more ideas to the table than yesterday? Fifth is excellence in execution. Ideas have no value unless they can actually be executed and implemented well and then improved so that we are constantly delivering at higher levels of customer satisfaction and employee satisfaction.

Infosys has always espoused a high standard of ethics in its interaction with all stakeholders but it was in 2000 that the company decided to formally codify the values in such a way that generates excitement and a shared ownership of the company core values. To engage a broad set of leaders in this process, the Infosys board members led the senior leadership team and a sample of employees representing different cross-sections of the company. They discussed their current understanding and concerns about the value system embedded in business processes and stakeholder relations. Consistent with Infosys's longstanding love for evidence, each member had to substantiate assertions with examples. Eventually, an iterative process arrived at a consolidated set of primary non-negotiable, cross-cultural and practical values that can stand the test of time. The team made these values easy to remember with the acronym C-LIFE, which stands for Customer Delight, Leadership by Example, Integrity and Transparency, Fairness and Pursuit of Excellence. To ensure that, as Infosys grew, the values would be instilled in the thousands of new employees systematically, this team identified mechanisms and systems to be put in place. These ensured on an ongoing basis the effective practice of the company core values in all processes. These included integrating values with HR systems, dealing with difficult situations that test values, and dealing with non-compliance. Examples include the creation of a whistleblower programme, a grievance review board, and Hearing Employees and Resolving (HEAR). To sustain these values in a positive way, the group created annual excellence award ceremonies that are telecast live to Infosys offices around the world. In this way, even the award ceremony celebrates a global culture of excellence, promoting meritocracy and highlighting leadership role models for all to follow.

Murthy believes that Infosys's values are what earned it admiration. He underlines one core value that he believed helped keep the founding team together for so long:

> We have always believed in putting the interest of the company higher than our personal interests because we have realized that doing so would indeed benefit us personally in the long term. From day one we wanted to run the business legally and ethically, to demonstrate that by putting the interests of the corporation above your own personal interest in the long term you will benefit. We were convinced that the softest pillow was a clear conscience. We were convinced about running the business using simple rules because simple rules are easy to communicate, easy to practice and easy to understand. Most importantly, you cannot cheat anybody with simple rules. Also, not using corporate resources for personal benefit was a dictum we practiced right from day one.

Murthy lives by this rule strictly even today, as Infosys Chief Mentor and Chairman. In 2004, for example, when travelling with his wife, a non-Infosys employee, he refunded the company the difference between the hotel cost of a single and a double room. When asked why he did this, he noted, 'The best way of communicating any message is walking the talk. You get the best credibility.' With such leadership emphasis on values, it's no wonder that 'Powered by Intellect, Driven by Values' is the company's slogan. Mr Murthy's leadership was clearly shared by others, as noted by K. Dinesh, another founder: 'The collective leadership [among the founders] in Infosys was for a cause that was a lot bigger than all of us. Infosys leadership is about having a dream, and executing that dream—always conscious of a larger cause that benefits others rather than the leaders themselves.'

'We were totally committed to our jobs and to one another,' Murthy observes, recalling an instance when he had told co-founder Shibulal not to go home until he had sorted out a problem bedevilling a particular project. Murthy had forgotten about his instruction and gone home himself. Four days later, he chanced upon Shibulal hard at work late in the evening. Upon being asked why he was working so late, Shibulal told Murthy, 'You asked me not to leave till the work was done.'

Another co-founder, N.S. Raghavan, reflects on the source of these all-important Infosys values: 'We have middle-class values. It is dignity of and respect for all people irrespective of their background. We don't do anything which is [harmful] to fairness in all our transactions. It's an ethical and moral means of making money, so creating money is not the essential thing. Money will automatically come.'

Infosys also has an instance when it fined its CEO for not reporting on time a change in his share ownership. Kris Gopalakrishnan had inherited 12,800 shares from his mother and the audit committee of Infosys imposed a fine of Rs 500,000 on Kris for 'inadvertently failing' to notify the company within one business day following the change in his shareholding.

Murthy defines a value system as 'a protocol or a set of protocols that a community uses in every transaction so that it enhances the trust, confidence, the comfort, energy and enthusiasm of every member in the community'. Infosys's C-LIFE captures the essence of this. Murthy elaborates:

> I think good habits [are those which] bring pleasure and happiness to you, but do not cost any money. Once you have such habits, you will not become a victim of money. If you do not become victim of money, then you can stand for integrity, honesty, decency and respect. This is what I truly believe in.

Infosys campus

By 2000, Infosys's corporate headquarters at Electronic City, Bangalore had expanded to a sprawling campus. With enviable leisure and technological infrastructure, this world-class headquarters was India's first large campus for a software company.

Today, Infosys in Bangalore has fifty buildings, spread over 80 acres. It's a melting pot of architectural styles from across the world. A food court draws inspiration from the Sydney Opera House. Infosys's state-of-the-art multimedia studio is housed in a spectacular glass structure, reminiscent of the glass pyramid at the entrance of the Louvre in Paris.

'We have a dream, a dream of providing the best workplace to the high-quality people who join us. Our employees see the campus as a great place to work, enjoy, they stay longer, productivity is higher, they appreciate the investment we made in providing facilities. When we get clients to our campus and take them around, they are amazed, see us as a premium player and set us apart from very many companies. Our competition says—do better than Infosys,' says T.V. Mohandas Pai.

'Yesterday, we moved from being a Bangalore company to an Indian company with a Bangalore base. Today, we are moving from being an Indian company with global reach to a global company headquartered in India,' said Narayana Murthy in 2000.

The Infosys family grows: 1,000 join in a quarter

In 1995, Infosys had less than 1,000 employees. For a company growing as rapidly as it was, that number was poised to increase exponentially. In 2000, the recruitment team added 1,000 new hires in a single quarter. From over 5,000 employees, the employee count almost doubled the very next year.

Adieu NSR

When Infosys's first employee Nadathur Sarangapani Raghavan retired in 2000, Narayana Murthy wrote a farewell note to his colleague, friend and co-founder of Infosys in the 1999–2000 Annual Report, saying:

NSR, as he is affectionately called, has several rare distinctions. He was employee number one at Infosys. He is the oldest amongst the founders. In his nineteen years at Infosys, NSR has taken up a variety of responsibilities. He has probably had the most eclectic career profile in this organization. He has handled HRD, Delivery, Education and Research, Planning and Finance, all with distinction. He was even the first-ever chauffeur of an Infosys vehicle–a rented Vespa scooter–ferrying me, the eternal pillion rider, across the streets of Bangalore during 1983! He is the only passable singer and restaurant quality cook among the gang of founders. I can go on and on because NSR has an inexhaustible set of endearing qualities. The most striking quality of NSR is his pleasantness. I have rarely seen him get upset about anything. He is best known at Infosys for his saying: 'You can disagree with me as long as you are not disagreeable.'

Infosys launches Finacle: the world's first fully web-enabled core banking solution

In 2000, Infosys led by Girish G. Vaidya launched the product that is known today as Finacle, an integrated core banking solution that leveraged Internet technologies to drive the operations of a bank. 'Banks are becoming a one-stop shop for financial services other than traditional core-banking services. But existing technology platforms fall short of the flexibility and interoperability needed to handle these diverse requirements; hence the need for a future-ready platform like Finacle,' said Nandan Nilekani at the launch.

NOTEWORTHY FACTS

- Infosys started developing its first core banking solution, BANCS 2000, in 1989. This was implemented at the first site in 1992.
- In 2000, Finacle had a footprint in fifteen countries. This number currently stands at fifty-three.
- Thirty-one out of Finacle's eighty-five customers are Tier 1 banks, ranked among the top 1,000 banks globally.

Infosys sets up Learning and Development Group, Infosys Leadership Institute

In January 2000, Infosys formally set up its Learning and Development Group (L&D). 'Training at Infosys, as some of our past recruits have discovered, is like doing your post-graduation and being paid for it'—this statement, which appeared in a 1991 recruitment ad, captures the spirit of learning at Infosys.

Infosys Leadership Institute (ILI) was created as a result of an assessment by Infosys using the Malcolm Baldridge National Quality Award (MBNQA) criteria that place the highest emphasis on leadership in driving business results. ILI was founded basically on three principles:

our company is our campus, our business is our curriculum, and our leaders are our teachers. In early 2001, the board launched the institute as the first building on Infosys's new Mysore campus to ensure that their legacy is sustained across future leaders. In 2004, the Learning & Development Group was combined with the Infosys Leadership Institute, which offers managerial and leadership training.

ILI developed a nine-factor model of leadership behaviours required for effective performance. This model was developed after careful research of the approaches followed by a sample eighteen global companies, and other relevant research. Each dimension, called a 'pillar', has its own unique importance to the development of leadership at the individual level. All of ILI's offerings were and still are aligned with this model as of today, including multisource (360 degree) feedback, courses, mentoring, job aides and various forms of experiential learning including action learning.

In October 2009, ILI was reorganized to provide heightened focus on leadership developmental needs of the seniormost and high potential leaders known as 'Tier leaders'. ILI's new focus is in ensuring personalized development is tailored to the unique needs of each leader; to ensure a sufficient bench strength of leadership talent to succeed senior roles; and to perform original research that is relevant to executing Infosys strategy and mitigating the risk of leader succession.

Global Education Centre (GEC)—the Taj Mahal of training centres

Infosys's Global Education Centre, one of the world's largest corporate training facilities, opened in 2005 in Mysore. The first GEC building (GEC I) can accommodate and train 4,500 employees at any given time. It's where the company's newest recruits go through an intensive fourteen and a half week long residential foundation programme. *Fortune* magazine visited the GEC in March 2006 and reported that gaining admission to the 'Taj Mahal of training centres' is harder than getting into Harvard. Only 1 per cent of applicants are selected at Infosys from over 1.3 million, as opposed to 9 per cent at Harvard.

In 2010, GEC II was inaugurated which increased capacity to develop 14,000 employees simultaneously. With this expansion, the

Mysore location is, to the best of our knowledge, the largest corporate education centre in the world in 2010. Speaking after the inauguration, Sonia Gandhi, chair of the United Progressive Alliance (UPA) and president of the Indian National Congress, said Infosys had proven that Indian companies are redefining world class excellence. On the same occasion Chief Mentor Narayana Murthy said, 'The Education Centre is a testimony of Infosys's commitment to building the competency of our employees.' He added, 'In addition, special programmes have been conducted at the GEC for students from Australia, Bhutan, China, Columbia, Japan, Malaysia, Mauritius, Panama, Thailand, the UK and the USA.' The objective of the Global Education Centre is to create an environment for lifelong learning.

Infosys and Microsoft's global alliance

In 2000, Infosys and Microsoft announced a strategic global relationship. 'Together, we can deliver world-class e-business solutions to our existing and future customers,' said Microsoft's Bill Gates on the occasion. Added Narayana Murthy, 'With over 1,200 professionals trained on Microsoft platforms and deployed globally, we can effectively leverage access to the very latest Microsoft technologies into business benefits for our customers. We believe that this relationship will expand our Fortune 1000 client base.'

NOTEWORTHY FACTS

- In 2004, Microsoft and Infosys announced a US$ 8 million IT transformation initiative, designed to help clients improve business performance and build competitive advantage. Later that year, a catalytic IT concept centre opened at Infosys's Bangalore campus, where clients could envision, architect and evaluate IT solutions through an informative and interactive experience.
- In 2010, Microsoft signed a partnership worth US$ 189 million over three years, with a possible expansion to US$ 240 million.

The dot com bubble bursts

In 2001, the industry was hit by the dot com crash. That year, a host of companies revoked job offers they had made to engineers about to graduate from technical universities. Infosys had recruited 1,500 engineers, and against all logic, decided to honour the commitment to hire them all, even though there was very little work. The tangible and intangible consequences were severe. Not only did Infosys take a hit to the books in a difficult year, but employee satisfaction also plummeted to unprecedented levels. The malaise showed up in internal Infosys employee surveys, and also in external measurements. Infosys slid down in many 'Best Company to Work For' lists and 'Best Employer' surveys conducted around 2001–02. Looking back, Murthy says:

> Many companies fired employees. HR managers of IT companies stood at the gates taking the employee identity cards and giving marching orders. We said, 'We cannot do this–it is not our employees' fault. It is our mistake.' We, the Infosys founders, would have paid salaries from our own pockets, but our accountants wouldn't let us. When you have so many people and so little work, they get bored and disappointed. But we had to live by our promises. The good part of that episode was that we came across as honest, decent people who live by our commitments. The goodwill we earned at the campuses is inimitable.

Although they had miscalculated their requirements in terms of employees, Infosys was one of the few IT firms to predict the downturn of the markets in late 2001. Murthy recalls:

> In October 2001, after surveying clients and other experts, we forecast that our growth in revenue for the fiscal year 2001–02 would drop to about 30 per cent–down from about 90 per cent the previous year. Our own industry analysts said that our sector would grow by 45 per cent, and some of our competitors predicted growth of more than 50 per cent. As it turned out, in 2001–02 our top line grew by 32 per cent, the sector growth rate was about 25 per cent, and our competitors grew by 20 to 25 per cent.

Move to a role-based structure

Infosys moved to a role-based structure in 2001. With the change, employees could identify potential roles and work towards them.

Promotions were based on merit and not on time spent in a particular role. This created multiple career paths and strengthened career planning. The new structure proved to be a great leveller. It spelt opportunity for employees who took the initiative and made performance paramount. This was an elaborate competency-modelling exercise of all roles within the organization structure, and collapsed fifteen layers into seven bands.

Infosys and Wharton School honour excellence in business transformation

In 2001, The Wharton School of the University of Pennsylvania and Infosys Technologies Ltd. jointly instituted the Wharton–Infosys Business Transformation Award (WIBTA). Since then, the award has honoured enterprises and individuals who have transformed their businesses, and impacted society, by leveraging information technology. The award is separately given for four regions: North America, Latin America, Europe and Asia Pacific. Technology leaders from over a dozen countries, like amazon.com and Samsung, have been celebrated in ceremonies held across the globe.

Mauritius disaster recovery centre

Infosys announced plans to set up its first disaster recovery centre at Mauritius in 2002, with a US$ 25 million investment. The centre, which became operational in 2004, serves as an alternate location in case of a disaster at any of Infosys's development centres. Replete with infrastructure, network connections, telecommunication facilities as well as back-up client data, it can take over client projects from across the globe in an emergency.

Infosys falls out of Best Employer status

The decade since 1992 had been a heady one for both the Indian software industry and Infosys. From March 1993 to March 2003, Infosys had a compounded annual growth rate of 65 per cent and its revenues had jumped from US$5 million to US$ 754 million. As it had grown, it had added people at an equally impressive rate, from a mere 250 new hires in 1992 to over 15,000 recruits in 2002. Infosys braced many a challenge as it transitioned from a small to a large company.

Rapidly changing HR policies bred confusion with both employees and managers. Middle and senior managers were made responsible by HR for communicating these changes effectively to employees. Some managers weren't as familiar with the details as required, and couldn't answer employee questions. Misinformation and rumours led to further discontent and lack of trust between some employees.

Infosys had always recognized that its employees or 'Infoscions' were at the heart of its impressive success. It had been one of the first Indian companies to grant stock options to its employees, creating thousands of dollar millionaires. It had previously been ranked no. 1 in the *Business Today* Best Employer Survey both in 2001 and 2002.

Consequently, it was a rude shock when in 2003, Infosys toppled out of the Best Employer list in the same survey. Its own internal employee satisfaction survey showed a variety of gaps. The results caused great commotion in the industry and reams of newsprint was devoted to analysing the reputational downfall of the 'poster child' of the Indian software industry.

As Infosys continued its heady growth, Hema Ravichandar, then Head-HR, needed answers to prevent crises like this one from recurring in the future. A major initiative was the establishment of the internal communications division which resulted in an improvement in the way policies were developed and communicated. A policy council was established, and employee attitudes were assessed more frequently. In addition, human resource generalists known as 'business partners' were embedded within each of the delivery units. As a result of the swift retrenchment, Infosys rebounded to regain a place on the Top Employers list.

The measures Infosys leaders had taken to improve employee satisfaction had been the necessary counterpart to the changes they had implemented in 2001 to improve business performance. Both were aimed at preparing Infosys for future competition as a large organization. But Hema felt the measures fell short of what would be required to cope with the challenges she foresaw on the horizon as Infosys continued on its high-growth path. Over the years, Infosys developed a deeper understanding of employee relations. Richard Lobo, Head of Employee Relations, HR explains, 'There are three ways in which we add value to the employee: learning value-add through training, emotional value-add through the work environment and financial value-add through compensation and benefits.'

Infosys enters BPM space with Progeon

Infosys entered the Business Process Management (BPM) market with a new subsidiary Progeon in April 2002. Since its inception, Progeon has focussed on end-to-end outsourcing and operates on the principle that true Business Process Outsourcing (BPO) is transformational: it should help customers change their business in four tangible ways—do it cheaper, better, differently, and eliminate work.

Today, ranked among the top ten third-party BPOs in India, Progeon operates in four countries—India, the Czech Republic, China and the Philippines—employing over 8,000 people.

Infosys establishes a subsidiary in China

Tapping opportunities and leveraging local talent in one of the world's fastest growing economies, Infosys formed Infosys Technologies (Shanghai) Co. Ltd, a wholly-owned subsidiary in China with an initial capital of US$ 5 million, in 2003.

Infosys assessed at CMMI Level 5

In 2003, Infosys was assessed at CMMI Level 5 across its development centres in India, and several client locations in the US. This was an important step in Infosys's journey to maintain world-class quality not just at its own centres, but also at client locations. The appraisal, conducted mainly on-site, was one-of-its-kind in the industry. The lead appraiser Ed Weller noted, 'Infosys is highly customer-centred and process-driven, with an uncompromising attitude towards high quality and on-time delivery.' In 2005, rounding off this achievement, Infosys's entire global operations were assessed at CMMI Level 5.

Infosys sponsors secondary ADR offering

In July 2003, Infosys became the first Indian company to sponsor a secondary offering and take the Indian shareholder to the global market. It completed a sponsored American Depositary Receipts (ADR) offering of 3 million equity shares listed in India into 6 million American Depositary Shares (ADSs) listed on NASDAQ. On the occasion Nandan Nilekani said, 'This is a larger event because it shows that the old trend towards outsourcing and offshoring has become mainstream, it shows that India has become the country of choice for this whole trend—and Infosys as the most admired company, the best employer, the best corporate citizen is at the vanguard of this new trend.'

Infosys's acquisition in Australia

In 2004, Infosys acquired Expert Information Services Pty. Ltd, one of Australia's leading IT services providers, for US$ 24.3 million. The company was renamed Infosys Technologies Australia Pty Ltd. The merger accelerated Infosys's market penetration in the country. Infosys Australia has recruited and developed Australian talent. It has worked with leading local IT companies on strategic opportunities and assisted government and industry bodies with strategic advice, thus bringing unprecedented opportunities for the local IT industry to grow and reach global markets.

Kris Gopalakrishnan says, 'We are looking at acquisitions as a way to fill in strategic gaps. In Australia we found a company that meets our requirements of performance, an Australian company with a significant back engine in India.'

Infosys Consulting launched

Bringing the power of the Global Delivery Model to a high-value service like consulting, Infosys Consulting Inc. was formed in April 2004. In less than two years, this US-based subsidiary of Infosys had worked with over twenty-five Global 1000 companies, helping its clients design and implement operational changes that make them fundamentally more competitive.

Led by American Stephen Pratt, who was named one of *Consulting* magazine's 'Top 25 Most Influential Consultants' in 2005, Infosys Consulting has over 100 consultants on board in the US, picked for their industry expertise and innovative thinking. Infosys also plans to hire 500 consulting professionals in the US and Europe and invest US$ 20 million in the venture over the next two years. Nandan Nilekani said, 'Around 2003 as our client relations became more complex and more sophisticated, with customers seeing us as mission critical transformation partners, we had to address our capability with high-end consulting skills to create next generation end-to-end business and IT solutions.'

Campus Connect: producing industry-ready talent

In July 2004, Infosys launched Campus Connect. An industry–academia partnership, it empowers engineering colleges to produce 'industry-ready' recruits. Whether it is publishing Infosys's technical courseware on the Web, or offering faculty an industry perspective through sabbatical projects, Campus Connect anchors programmes that significantly enhance the quality of IT education. Beginning with India, the initiative has now spread to China. Its biggest contribution so far is in sharing and rolling out Infosys's flagship Foundation Programme—an intensive entry-level training course for new employees—in hundreds of colleges across India.

NOTEWORTHY FACT

- Between 2004 and 2005, Infosys processed over 1.4 million job applications and conducted more than 47,000 interviews. Only one per cent of the applicants made it to Infosys!

Brand with a conscience

In 2004, Infosys was among seven international companies, and the only Indian organization, chosen to be in the first annual list of 'Top Brands with a Conscience'. The list was compiled based on principles of humanity and ethics rather than financial worth and published by the Medinge Group, an international collective of brand experts who meet annually. Companies were evaluated on parameters ranging from the evidence of ethical programmes and human implications of the brand to the ability of the brand to take risks in line with its beliefs. According to Narayana Murthy, 'Brand is a trustmark.'

The billion dollar milestone

Twenty-three years after it was started, Infosys crossed the billion dollar mark, reporting revenues of US$ 1.06 billion in FY 2003–04. As congratulatory messages poured in from leaders around the country, the Infosys family, scattered across the globe, came together on a single day to celebrate this milestone. Anecdotes, words of wisdom and motivational messages delivered by the senior management, founders, Infosys's first customer, early investors and children of employees made it a truly memorable occasion. As did a special one-time cash bonus for employees!

NOTEWORTHY FACT

- Infosys announced a 3:1 bonus and a special one-time dividend of Rs 100 per share in 2004.

Infosys turns twenty-five, revenues cross US$ 2 billion

In its twenty-fifth year, Infosys also crossed the revenue milestone of US$ 2 billion. 'It took us twenty-three years to reach the revenue milestone of one billion dollars. The next billion dollars took us only twenty-three months to achieve,' reported the Letter to the Shareholder in the Infosys Annual Report 2005–06.

NOTEWORTHY FACT

- In 2005, global credit ratings provider Standard and Poor's assigned Infosys a credit rating higher than the agency's sovereign rating on India. Infosys obtained 'BBB' local currency and 'BBB-' foreign currency rating. It was the first company in India to obtain a credit rating higher than India's sovereign rating (BB+/Stable/B). According to Standard and Poor's, this reflects Infosys's very conservative financial profile and policy, which feature ample liquidity, a strong operating cash flow, and a debt-free balance sheet.

- In May 2005, Infosys initiated the largest international equity offering from India, for US$ 1 billion. As part of this ADS offering, Infosys offered 3.2 million shares to Japanese investors through a public offer without listing (POWL). This was the first POWL issue by an Indian company. It not only awakened Japanese interest in India, but also opened the market for Indian companies.

Over 100,000 employees

The employee count passed the 100,000 mark in 2009. As the Infosys family grows, new recruitment records are set; 2,076 Infoscions joined on 26 June 2006—the largest-ever number to join Infosys on a single day. At present, there are over 114,000 Infoscions globally, and we anticipate hiring an additional 30,000 employees in the next twelve months.

Infosys today has employees of eighty-one nationalities and is committed to creating a diverse and inclusive workplace. Infosys is the first Indian IT company to set up a diversity office for promoting its diversity and inclusivity vision. The Infosys Diversity Office suggests, 'A diverse workplace, as we define it today, is based on gender, culture, the differently abled, work experience and family status. By an inclusive environment, we mean creating a place free of barriers in which every employee has the opportunity to participate, contribute and develop freely and equitably.' The diversity office will focus on bridging differences by enhancing commonalities among the diverse work pool.

*

As we approach the thirtieth year in Infosys's history, we're proud of what we've achieved as a company. We go forward fully assured that while our business models, our customer value propositions and our geographic footprint will continue to evolve, our values are steadfast and unwavering. The same values our founders practiced, and later Infoscions codified into C-LIFE, are part of our legacy that threads through everything Infoscions do for all our stakeholders worldwide.

Bibliography

Manfred, F.R., De Vries, Kets, Agrawal, Anupam and Florent-Treacy, Elizabeth (2006). *The Moral Compass: Values-based Leadership at Infosys*, Fontainebleau: INSEAD.

Nanda, Ashish and Delong, Thomas (2002). *Infosys Technologies*, Boston: Harvard Business School Press.

CHAPTER 2

OBJECTIVELY MEASURING LEADERS

MATT BARNEY, PHD AND SIDDHARTH PATNAIK, PHD

'To measure is to know.'

—*Lord Kelvin, mathematical physicist, nineteenth century*

Emperor Wu (156–87 BC) of the Han dynasty in China was the first in the world to use systematic measurement procedures to evaluate people. (Like Infosys, the early Chinese wanted to make sure people could perform at their jobs before selecting them!) But in the last 4,000 years, significant advancements have taken place to dramatically improve measurement and evaluation of all professionals, including leaders. Is it possible that measurement systems have now evolved to the point where they are as sophisticated as the physical sciences?

The work of a Danish statistician during World War II was a pioneering effort towards the objective measurement of people. In 1944, Georg Rasch devised a method for human measurement that met the rigorous standards that had propelled other sciences for centuries. It is thanks to Rasch and his contemporaries that over the last sixty years engineering-worthy instrumentation has become available to assess leaders. Since his original innovation, Rasch's approach has been used successfully in everything from physician certification testing, professional golf proficiency, language proficiency and musical skill assessment to movie preferences and wine judging. At the Infosys Leadership Institute (ILI) we use the Rasch family of psychometric methods to effectively gauge the attributes relevant to selecting and growing leaders, and to evaluate our investments in leaders at Infosys.

The information provided by Rasch Measurement is substantially more accurate and precise than earlier approaches. One important feature of the Rasch approach is that it is extremely easy to understand. Infosys leaders can use the Rasch Measurement for their development in the same way that they think about measuring temperature with thermometers, or distance with rulers. Just as we infer the temperature from the length of mercury in a glass tube—an indirect measure of heat—we can gain information about leader knowledge, skills and abilities from their behaviours. In Infosys's 'Leadership Journey Series', a battery of advanced leader assessments, we use multisource computer-adaptive instruments. Multisource surveys, also known as 360 degree surveys, are best analysed with the Many Facet Rasch Model (MFRM) that removes various biases, such as rater severity and leniency, from each measure to make sure the information is fair, accurate and precise (Linacre, 1994a).

Because we've never met a leader who enjoys taking long, tedious questionnaires, surveys or tests, we use computer-adaptive technology to ensure that the assessments are as short and focussed as possible (Linacre, 2000). Computer-adaptive measurement, which has been relatively widespread for forty years in medical and educational applications, is relatively new to be applied to leader selection and development. There are several important practical benefits to the computer-adaptive approach to measurement.

First, assessments are between 20 and 90 per cent shorter than they would be with traditional computer-based or paper-and-pencil-based approaches. In one medical example, a measure that took over fifty questions in a traditional assessment achieved the same precision with only five questions for 70 per cent of the patients through computer-adaptive measurement (Ware, Bjorner and Kosinski, 2000). Since adaptive tests are shorter, we avoid survey fatigue and future resistance to filling out surveys. At the same time, we're able to measure more things in the same or less amount of time as compared to earlier methods. This is why computer-adaptive measurement can be more informative, since it is able to capture more information in the same or less amount of time.

Second, for high-stakes environments such as certification testing or pre-hire employment screens, the item banks are substantially more secure with computer-adaptive measurement. Since each person gets a tailored measurement experience based on questions whose locations (difficulty) are known, each person gets a unique set of questions. When you have a very large 'bank' of items, it is very unlikely that any two people will get exactly the same questions. Similarly, for unsupervised assessments over the Internet, item banks are the only reasonable way to maintain item security. While questions can still be misappropriated with unproctored tests, in this case it is much harder to steal them than in scenarios where everyone gets the same questions. When using traditional means, it is not unusual to find test questions and answers for free or up for sale on the Internet; computer-adaptive methods make this much more difficult. With computer-adaptive testing (CAT), we can use a procedure that re-tests leaders when they're in a proctored environment—in the final set of interviews—to verify that they are the same person as in the pre-interview assessments.

Third, computer-adaptive measures are actually more precise, fairer and more accurate than alternative approaches, at least when the MFRM approach is used. They are more accurate because only those questions that meet Rasch's stringent standards get used. Rasch represents a targeted 'ideal' that we aim towards to make sure our questions are close enough to be practically useful. They are also more precise because unlike traditional approaches, the adaptive algorithm can be set to cease asking questions only after all estimates have sufficiently small amounts of error. Rasch-based CATs are also fairer because with Linacre's MFRM, rater severity (rarely giving high ratings), leniency (mostly giving high ratings) and other forms of bias can be systematically removed or omitted from the estimate of the leader, to make sure they're entirely undistorted. To the best of our knowledge, we believe that in 2010 we are the only practitioner–scientists globally who use these advanced methods for leader development.

Table 1 gives an overview of the main benefits of Rasch Measurement over the two alternative approaches. One limitation of the Rasch Measurement approach in contrast to the other two is the fact that not all data meets the stringent standards of Rasch, and we end up 'throwing out' relatively more questions than in the other two approaches. Some data that doesn't meet Rasch's stringent quality control standards must be removed like rotten apples so that they don't spoil the bunch. Classical Test Theory (CTT) and Item Response Theory (IRT) are more efficient in this regard; however, given that there are a large number of benefits that only Rasch makes possible, at ILI we are comfortable with accepting this small limitation in lieu of a much bigger payoff in the other areas.

Table 1: Rasch Measurement Contrasted with Classical Test and Item Response Theories

	Rasch	CTT	IRT
Amount of scrapped raw data	Medium	Low	Low
Minimum sample size of leaders required to calibrate	30[1]	300[2]	250[3]
Sample-distribution free	Yes, verified with mathematical proof	No, different norm groups produce different scores	Claimed, but not verified with mathematical proof
People and questions on same 'ruler' for clear feedback	Yes	No	No
Rater severity and leniency bias removed	Yes	No	No

[1]Linacre, 1994b
[2]Nunnally and Bernstein, 1994
[3]Embretson and Reise, 2000

Perhaps the most important practical reason ILI chose to use the Rasch Measurement method is the power with which we can give feedback to leaders with Rasch. Other approaches are complex, and require leaders to interpret norms, percentiles (with CTT) or even more complex information (with IRT). Neither CTT nor IRT can give information that is just like a thermometer or a ruler. Only a Rasch approach uniquely produces information where leaders and questions are on the same underlying ruler. The most important aspect of the feedback is it helps focus busy leaders only on those actions that are neither too easy nor too hard, but are 'just right' given their current level of proficiency.

Figure 1 shows an example of the Rasch Measure, where the highlight focuses leaders on areas most fruitful to grow their 'Individualized Consideration', a Rasch measure based on the well-studied Full Range Leadership Model (Avolio and Bass, 1995), created and validated by ILI. In the figure, you can see that this person ('Hugo Munsterberg') has already mastered behaviours such as 'spending a significant amount of time coaching his/her people' and 'tailoring the rewards specific to each individual employee'. But the areas he needs to work on are highlighted: 'systematically harvesting examples where direct reports did a good job' and 'customizing the learning and development support to the unique needs of each person'. Lastly, there are several areas that are too hard for the leader right now, such as 'counselling leaders', and he should master these easier tasks first, before trying these more intimate, emotional areas of individualized consideration.

Individualized Consideration

Assessment Completed: April 15, 1913

Hugo Munsterberg

Score: 75/100
The areas in grey below are the best areas for you to focus on developing.
Areas below the grey highlight are areas you've mastered; while areas above
the grey are best addressed in the future, as they are more difficult to master.

Individualized Consideration

	Item	
100	demonstrates that he/she trusts employees	Areas for Future
99	counsels employees when need	
89	shows genuine caring for each employee as a unique individual	
76	customizes the learning and development support to the unique needs of each person	Focus Area
76	systematically harvests examples where direct reports did a good job	
69	tailors rewards to the specific preferences of each individual employee	
32	spends a significant amount of time coaching his/her people	Areas Mastered
7	acts in ways that suggests he/she is entirely self-centred	
1	ignores employee preferences when delegating assignments	

Figure 1: Example of Rasch Feedback for Leaders

Infosys's Nine Dimensions of Leadership

All of ILI's work is based on a 'nine pillar' model of leader behaviour, shown in Table 2. Nine behavioural areas form the basis for all assessments, selection procedures and developmental interventions for the entire institute. Table 2 below shows the definitions of each dimension. Subsequent chapters in this book discuss each of these dimensions in detail.

Table 2: ILI's Leadership Dimensions

Leadership Dimension	Definition
Strategic	Establishing and committing to a long-range course of action to accomplish a long-range goal or vision that sustainably gives Infosys an edge. Continuously creating new differentiators and challenging assumptions made about current strategies in order to continually move ahead of competition.
Relationship/ Networking	Developing, maintaining and leveraging long-term internal and external relationships/networks. Building effective relationships beyond transactions with all internal and external business partners to the point of being a completely trusted advisor.
Talent	Selecting, developing and managing the performance of a team capable of executing the vision. Attracting, developing and retaining highly capable individuals to build the leadership pipeline are central. Similarly, creating an effective work climate to drive performance and requisite learning is critical.
Change, Transition and Adversity	Managing through the inevitable sources of resistance that comes with transformational leadership. Devising change strategy and creating processes and systems that mitigate the risk of adoption of new innovations are key.
Operational	Leading operations involve systematically applying a portfolio of methods that achieve high degrees of efficiency, productivity and quality. Institutionalizing a culture of achievement, proactive prevention of defects, process innovation and improvement in order to realize goals around delighting customers consistently and sustainably.
Content	Creating and leveraging deep domain expertise required for success in your role. This is critical to energizing one's strategy and team. Content leadership is about possessing and creating knowledge and mental models in one's core discipline to outthink and outlead the competition.

Leadership Dimension	Definition
Entrepreneurial	Incubating new business ideas, models and working arrangements in new markets, new product segments and services to drive growth.

In 2010, ILI began to use the 'Leadership Journey' series of assessments to select both new 'Tier' leaders, our term for high potentials, and also lateral hires for senior roles. Using a subset of the Leadership Journey series, these will use assessments of personality traits, cognitive ability (called 'learnability' at Infosys), and values that predict leader performance and succession.

Because of Infosys's longstanding commitment to evidence-based decision making, the useful measurement of our leaders is important to us. We want to make sure that the advice we give leaders about their development is the best possible, and we want to make sure that what we do to grow them actually seems to pay off. Because we've invested in these advanced methods, we are positioned to help our leaders grow—with demonstrable results far better than alternative approaches could. Importantly, this provides a very solid foundation for our ultimate measures. In the near term, ILI's purpose is to increase the probability of our leaders realizing strategic goals, or in other words performing. But in the end, our value is measured in the degree to which the institute successfully mitigates the risk of succession of the Infosys Board of Directors. Our forecasting models, based on the latest science, are intended to help inform broad, portfolio-based decisions about leader and leadership investments. It is because we've gone to such trouble to create instrumentation that we feel our research and succession practice will be set up for success for many years to come. For a start, we've used these 'Leadership Journey Series' assessments to select the leaders covered in the subsequent chapters of this book—so that the people whose advice we're recommending are demonstrably effective in each area.

Bibliography

Avolio, B.J. and Bass, B.M. (1995). 'Individual Consideration Viewed at Multiple Levels of Analysis: A Multi-level Framework for Examining the Diffusion of Transformational Leadership', *Leadership Quarterly*, 6, 199–218.

Bass, B.M. (1999). 'Two Decades of Research and Development in Transformational Leadership', *European Journal of Work and Organizational Psychology*, 8(1), 9–32.

Day, D.V. and Halpin, S.M. (2001). 'Leadership Development: A Review of Industry Best Practices', US Army Research Institute of Behavioral and Social Sciences, retrieved 25 October 2010 from http://www.au.af.mil/au/awc/awcgate/army/tr1111.pdf.

Embretson, S.E. and Reise, S.P. (2000). *Item Response Theory for Psychologists*, Mahwah, NJ: Lawrence Earlbaum and Associates.

Harvey, J. and Mogey, N. (1999). 'Pragmatic Issues When Integrating Technology into the Assessment of Students', in S. Brown, P. Race and J. Bull (eds.), *Computer-assisted Assessment in Higher Education*, London: Kogan-Page, 7–20.

Infosys Leadership Institute Faculty (2002). 'Developing Leaders @ Infosys', *Praxis-Business Line*, June, 38–43.

Krishnan, S.K. and Varkkey, B. (2004). 'Nurturing Fast Track Leaders: A Concept Paper', retrieved 26 April 2006 from http://stdwww.iimahd.ernet.in/~sandeepk/Fasttrack.pdf.

Linacre, J.M. (1994a). *Many-Facet Rasch Measurement*, 2nd edn, Chicago: MESA Press.

Linacre, J.M. (1994b). 'Sample Size and Item Calibration (or Person Measure) Stability', *Rasch Measurement Transactions*, 7 (4), 328, http://www.rasch.org/rmt/rmt74m.htm.

Linacre, J.M. (2000). 'Computer-adaptive Testing: A Methodology Whose Time Has Come', MESA, Memorandum no. 69.

Nunnally, J.C. and Bernstein, I.H. (1994). *Psychometric Theory*, New York: McGraw-Hill.

Reise, S.P. and Yu, J. (1990). 'Parameter Recovery in the Graded Response Model Using MULTILOG', *Journal of Educational Measurement*, 27, 133–44.

Ware, John E., Bjorner, Jakob B. and Kosinski, Mark (2000). 'Practical Implications of Item Response Theory and Computerized Adaptive Testing: A Brief Summary of Ongoing Studies of Widely Used Headache Impact Scales', *Medical Care*, 38 (9), 73–82.

CHAPTER 3

STRATEGIC LEADERSHIP

Rajeswari Murali and Matt Barney, PhD

'On a hot summer morning in 1995, a Fortune10 corporation had sequestered all their Indian software vendors, including Infosys, in different rooms at the Taj Residency hotel in Bangalore so that the vendors could not communicate with one another. This customer's propensity for tough negotiations was well known. Our team was very nervous. First of all, with revenues of only around $5 million, we were minnows compared to the customer. Second, this customer contributed fully 25 per cent of our revenues. The loss of this business would potentially devastate our recently-listed company. Third, the customer's negotiation style was very aggressive. The customer team would go from room to room, get the best terms out of each vendor and then pit one vendor against the other. This went on for several rounds.

Our various arguments why a fair price—one that allowed us to invest in good people, R&D, infrastructure, technology and training—was actually in their interest failed to cut any ice with the customer. By 5 p.m. on the last day, we had to make a decision right on the spot whether to accept the customer's terms or to walk out. All eyes were on me as I mulled over the decision.

I closed my eyes, and reflected upon our journey until then. Through many a tough call, we had always thought about the long-term interests of Infosys. I communicated clearly to the customer team that we could not accept their terms, since it could well lead us to letting them down later. But I promised a smooth, professional transition to a vendor of the customer's choice.

This was a turning point for Infosys. Subsequently, we created a Risk Mitigation Council which ensured that we would never again depend too much on any one client, technology, country, application area or key employee. The crisis was a blessing in disguise. Today, Infosys has a sound de-risking strategy that has stabilized its revenues and profits.'

—*N.R. Narayana Murthy, Infosys Chief Mentor and Chairman,*
at a pre-commencement lecture at the New York University,
Stern School of Business, 9 May 2008

As Infosys grew from revenues of a few millions in the 1990s to a $5 billion company in the first decade of the 2000s, it was instances such as this that helped define what strategic leadership should be in the organization.

This chapter has three major sections. First, we will briefly review the major theories related to strategy. Second, we will review Infosys's strategic milestones in order to understand how it evolved. Finally, we will review specific actions and lessons learned by Infosys leaders who have scored high on Strategic Leadership, as measured by the Leadership Journey Series.

Major Strategic Leadership Approaches

The literature has many theories about strategy, and we will review several major models that suggest how companies create unique value for their stakeholders. While each theory has a different focal point, analytical toolset and deployment approach, all:

- consider how companies win in the marketplace. Some go beyond just the firm level of analysis and also propose industry, national and global strategies for creating value.
- define winning at least partially in financial terms such that a firm sustains above-average returns, beyond the costs including cost of capital invested.

Together, all strategy theorists suggest that effective leaders secure 'economic profits' or 'rents' in excess of those earned by competitors by devising a unique approach to creating value.

Structure-based Strategy

Harvard Business School professor Michael Porter has written extensively on strategy for more than forty years. One of his earliest and most influential strategic leadership analytical frameworks designed to examine industry-level strategy is known as the Five Forces Analysis (Porter, 1979). Based on work in economics, Porter suggests that five forces determine the competitive intensity and overall profitability of a market. The first three are 'horizontals' such as the threat of substitute products, the threat of established rivals, and the threat of new entrants; whereas the other two are 'verticals'— the bargaining power of suppliers and customers. In practice, many leaders use Porter's forces with an analysis of a company's strengths, weaknesses, opportunities and threats (SWOT). Porter's work suggests that the source of strategic competitive advantage is the presence of structural barriers to one of the five forces, such as patents or capital investments that prevent new rivals from entering the marketplace.

Porter further builds out his theory in detail at the firm level with three 'generic strategies' that transcend industries (Porter, 1985). His generic strategies suggest that firms can choose one of the below:

1. *Low-cost leadership*: Much like Wal-Mart's famous supply chain that enables them to consistently undersell competitors while growing.
2. *Differentiation*: Like Apple, a firm pursuing this strategy seeks to be systematically unique in ways that large numbers of customers desire. Apple's iPad and iPhone are just recent examples of a long-standing Apple approach to innovating beyond competitors.
3. *Focus*: Like McKinsey, this strategy narrowly chooses a small scope of a very few segments and intentionally does not service other markets.

Core Competence

Whereas Porter takes a macro perspective on strategy, C.K. Prahalad and Gary Hamel took a firm-level view (Prahalad and Hamel, 1999). They suggested that the source for competitive advantage in the long run is the ability to build better offerings, unanticipated products and services more effectively than competitors. In this way, the real source of advantage is in the leader's ability to leverage existing capabilities that are superior to the competition. This includes not only delighting existing customers better than competitors, but also consistently creating new, better or lower cost offerings than any other market participant. They suggest there are three tests to whether or not a firm has a core competence:

1. Does it give potential access to many markets, products and services?
2. Will it deliver significant benefits to the end customer (e.g. 'delighters' that they aren't necessarily asking for, desire and cannot get elsewhere)?
3. Is it difficult for competitors to mimic?

Resource-based View

The third model we will review had its genesis in the 1950s where it had secured interest among strategy experts long before Porter and Prahalad (e.g. Penrose, 1959). All three approaches—the structural, competence-based, and the third, resource-based approach to strategy—share similarities, in that each examines the mechanisms by which value flows from the supplier to the customer. Porter's notion of a 'value chain' and Prahalad and Hamel's 'core competence' are quite similar to our third theory, the 'resource–based' view of the firm (Porter, 1985; Barney, 1991). A 'value chain' disaggregates a company into the components of its work that are the potential sources of differentiation. Porter (1985) suggests a firm gains competitive advantage by performing these activities cheaper or better than the competition. Figure 1 shows Porter's 'generic value chain' that can also be used to understand the resource-based view of the firm.

The resource-based view (RBV) of the firm suggests that leaders create good strategies in so far as they have unique capabilities in their organizations that derive their value from resources that competitors do not have. These capabilities are described as processes—bundles of the work activity described earlier by Porter (Eisenhardt and Martin, 2000). The RBV became popular in the 1990s with Jay Barney's insight

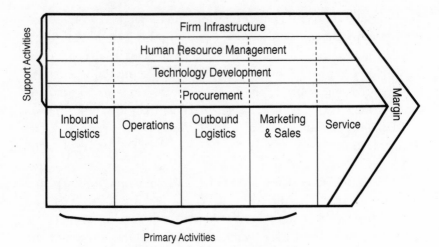

Primary Activities

Figure 1: Porter's Generic Value Chain

that four factors would give companies competitive advantage, if a firm possessed resources with the following attributes, known as VRIN (Barney, 1991):

1. *Valuable*—The resource had to be valuable
2. *Rare*—The resource must be in short supply in the marketplace
3. *Inimitable*—The resource can't be mimicked at all, or at least easily
4. *Non-substitutable*—The resource must be difficult to substitute with some other asset

RBV proponents suggest that leaders that can secure advantage by acquiring or developing these resources. This includes attracting talent, procuring unique innovations, or creating better capabilities with VRIN attributes.

Critics point out several concerns with the RBV. First, they note that VRIN resources are especially hard to find or grow, largely because they are intangible, causally ambiguous or the result of complex social processes (Priem and Butler, 2001a, 2001b). Second, they note that the way RBV researchers define 'value' is self-referential (tautological), meaning that it was defined as valuable in the marketplace, and then RBV says that differential marketplace returns suggested that it was valuable.

Research at the Infosys Leadership Institute suggests a possible remedy, however. The Cue See model is a framework that helps establish strategy and then cascade targets across the firm's 'value chain'. The targets are set to be both necessary and sufficient to realize the ultimate firm level goals. The Cue See model suggests that if a single asset, or combination of assets, has a strong probability of consistently achieving or exceeding these strategy-set process targets, far beyond the competition, then they can be useful to the firm in securing competitive advantage (Barney, 2009a, 2009b). In this way, value refers to the utility, or use value, of a given capability to realize a specific set of process goals whose ultimate result is valued by a paying customer in the marketplace (Lepak, Smith and Taylor, 2007). The Cue See model modifies the RBV by suggesting specific requirements imposed on all organizational processes, given a particular business strategy. Rather than traditional RBV definitions of value as in the liquidation value of an asset (or a combination of assets) in the marketplace, the Cue See model suggests that the assets must consistently produce superior quality, cost, quantity or cycle time results that ultimately delight customers who pay for the offering. Consistent with both the RBV and the core competence approach, Cue See suggests that if a firm can secure any resource (e.g. information, employee, machine) that consistently realizes quality, cost, quantity or cycle time targets in processes and competitors can't secure, mimic, or somehow achieve the same results, competitive advantage can be achieved.

The benefit of the Cue See model to the strategy literature is that it integrates the methods, tools and theories from strategy and builds a bridge with the industrial/systems engineering and quality science methods, thereby improving strategy execution. For example, Lean and Six Sigma improvement methodologies are well suited and noted for being effective at both designing new processes and products required to realize specific targets (e.g. design for Six Sigma) or improving a specified outcome like quality (e.g. Lean, Six Sigma DMAIC).

Intended versus Emergent Strategy

Harry Mintzberg (1987) provides an alternative, emergent approach to strategy in contrast with the other more structured approaches. His contention is that strategies can form as well as be formulated over time, as uncertainty resolves itself and new ideas emerge.

Mintzberg argues that a strategy may evolve, or it could be a deliberate set of decisions followed by implementation. However, when completed plans do not provide the expected results, leaders are left with unrealized strategies. Mintzberg makes a connection between thought and action; he notes that crafting strategy requires both thoughtful reflection and opportunistic action. Given that markets are uncertain and that opportunities emerge, Mintzberg's approach allows for leadership flexibility to determine new opportunities to create value.

The research by Mintzberg and others suggests that effective strategies could be devised by combining deliberation and control with flexibility and organizational learning. It suggests that strategy development in a large organization might be best done by using the 'umbrella approach' where senior management sets out the broad themes but leaves strategy specifics to leaders at lower levels in the organization. This approach blends an organization-wide strategic approach with market, product and geographic nuances best addressed by leaders closer to the details. Additionally, this approach allows lower-level leaders to leverage peripheral vision, detecting emerging patterns and strategizing accordingly.

Science and Practice of Strategic Leadership

Consistent with the literature, Infosys possessed one unique core competence, as the original creator of the Global Delivery Model. The original strategy of the company was to have smart, values-driven software experts in India charge discounted prices for customers in the developed world. From Porter's perspective, Infosys was able to initially compete based on low cost and twenty-four-hour programming support in a specific focussed niche: software outsourcing. From a core competence and resource-based view of the firm perspective, since Infosys was, in the beginning, one of the only firms that had demonstrated consistent customer delight with a labour arbitrage model, it had demonstrated that it could uniquely deal with the infrastructure, skill and governmental constraints of India to leverage the low-cost high-skilled work force in the service of global customers. From Mintzberg's research on emergent strategy, Infosys has recognized opportunities as patterns emerged, and appropriately evolved the strategic initiatives.

After many years of revision, the following behavioural definition of strategic leadership for Infosys has emerged:

Leaders must:

- create strategies that are consistently ahead of the competition
- proactively adapt his/her vision of the future in advance of marketplace changes
- devise ingenious approaches to create unique value for external or internal customers.

Facility Differentiators—Amazing Campuses

Early in Infosys's history, when the founders decided to focus on the US and other developed markets, then CEO Narayana Murthy consciously decided to build facilities that would reframe Infosys and even India in the eyes of the customers. In particular, ILI's headquarters were the first to be built on the campus near the global headquarters in Bangalore, to be on par with the campuses of General Electric's famed Crotonville.

You will recall from the chapter on Infosys's history that beautiful buildings were one manifestation of a long-standing company strategy to gain respect in the eyes of all stakeholders. Infosys always sought to 'become a globally respected software company providing best-of-breed software solutions delivered by best-in-class people'. Infosys's many

The Infosys Leadership Institute headquarters building in Mysore

ILI Mysore has resort-like accommodations for the customers and leaders who visit the campus, and especially for the 36,000 new engineers who will be hired in 2010

spectacular campuses were conceived not after Infosys became large but rather in the 1990s when the cost of the campus was more than the company's annual income. The vision was to create an atmosphere where the infrastructure gave the clients the confidence that Infosys was on par with the best in the world, and to create a work environment where Indian software professionals could thrive in an increasingly competitive labour market. High speed connectivity, captive power generation and state-of-the-art customer care centres ensured that the offshoring experience was seamless to customers globally with well-cared-for employees.

Infosys, Bangalore

Infosys, Bangalore

Infosys's resort-like settings are designed to nurture employees with an inspirational ambience beyond even what other global organizations provide. At Mysore where ILI is headquartered, employees of all levels enjoy recreational facilities such as basketball courts, swimming pools, a health club, a music centre, a yoga room, cricket, track and field sports, rock climbing, an eight-lane bowling alley, a fitness centre with a special enclosure for aerobics, an amphitheatre and a four-theatre movie multiplex. Infrastructure needs are addressed with designated buses for transportation, medical facilities, a bank, ATMs and a travel counter. The sheer scale of the Mysore facility is another aspect to Infosys's differentiation. In 2009, Infosys launched the largest building in post-Independence India on the Mysore campus, with an area of over 1 million sq. ft, to teach new engineers. As many as 15,000 students can be taught simultaneously on this campus when the need arises. This is a key part of the overall positioning of the organization and facilitates scaling up in human resources to meet changing market needs. And Mysore isn't the only Disney-like campus that Infosys has. The pictures demonstrate a striking contrast between Infosys's levels of excellence and what some foreign customers are used to thinking about India.

The Flat World Advantage and the Global Delivery Model

While Thomas L. Friedman was interviewing Nandan Nilekani, then Infosys CEO, Nilekani noted that 'the playing field is being levelled' (Friedman, 2005) because of rapid globalization and the growth of China and India as significant players. This resonated with Friedman and he used it as the inspiration for his bestselling book *The World Is Flat*. Infosys leveraged the publicity that it got from Friedman's work to clearly articulate the benefit from its Global Delivery Model to its customers.

Consistent with Mintzberg's recommendations, Infosys leadership emphasized that excellent software and related services could be delivered to customers anywhere in the world, which was at once a key differentiator, brand and strategy. The idea was to consistently increase productivity and returns by using technology intelligently to leverage a global talent pool, providing labour arbitrage.

Infosys's operational effort was on intelligently breaking down and distributing the work. Customer-facing tasks needed to be done in collaboration and in the same geography with the customer, while software work could be done offshore but meeting the highest standards of quality. To execute these seamless operations with flawless customer support, centres were opened in locations beyond India—in Mexico, Latin America, Poland, Czech Republic and China—to meet the needs of global customers.

Strategy Execution and Scorecard

Strategic leadership requires that the strategy adopted is actually translated into operations. In 2002 Infosys adopted a scorecard approach to ensure that the strategic imperatives were broken down into the appropriate deliverables for all levels of the organization. The balanced scorecard is a framework created to help clarify the lead indicators of strategy execution, so that they can be managed in the service of financial and customer outcomes (Kaplan and Norton, 1996).

Infosys, in fact, became the first IT consulting and services company worldwide to be recognized in the Balanced Scorecard Hall of Fame for executing strategy. The award was based on five key principles:

(1) mobilizing change through executive leadership; (2) translating strategy into operational terms; (3) aligning the organization around its strategy; (4) motivating to make strategy everyone's job; and (5) governing to make strategy a continual process.

At Infosys, during the annual planning process, previous strategies are revisited and realigned as needed. New strategic themes, objectives and initiatives are identified with active participation from all members of the senior management team including the Infosys Board, keeping in mind corporate intelligence garnered by an independent team to include internal and external views. The strategic initiatives, across themes, are then prioritized based on their impact to objectives. The portfolio is then managed through an internal portal (Infy Plus) by the corporate planning group.

Infosys's scorecard is the underlying mechanism that allows the organization to integrate strategy formulation, execute across its various units, link key performance metrics and ensure optimization of budgetary plans against strategy. The key steps followed in the scorecard development process are as follows:

- Every strategic objective has a set of lead and lag indicators identified to create a set of metrics.
- All potential metrics are suitably evaluated to ensure that they will facilitate company strategy implementation.
- These metrics are filtered through an assessment process. They may be financial or non-financial.
- The corporate scorecard is then converted into an alignment matrix for all members of the executive team to drive clarity on primary and shared goals.

This process facilitates monitoring on a quarterly basis. The review structure also enables timely corrections, creating a nimble senior leadership decision-making process. These control structures have enabled Infosys to deliver consecutive quarters of top- and bottom-line guidance to the market successfully both through the growth periods and the recessionary ones. But ILI is also examining solutions to some of the limitations of the balanced scorecard including lack of verifiability of root causes, and improving the meaningfulness of goal cascading to all levels of employees.

Predictability, Sustainability, Profitability, De-risking (PSPD)

As Infosys faced challenges it became apparent that it needed to buffer itself from customer, competitor and other risks to continue successfully on a planned growth trajectory. Infosys arrived at a governing rule for its risk reduction strategy, abbreviated as 'PSPD', so all leaders could work together toward the organizational goals in synchrony. Chief Mentor Narayana Murthy describes PSPD as:

> A good forecasting system for sales based on data gathered from the trenches ensures Predictability (although predictability of costs is also needed to have predictable profit streams). Sustainability is achieved by energetic and motivated sales people who pound the pavement and make sales happen; by production people ensuring that quality products are delivered to the customer on time; and by billing and collecting on time. Every enterprise must focus on high Profitability in order to ensure the best returns for its shareholders. Indeed, the long-term success of a corporation depends on having a model that scales up profitably. Finally, the corporation must have a good De-risking approach that recognizes, measures and mitigates risk along every dimension. The Degree of Affordable Risk (DAR) is a composite measure of the risk threshold of a corporation. Every corporation must measure its DAR, constantly improve its DAR.

The Risk Mitigation Group was set up after the incident introduced at the beginning of this chapter. The first commitment was to ensure that henceforth, Infosys as an organization would never again depend too much on any one client, technology, country or application area. The de-risking strategy has over the years helped the company stabilize its revenues and profit.

Another significant strategic decision that emerged as part of the continuous risk abatement focus was the investment Infosys made with numerous customers at the turn of the century when it aggressively pushed for Y2 K opportunities. The company realized that it was committing valuable resources to the effort that had a limited timespan; however, what it planned and successfully leveraged was the demonstrated value of offshoring. Some of these clients would not have experimented with it any other way and by consciously building trust and credibility Infosys was able to convert them for the long term. Most accounts that were started before the Y2K problem have now grown to $25–50 million in revenue.

Similarly, during the dot com bust in 2002, Infosys consciously maintained its work force despite the recessionary pressures, anticipating the market to open up rapidly after the downturn. When this happened the company was able to ramp up quickly to meet demand. This was repeated in the recent 2008–09 downturn where Infosys was the only IT company that did not lay off its employees but additionally honoured the 18,000 offers it had made to fresh graduates after campus recruitment.

The Emergent China and Australia Strategy

Infosys had been contemplating setting up an office in China, when fortuitously, Chinese Premier Zhu Rongji travelled to India in 2002 and was visibly impressed on visiting the Infosys campus. Learning about the interest from Infosys to enter China, he enthusiastically gave an on-the-spot approval. Infosys leveraged this opportunity and planned for a development centre in Shanghai. This city was the preferred choice because it had the infrastructure and the availability of engineering talent and it was felt that the company could replicate the Bangalore offshoring model here. The strategy to ensure success for the China subsidiary has been an evolving one: initially the focus was on making it a development centre for local business, but as Infosys struggled to penetrate this market it has slowly shifted to attract business from multinational corporations working in China. Since MNCs need to have a local Chinese joint venture partner, they are also comfortable working with IT support that is local. Infosys in turn has been able to build on its long-standing relationships with these MNCs in the US and Europe and offer them facilities in China. This subsidiary helps further the company's long-term strategy to access talent wherever it is available and needed.

The Australia subsidiary story is also one of taking advantage of opportunities that present themselves at certain points in time. Infosys had entered Australia in a small way, starting work with Telstra. As this business grew, in 2003 the chance presented itself of acquiring Expert Information Services Pvt Ltd with its existing work force of about 450 employees. This has enabled the Australia subsidiary to be a strong strategic arm for Infosys, with a local front end entity (sales and support) able to fully leverage the back end development work from India. The strategy was emergent and Infosys has piggybacked on the advantage to scale up its offerings in New Zealand and other APAC countries.

Infosys leaders have also shown their strategic leadership in initiatives that they have led within their individual domains. Using the Leadership Journey Series assessments, we identified three highly rated leaders who shared their approach to strategic leadership.

Domain-specific Verticals—Retail as a Pioneering Unit

U.B. Pravin Rao, Retail Vertical head and leader of the pioneering team that envisioned how Infosys would create its industry verticals, recalls the excitement in 2001 when this unit was launched as a pilot.

Infosys at that time already had long-term relationships with a few global retail clients. However, the focus up to that point was only around offering technology solutions to these customers. The new vertical structure provided an opportunity for Infosys to leverage and demonstrate its domain skills as well. In order to buffer the team's domain credentials in the near term, Pravin says that they consciously broke away from the 'grow from within' philosophy and decided that they should quickly acquire talent with deep retail industry expertise. While the efforts were underway, leaders like Patrick Ogawa, Anantha Radhakrishnan and Balaji Yellavalli, who had prior retail experience but were working in other parts of Infosys, were drafted into the Retail team to strengthen the domain expertise. Simultaneously, the unit also decided to start building intellectual property with its own unique retail offerings, appointing a Retail Solutions Council for oversight. The retail solutions were the best way to demonstrate deep domain understanding to the client and it started paying rich dividends. This complete verticalization by the Retail team gave it the first mover advantage as compared to its Indian competitors, TCS and Wipro.

However, Pravin and Manish Tandon (Group Engagement Manager for that period in Retail) pointed out that it is important to thoroughly understand the needs of the customers and create the strategic positioning appropriately by offering multiple levels of solutions to clients. 'Vanilla' or undifferentiated offerings do not work as clients are at different stages of adoption when it comes to IT outsourcing. In 2005–06, they found that while retail solutions was a big hit with retail clients, they were not able to make much headway in growing the CPG (consumer packaged goods) segment. On deeper analysis, they realized that the consumer packaged goods industry was just then getting into outsourcing, unlike the retail segment, and was therefore not ready for advanced offerings. Realizing this, the Infosys team reverted back to the American Development model (ADM). Once the clients built their own experience with outsourcing and saw its benefits they would automatically be open to more offerings. Today, in the CPG space, they have moved beyond ADM and have been able to sell CPG-specific solutions.

Strategic Change for Growth in CME and IMS

In 2002 when Anand Nataraj joined the Communications, Media and Entertainment (CME) unit it was called Communications and Product Services (CAPS) and had already achieved the distinction of having the highest number of new account openings in Infosys. However, as they analysed the growth potential of these accounts, they found substantial variation. It was clear that the group was diluting its energy, working on anything and everything. Consequently, in 2003, Anand and his sales team decided to refocus. Anand spearheaded the initiative to go after 'must have' high potential accounts. These were the most attractive, high-growth accounts that Infosys simply would differentially invest time and energy in. All other opportunities were only worked on by way of a request for proposal (RFP) response. This purposeful focus paid off because telecommunications companies were also consolidating simultaneously—for example SBC acquired Bell South which in turn acquired AT&T. This strategy saw the CME group grow from $60 million in 2004 to $580 million in 2008. Under Anand's leadership, the Infosys footprint in the CME space has expanded from being present in just one major operator, when he joined, to being present, when he moved on to his new role as unit head of Infrastructure Management Systems (IMS) in 2008, in:

- seven out of the top ten CSPs worldwide
- five out of top six NA telecom companies
- four out of the six top European telecom companies
- the top three cable companies and the top two ISPs.

As unit head of IMS, Anand looked at consolidating and growing IMS, 'moving from IMS 1.0 to IMS 2.0'. He did a complete analysis of existing capabilities and market positioning, especially as it relates to branding. In his quest to improve IMS branding, he is ensuring that strong relationships are built with deal consultants and analysts from Gartner–Forrester and is trying to position end-to-end Infra Transformation solutions to customers. From a capability perspective for strategic advantage, he is focusing on creating differentiators by enabling a culture of innovation, entering into new technology spaces such as Virtual Desktop Infrastructure (VDI) and cloud computing, and scaling up education through the IMS Academy. This strategy over the past two years has seen IMS revenues growing from 4.9 per cent of Infosys revenues in FY 2008–09 to 7.2 per cent of company revenues in FY 2009–10.

IVS Specialization Strategy

Manish Tandon moved into Independent Validation Services (IVS) as unit head in 2008 at the time when the economies of the world were heading towards a recession. Even as he was getting ready to join the group he realized that they needed to reposition fast as the market was being commoditized by a multitude of smaller players. IVS had the potential to grow rapidly and be a major unit in Infosys but in order to continue to maintain margins it needed to do things differently.

The first step in leadership in his mind was a clear articulation of vision in the near term. The salient features were that IVS needed to build and grow specialized services, counter commoditization and create verticals along domain lines. The specialization story could be built along several dimensions: horizontal testing solutions, verticalized functional testing solutions and package specific testing solutions. Each of these specialization types would lead to enhanced differentiation, much better customer value in terms of quality of output, cost and faster time to market, and hence much better price points at which customers were willing to buy these services. Here are some examples of each of the three dimensions mentioned above that will illustrate that strategic perspective:

1. A great example of a horizontal testing solution was a patented tool called Clearware that was created for data warehouse (DW) and business intelligence (BI) testing. This tool not only helped customers validate the output of their BI and DW projects but also created a mechanism for managing ongoing data quality issues in their production environment.
2. An example of a verticalized functional testing solution is e-commerce testing. Infosys found that 70–80 per cent functionality in a typical retail e-commerce site was the same and hence built a pre-packaged test suite to positively impact speed to market which is vital for any e-commerce site.
3. Finally creating automated regression test beds for standard package solutions SAP, Siebel, Peoplesoft and Finacle (Infosys's banking product) is an example of adding higher value to the client context in testing services.

As Manish reiterates, it is not enough to have strategy; implementation is the key. IVS in the last year, despite the recession, had a smaller drop in its revenue productivity because of the rapid move into specialization. The results in the current financial year that IVS has achieved have been quite impressive and they continue to see momentum of client demand for these services, significant differentiation against competition leading to better win rates, industry recognition in terms of patents and recognition and finally shareholder recognition because of enhanced growth and improved revenue realization. Manish modestly adds that the full benefits are yet to be realized, but he is optimistic.

*

Infosys has over the years shown dynamism in taking advantage of changing market conditions to move its long-term strategy forward. This was amply illustrated in the marketing push around 'How to Win in a Flat World'. The organization has constantly reorganized itself as the need has arisen and the nuanced approach to an emergent strategy is visible as we talked to the leaders on their sectoral goals. The strategies are not merely academic exercises—they are matched with equal focus on execution. The alignment of strategic imperatives to cohesive ground level planning and monitoring mechanisms is stressed through the processes that the organization has institutionalized, be it PSPD or the adoption of the balanced scorecard.

Bibliography

Barney, Jay (1991). 'Firm Resources and Sustained Competitive Advantage', *Journal of Management*, 17, 99–120.

Barney, Jay, Wright, Mike and Ketchen, David J. (2001). 'The Resource-based View of the Firm: Ten Years after 1991', *Journal of Management*, 27, 625–41.

Barney, Matthew F. (2009a). 'Leading Scientifically: Introducing the Cue-See Model for Evidence-based Leadership', Invited address, Society of Psychologists in Management (SPIM), San Diego, California, February.

Barney, Matthew F. (2009b). 'Enhancing Utility Analysis to Influence Your CFO: Introducing the Cue See Model', Poster at the 2009 Annual Society for Industrial–Organizational Psychology (SIOP) Conference, New Orleans, LA, April.

Eisenhardt, Kathleen M. (2000). 'Dynamic Capabilities: What Are They?' *Strategic Management Journal*, 21, 1105–21.

Friedman, Thomas L. (2005). *The World Is Flat: A Brief History of the Twenty-first Century*, London: Penguin.

Ireland, Duane R. and Hitt, Michael A. (2005). 'Achieving and Maintaining Strategic Competitiveness in the Twenty-first Century: The Role of Strategic Leadership', *Academy of Management Executive*, 19 (4), 63–77.

Kaplan, Robert S. and Norton, David P. (1996). *The Balanced Scorecard: Translating Strategy into Action*, Boston: Harvard Business School Press.

Lepak, David P., Smith, Ken G. and Taylor, M. Susan (2007). 'Introduction to Special Topic Forum Value Creation and Value Capture: A Multilevel Perspective', *Academy of Management Review*, 32 (1), 180–94.

Mintzberg, H. (1987). 'Crafting Strategy', *Harvard Business Review*, July/August, 66–75.

Penrose, E.T. (1959). *The Theory of the Growth of the Firm*, New York: Wiley.

Porter, M.E. (1979). 'How Competitive Forces Shape Strategy', *Harvard Business Review*, March/April, 91–101.

Porter, M.E. (1985). *Competitive Advantage*, New York: Free Press.

Priem, R.L. and Butler, J.E. (2001a). 'Is the Resource-based "View" a Useful Perspective for Strategic Management Research?' *Academy of Management Review*, 26 (1), 22–40.

Priem, R.L. and Butler, J.E. (2001b). 'Tautology in the Resource-based View and the Implications of Externally Determined Resource Value: Further Comments', *Academy of Management Review*, 26 (1), 57–66.

Prahalad, C.K. and Hamel, G. (1990). 'The Core Competence of the Corporation', *Harvard Business Review*, May/June, 2–15.

CHAPTER 4

CHANGE LEADERSHIP

PRADEEP CHAKRAVARTHY

> 'The ugliest caterpillar emerged from the chrysalis as the most beautiful butterfly.'
>
> —*Pradeep Chakravarthy, 2010*

The verb 'change' means 'to cause to be different and to give a completely different form or appearance to; transform' (Free Dictionary, 2010). In this process the organism or organization transforms its very essence and loses its original nature. The process of change may or may not be an improvement depending on the perspective of the passive observer or the entity being changed. Change in the context of organizations can no longer be treated with the mystery and wonder of what goes on within a cocoon or a chrysalis. Globalization, work force diversity, disruptive technologies and increasing complexities of business require companies to change constantly. This is so obvious that it has become a cliché. Nevertheless, practitioners of corporate change initiatives in Fortune 1000 companies in the US, for example, report success rates of well below 50 per cent, sometimes even as low as 20 per cent (Lucey, 2008). Ernst and Young (1992) suggest that as many as 75 per cent of transformational efforts fail to realize the results they originally sought, in the timeframe desired. The failure rate in the UK is similar (ZDnet, 2010):

- Companies surveyed in the UK lose £1.7 billion a year from failed change initiatives
- One-third of business process changes fall short of expected benefits
- One-fifth of businesses do not measure change management performance.

At the same time, the very definition of leadership has often included the activity of bringing about a new order of things. In this chapter, before we examine how leaders in Infosys have managed change, we will review some significant trends in the scientific study of business change.

Research on change in organizations has looked at the issue from two angles, one from an individual perspective of what an individual needs to do to be able to manage change successfully and the other from an organizational system perspective. Organization-level research focuses on what the organization as an entity must do to fully diffuse innovations throughout the enterprise.

Individual-level Change Models

Organizations today try to recruit and retain individuals who are willing to change constantly. Paradoxically, some of the highest achievers are also the first to oppose and resist change that the organization sees as essential for its own success. In an interesting comparison between biological theories of change and organizational change process, Van De Ven and Marshall (1995) compared biological change to organizational change. Biological theories assert that change in living organisms is either cumulative (every change continues to retain some elements of the past stage that are vital for the survival of the organism) or conjunctive (there is a common underlying process).

Biological theories of change also suggest that change may be within the organism itself. If change is so natural, why is change for humans still so difficult? Alvin Toffler's concept of 'future shock' provides one explanation (Toffler, 1970). Toffler argues that 'future shock is the shattering stress and disorientation that we induce in individuals by subjecting them to too much change in too short a time'. This fatigue of 'too much too soon' is compounded by what Darryl Conner (1993) calls the 'beast' within us. The 'beast' is the mental process that projects what we think will happen because of the change and, in the absence of information, assume the worst. The change itself is often not as intimidating as the possible consequences that are imagined to be mostly negative. Conner suggests that this mental state is affected by the following variables:

- Perceived threat to job security, power or position
- Trust in the management
- Information on future plans
- Influence of colleagues
- The individual's own need for achievement

Conner suggests that these factors cause resistance at the individual level of analysis. Very high levels of resistance to change from the individual often lead to reduced motivation, inertia and non-compliance. When it is particularly severe, resistance can manifest itself in the form of sabotage. Sabotage can take many forms, ranging from telling others not to change to leaving the organization, and can result in clinical depression. A study by Cap Gemini (ZDnet, 2010) focussed on the causes of failed organizational change. Their results suggest that 46 per cent of the executives cite the failure to achieve a project's original objectives, and 41 per cent cite the inability to achieve buy-in from employees.

Another line of research has focussed on individual-level factors across diverse geographies and industries (Peus, Frey, Gerkhardt, Fischer and Traut-Mattausch, 2009). This research suggests, first, that an individual's trust in the sense of justice is a significant influence on the level of resistance to change. Justice includes a) fair criteria; b) a fair process of communication; c) appropriate rewards for effective behaviour; and d) a clear connection between the output and the input.

Second, the research shows that the flow of information is important. All information, even unfavourable news, is important. Further, all information must link clearly and succinctly with the vision of the organization to ensure that the change remains obviously relevant to realizing ultimate goals. The researchers suggest that the most successful changes incorporate three channels of information flow:

- monologue: top-down communication
- dialogue: conversations with immediate superiors
- background: informal conversations with peers.

Organizational-level Change Models

Research and writing on change has also focussed on change at the level of an organization or a larger team composed of individuals. Researchers have developed a variety of models that account for successful change in an organization. Some are derived from empirical research and many are constructed from anecdotal field studies that we hope will be later tested empirically. Using a model, especially one that has been empirically tested, ensures that change leaders increase the chances of their success. Table 1 gives an overview of some of the major models of organizational change.

Table 1: Models of Change Variables in Organizational Change

Model	Variables	Variable Interdependency	External Environment	Assumptions
Force Field Analysis (1951)	Driving forces, restraining forces	Driving and restraining forces occur simultaneously	Either force may be due to environmental drives or restraints	Disequilibrium occurs during change; equilibrium is re-established
Leavitt's Model (1965)	Task, structure, technological and human variables	The four variables are interdependent (a change in one affects the others)	Not represented in the model	Change in the variables is undertaken to affect the task variable (products and services)
Likert's System Analysis (1967)	Motivation, communication, interaction, decision-making, goal-setting, control, performance	The levels of variables are measured independently on a survey	Not directly represented in the model	Four different types of management systems are identified based on the seven variables: participative, consultative, benevolent-authoritative and exploitative-authoritative
Weisbord's Six-Box Model (1976)	Purposes, structure, relationships, leadership, rewards and helpful mechanisms	The interconnections between the boxes, or variables, are not explicit	The environment has an influence through organizational inputs and outputs; the fit between the organization and environment is considered also	The larger the gap between the formal and informal systems within each variable, the less effective the organization

Model	Variables	Variable Interdependency	External Environment	Assumptions
Congruence Model for Organization Analysis (1977)	Inputs: environment, resources, history, strategy; throughputs: task, individual, formal organizational arrangements, informal organization; outputs: individual, group and system	Organizations are dynamic; interactions occur at the individual, group, and systems levels across the internal (throughput) variables	The external environment provides feedback related to the inputs and outputs	Assumes open systems theory, formal and informal systems, the fit or congruence between the internal variables
McKinsey 7S Framework (1981–82)	Style, staff, systems, strategy, structure, skills and shared values	Variables are interdependent; the illustration is termed the managerial molecule	Not directly represented in the model, although other non-crucial variables exist	Variables must all change to become congruent as a system
Tichy's TPC Framework (1983)	Inputs: environment-history, resources; throughputs: mission/strategy, tasks, prescribed networks, people, organizational processes, emergent networks; outputs: performance, impact on people	All variables are interrelated, although some relationships are stronger and some are weaker (reciprocal)	The environment is included through organizational inputs and outputs and the feedback loop	All variables are analysed from a technical, political and cultural perspective (the strategic rope metaphor)

Model	Variables	Variable Interdependency	External Environment	Assumptions
High-Performance Programming (1984)	Timeframe, focus, planning, change mode, management, structure, perspective, motivation, development, communication, leadership	The levels of variables are measured independently on a survey	Not directly represented in the model	Four different levels of organizational performance are identified based on the eleven variables: high-performing, proactive, responsive, reactive; these are associated with empowering, purposing, coaching and enforcing leadership behaviours respectively
Harrison's Diagnosing Individual and Group Behaviour (1987)	Inputs: resources, human resources; throughputs at the organizational, group and individual levels (lengthy titles); outputs: group performance, individual performance, QWL outcomes	Main lines of influence and feedback loops; all relationships are directional with the exception of one reciprocal relationship between two variables	Minimal boundaries between the organization and external environment	Assumes open systems theory, emphasis on three levels of performance, including organizational performance and QWL outcomes
The Burke–Litwin Causal Model of Organizational Performance and Change (1992).	Open systems model depicting twelve variables or factors	All variables are interrelated, depicting reciprocal relationships. However, the model implies a top-down causal chain	The external environment is included as an input variable with a feedback loop from the performance variable (i.e. outputs)	Assumes open systems theory, emphasis is on diagnosing transformational and transactional dynamics. The first model to assert causality

Model	Variables	Variable Interdependency	External Environment	Assumptions
Organizational Intelligence Model (2008)	Open systems model depicting eleven variables or factors.	The top part of the model depicts strategic factors that influence key indices that drive employee engagement and performance. While the variables are interrelated, the model asserts a top-down causal chain	The external environment is included as an input variable	It's not enough to measure employee engagement alone. The model emphasizes and serves as a framework to assess the strategic factors (i.e. secondary drivers) and primary drivers of employee engagement and performance

Table reproduced with permission from Falletta, S. (2008). *Organizational Diagnostic Models: A Review and Synthesis*, Sacramento, CA: Leadersphere White Paper.

Since it is one of the most evidence-based models, the approach by Burke and Litwin (1992) is especially important to understand. They identify some of the key factors that influence change:

Table 2: Change Factors According to Burke and Litwin

Variable	Conceptualization (i.e. descriptions)
External Environment	Any outside condition or situation that influences the performance of the organization, including marketplaces, world financial turbulence, and political/governmental risks
Leadership	Executive behaviour that provides direction and encourages others to take needed action; includes followers' perceptions of executive practices and values and leaders' role modelling
Mission and Strategy	What top managers believe and have declared as the organization's mission and strategy, as well as what employees believe is the central purpose of the organization; the means by which the organization intends to achieve its purpose over time
Culture	The collection of overt and covert norms, values and beliefs that guide organizational behaviour and that have been strongly influenced by history, customs and practice
Management Practices	What managers do in the normal course of events with the human and material resources at their disposal to carry out the organization's strategy
Structure	The arrangement of functions and people into specific areas and levels of responsibility, decision-making authority, communication and relationships to implement the organization's mission and strategy
Systems	Standardized policies and mechanisms that are designed to facilitate work and that primarily manifest themselves in the organization's reward and control systems (e.g. performance appraisal, management information systems, budget development and human resource allocation)
Climate	The collective current impressions, expectations and feelings of the members of local work units, which in turn affect members' relations with supervisors, with one another, and with other units

Table reproduced with permission from Falletta, S. (2008). *Organizational Diagnostic Models: A Review and Synthesis*, Sacramento, CA: Leadersphere White Paper.

In the end, models are only a lens to view the organizational landscape from a distance and give a different perspective that can be taken to mitigate the risk of the harvesting benefits. Each organization may have different dynamics. Individuals also shape the changes and within large organizations, with different geographical and service structures, the permutations and combinations can border on infinity. There also seems to be a gap between knowing and doing, despite such elaborate models. Lucey (2008) suggests that there are ten factors associated with poor organizational change; these are cited in Table 3.

Table 3: Factors Affecting Change Failure

Reason	%
Implementation took longer than planned	76
Major unanticipated problems occurred during implementation	74
Coordination of implementation activities was not effective enough	66
Competing activities and crises distracted attention from implementation	64
Skills and abilities of implementation team were lacking	63
Training and instructions to lower level employees were not good enough	62
Uncontrollable factors in the external environment affected the change	60
Leadership and direction by department managers was not good enough	59
Key implementation tasks and activities were not defined in enough detail	56
Information systems used to monitor implementation were not adequate	56

Change Leadership at Infosys

But how has Infosys applied these sciences? Next, we will examine leaders' experiences of the three types of change in the Infosys leadership framework:

1. **Change leadership** is about managing through resistance such that benefits can be fully harvested
2. **Adversity leadership** is about managing crises

3. **Transition leadership** is about acquiring and integrating new lines of business

Using the Leadership Journey Series discussed in earlier chapters, we identified five Tier leaders who are especially effective at leading change. Our purpose in interviewing them was to help other leaders gain insights into how you can learn from their experiences.

In sharing their experiences, three distinct themes emerged. The first theme was how the individual leader viewed change and how this powerfully impacted their ability and success to influence others to change. This theme was predominant, especially in the examples given by Nandita Gurjar, who unlike the other leaders had to manage change across the entire organization globally, at the highest level of impact and intensity in her role as the global head of HR.

The second theme involved changes at the level of a business offering. Infosys has business units that focus on domains such as the banking or manufacturing industries as well as units that focus on services across industries such as testing. B.G. Srinivas has had the rare experience of heading both a service (Enterprise Solutions or ES) and a unit (Manufacturing). His experiences in implementing and Managing change span both these kinds of sub-units at Infosys.

The third aspect was globalization, in particular, the increasing growth of Infosys into countries and cultures different from Infosys's roots in India. BG recounted his experiences in Europe while Suryaprakash (Sury) recounted his in China.

The Individual's Mindset

All the leaders interviewed agreed that much of the passion and energy that change requires had to come from within themselves. Each of them admitted that before they started on the change initiative, they took a lot of time to get educated on what the change was and became personally passionate that it was going to help. 'Either you get convinced or convince the other person it is not needed' was a theme heard from nearly all the leaders. Is this always practical? Can we get convinced all the time? The answer from the leaders was a yes, and for those who were not convinced, the data point they searched for was the overall benefit to Infosys. Once the benefit to Infosys was established, each leader put his/her concerns and doubts on the backburner and embraced the change wholeheartedly. For example, when a move to verticalize was announced, BG was not really for it but once he realized his organization needed it, he was fully supportive. He came into the meeting and said, 'We are going to go ahead and it will give us the best. Verticalization will happen and none of us will question this again.' He was behind it and expected his employees to be behind it as well. In BG's case, he was both a person impacted by decisions from superiors that changed his work, and also an agent of change to implement these improvements throughout his areas of responsibility. Manoj Narayan says he asks himself four questions before launching a change initiative:

- Am I, as a person, convinced about the need to change?
- Do I understand why and what needs to change?
- How are we to create meaningful change?
- How will I make it work?

'The answers to these questions determine the passion I will invest. It applies to internal as well as client situations,' he adds.

In Nandita's experience, people typically don't like change and they express this initially, even if it means good for them in the long term. Some get convinced by reasoning and data, while others require others' emotional support over a period of time. Problems occur when people shy away from the emotional support needed. All leaders agreed that after deploying a change, it was advisable to check individually with as many stakeholders as possible if things were going well and especially with those who were very reluctant to change.

When change is implemented, effective leaders are prepared for resistance. The very best anticipate the sources of resistance so that they, as the change agent, may see something others have not, and act accordingly. It is therefore essential that they are completely emotionally committed to the importance of the change. If this does not occur, the change leaders who are supposed to implement the change will not passionately overcome the inevitable resistance, and the change is less likely to succeed. To this extent, Nandita distinguishes impactful change from the revisions and creations of policy. 'Equating both together trivializes the former,' she says. Elaborating on this, she says she believes leaders need to distinguish between impactful change that will drastically alter the way an organization functions vis-à-vis a yet-to-emerge environment and smaller, more transactional changes that deal with the day-to-day operations. Both are important according to Nandita, but the former are more vital for the success of the company and are more difficult to champion and implement since they are for a future environment that may be difficult to envision for many in the organization, who believe 'things will continue to always be the way they are today'.

Manoj is a change agent who has managed complex engagements that have changed the way clients have worked. He was instrumental in winning a large managed services deal at a time when Infosys was exclusively working on staff augmentation projects. It was negotiated with a leading international bank on a project-by-project basis by contracting with 120 different IT services subcontractors. The client did not see the need for this at first and one of the first things that needed to be done was to create a sense of urgency of why this would be useful for the client's profitability in the long run. 'We followed data with several joint workshops and finally the client trusted our ability to manage the programme,' Manoj recalls. Creating a sense of urgency and following that with trust-enhancing measures are therefore important especially when the other person is not as adept as the change agent in proactively envisioning the future.

In Sury's case, his mental model needed to adjust to cope with global and cross-cultural issues. Sury's mindset changed when he assumed responsibilities for China, since there was an added culture variable. 'To be successful, I realized I had to change my mindset first. It was difficult for me to stop thinking of only delivery where the mindset was to get every delivery parameter right. I had to get into an executive leadership mode where everything on my platter was important, but some more so than others and demanded immediate attention and resolution,' he says. Sury reports that he had to prioritize in different ways to cope with leading change in China. He notes, 'Having accepted that at an individual level, made it easier for me to prioritize and progress.' The crux of Sury's learning is that it is vital for the leader to change their own mindset first and then develop a mental model to process information and prioritize tasks that are appropriate to the role and culture of the operating environment.

Leading by personal example is another key success factor. Manoj says this is true, especially when you create a new offering or framework that is intended to be used by a larger group. 'I have got my hands dirty by selling and winning deals through new offerings and in the process mentored and trained people to take up solution lead engagements,' he says, echoing a key precept of the Infosys value system, leadership by example.

For BG, his attributes of tenacity and persistence were important for him in resolving constraints. He recognized the need to get into consulting in order for Infosys to increase the value it creates for customers. He felt Infosys had to be a consulting-led unit. He realized that solely depending on lateral hires is not sustainable and began the Enterprise Solutions (ES) Academy to grow the next generation of talent. To sustain this change, BG influenced a separate pay and promotion structure; this was virtually unheard of at Infosys at the time. He led these changes effectively because he was persistent, and individually convinced people by discussing the future growth prospects for the successful adoption of the changes. The successful management of such changes also increased his reputation of getting things done. This reputation was an asset in future change initiatives when people would trust him more.

Citing another example for the need to be persistent, Gopal Devanahalli says he had an opportunity to be involved in a recent acquisition that Infosys carried out in the US. Gopal recalls, 'The process of acquisition spanned over twelve months. During this period the business environment dramatically changed because of the recent financial meltdown. Also the new company had a completely different business model from Infosys. All these factors made the acquisition extremely complex and a lot of traditional thinking had to be questioned.' Gopal feels that the key factors involved here were: persistence through the twelve-month-long process in ensuring interest and excitement on both sides; getting the stakeholders at Infosys to look at the possibilities by showcasing the right data and analysis; and having an open mind to look at a different business model.

The challenge for any leader is to balance aggressively adopting changes in the workplace, while not disturbing other existing pieces of work and not disengaging the workforce. Both Anand Nataraj and BG have been in this predicament when they had to discreetly support another change agent. In these cases, they needed to maintain a fine balance between enabling the leader to manage the change without becoming someone who that leader had to keep coming back to for help. On occasion, this may even mean a stern message of projecting the leader as the 'captain of a ship' and telling persistent dissenters to make a choice. In such situations, the leader who is helping their direct report (who is managing the change on their own) should keep checking if

(i) The person feels threatened with any possible negative impact either personally or professionally
(ii) There is conformance to the change
(iii) There is always value to the client
(iv) They are projecting their direct report as a leader to the larger community through small but important gestures such as introductions in mails, attending certain critical meetings (though the role holder may not be eligible to attend them) and coaching them to participate in such meetings effectively.

All Infosys leaders who were interviewed either implicitly or explicitly concurred that persistence was a key individual trait that was critical to being a successful change agent. Nandita goes so far as to say that this is more important when scale of implementation in change implementation is a complicating factor. She notes, 'Getting an elephant to dance is not easy.' In large-scale reorganization programmes like the IRACE (Infosys Role and Career Enhancement) transformation programme implemented in 2009, there is much more need to convince and reconcile agendas, often for very senior, experienced members. The influence at senior levels could take up to a year and consume 40 per cent of the effort. It is also essential for the benefits to be fully realized. In Mandeep Kwatra's case, emphasizing the business context for the need to change was essential in successful implementation of many initiatives. Understanding the technology implications were important but in his case, clearly articulating the business benefits substantially improved both the execution, the morale of the team as well as the delight of the client. Most leaders also indicated that they were able to convince others of implementing a change if they highlighted the business rationale.

Like Nandita, Rajeswar Rao gives another perspective on his own internal need to change during a new campaign. Rao believes that being humble when initiating change is important, since it is not just one person who makes a difference. His experience leading change in the past decade that he has worked in Infosys has largely been positive because of those around him who had high levels of aspirations and energy. For Rao, 'getting into the mindset that I was only a facilitator' ensured that he was more nimble in adapting and successfully solving issues that cropped up in implementation. He recollects, 'It helped to constantly remind myself that the best ideas are not always mine and the wisdom of the group is greater than that of each one of us.'

Changes within a Business Unit

Infosys has adapted different organizational structures over the years, from geographic to business line to today's matrixed structure. These sorts of structural changes can be among the most difficult to implement in spite of inevitable resistance, so the experiences of other leaders is especially instructive in this area.

BG is among the leaders responsible for the outstanding growth of Enterprise Solutions (ES) which today accounts for 25 per cent of Infosys's revenues and is among the largest employers with more than 13,000 Infoscions. ES was started in 1998 and launched in 1999. Soon after, its then head resigned. Chandrashekar Kakal was a senior leader and BG was recruited from another multinational to head the unit. As a new employee, he worked very consciously to build relationships and learn the Infosys culture as an early priority.

ES had 150 people at its inception. BG was very clear that ES's package services would be one of the largest contributors for the company's revenue and therefore believed that ES should be organized on the basis of different package services. ES was consequently reorganized into packaged services such as SAP, Yantra (later acquired by Sterling), supply management, Oracle and the TIBCO alliance. All of these teams were not called practices then but creating these groups made for a sense of focus for the groups and greater financial accountability.

For each group BG set clear stretch targets that were based on what the team could achieve. In most cases, targets were set individually with care that the individual was not overwhelmed and yet had a target that was not too easy. Rather than setting the target himself, BG would often ask his team members, 'What would be a stretch target for you?

Will it excite you? If not what excites you?' to get them involved in the target-setting.

The focus and clear, collaboratively set stretch targets helped in making some early small wins. These wins improved the team's confidence levels and therefore reduced resistance to change later. For example, at one time ES had only two or three PeopleSoft professionals but the team still bid on a large multi-million euro proposal. The team even got invited to the final round. ES didn't win but gained a lot of confidence to successfully bid for larger proposals in the future. In this way, BG led his team to consider failure as a part of change, and to be resilient and learn from failures.

Expanding on this, Gopal recalls his first change initiative in Infosys in 2005. He had to come up with a new way of structuring the sales organization to focus on large prospects. Gopal involved people from different units to debate the model that needed to be adopted, then had a few workshops with the sales leadership as well as the unit leadership team to explain the model and take their inputs to improve the model. The new structure was conceptualized and implemented in a short timeframe of six months. In Gopal's view this was possible because:

(i) Gopal personally understood the sales organization extremely well as he was part of it
(ii) it impacted a specific group (the sales group)
(iii) feedback was sought and incorporated at different stages, and
(iv) there was a strong executive sponsor for the change.

BG's simple, consistent messages with clear targets that were set consultatively were followed up with several communications reinforcing the focus of the change. The communications reminded the team of the need for change and nurtured the development of new team norms. Such communications made the messages much more ingrained in the team. BG was talking a lot about growth and that was his consistent message. It was always growth and nothing else was emphasized. His communication was therefore simple yet effective and uncluttered. He reiterated the focus on '70 per cent growth for the coming year with sustainable margins'. His employees could see his vision of becoming a 1 billion euro unit, even though at that time the unit was worth only 600 million euro.

BG led the structural changes in light of the message of the need for growth. The new model ensured that Group Engagement Managers (GEMs) had a lot more bandwidth to work with clients since another, more senior person took care of deal approvals. With BG's new model, four large deals, of 100–200 million euro each, were won. The model was clearly adding to the significant growth goals of BG's team. These bigger wins helped cement the popularity of the new model in the eyes of the team. Going back to the organizational models we discussed earlier in Table 1, this becomes a fine example that shows the use of interdependencies. The model also worked since it was not micro-managed by BG. He built his credibility with his team by getting quick approvals and making things easy for the team's new deals to be approved. Otherwise, he was more in the background, playing a supportive role and letting his leaders take credit for the model's new successes.

Anand used a similar approach as the one used by BG to lead change. When Anand assumed control of his unit, there were issues both with his new clients and his new team. With the markets, the rest of the organization was growing but his unit was not. The key measure in those days was the number of new accounts opened. Anand notes, 'After I joined Infosys and understood the culture, I did some analyses of the data. It appeared that although the metric made people open new accounts, it was not translating into higher revenue. This was because the scale and longevity was lower. It became apparent that consolidation was important. I was able to convince key stakeholders because of data and analysis.'

Anand demonstrates the importance of having data and facts to influence change; this is also part of the contrast effect noted in the chapter on relationship and networking leadership.

Anand focussed on a short list of 'must have' accounts, and the rest became accounts Infosys would service if the clients called and specifically asked for Infosys support. In this way, Infosys won several large multinational clients. In one case, Anand asked one employee to 'exit gracefully from an existing $50,000 account, much to his surprise'. Initially, the employee resisted, noting 'this is my first step to reaching my $3 million target'. Anand used data to convince him that the amount of time he had to spend on the account was simply not worth the effort. Anand's influence paid off because as the customer's contract was approaching expiration, 'though we were well placed to win them back, we did not apply. The individual with the increased time was able to focus and win larger accounts.' Anand's example teaches the lesson of opportunity cost—doing lower-value work today means we have to forego more valuable work later. Opportunity cost is often an impetus for leaders to make appropriate changes.

Anand's example demonstrates that all stakeholders, superiors, peers, customers and subordinates need to be aligned around the various types of change. Anand says, 'The buy-in should ensure it is an area of priority not just for you but for others as well, across the hierarchy. The change will be more effective with clear criteria for movement and coaching even to the extent of helping the person prioritize.'

Anand also notes the importance of enlisting all the people on the team to help influence changes. He recalls, 'When I joined a new business unit, revenues were low and so was our image amongst internal clients. We were never invited to deals and even if we were we never won any. It was seen as the head of the unit's problem and the first thing I did was to call the team together on this and convince people why it was their problem as well. We got several action points from a brainstorming exercise and picked the top three and simplified them so that they were easy to remember and identify with.'

Anand's team was focussed on three areas:

1. Branding
2. Developing end-to-end solutions and capabilities
3. Scalability

For the first, Anand's team created a simple, easy to remember, colorful presentation. He says, 'The key slide had a jigsaw of how parts of the strategy would fit into each other and what would be done for each person.' His team's focus paid off and branding by analyst reports improved significantly along with actual increased business.

In the other two areas, regular reviews and action plans helped further implement his changes. Within a year Anand's team was 'growing at 18 per cent in a tough market'—significantly faster than the competition. In two years, the number of deals that Anand's team were invited to bid on went from three to sixteen. Rewards and recognition were important in helping Anand's team weather the stormy changes.

Anand vigilantly monitored these results so that he could answer the employee's question, 'What do I get from the change?' He ensured that 'this was added to the goal sheet and then reviews were regular as was the celebrating of success, however small'.

Anand also reflected on the need for his operational excellence to improve. He remembers, 'Our ISOP (Infosys Scaling of Outstanding Performance, discussed in the chapter on operational leadership) scores were low for two years. Finding out why revealed that only three people were actively involved in the application process.' To drive these changes, Anand engaged his senior leaders; he 'had senior members as track leads and each of them could choose a smaller team. We also ensured there was collaboration within the team. The track leader reported to the sponsor but there was a high degree of freedom in how people did what they agreed to do. The lead acted as a role model even in seemingly small actions like preparation for meetings and updating trackers.' Anand made sure that small successes were celebrated with accolades for those who had collaborated on operational changes, and role-modelled other desired behaviours. Anand's team focus paid off, winning a 50-point improvement in the subsequent ISOP assessment.

Global Change

BG, Sury and Nandita all had experiences initiating and managing change across different geographies. When BG assumed leadership of the Europe business in 2004, it had a steady growth rate, but was only 13 per cent of Infosys revenue. BG had replaced a very popular and likable leader who had recruited most of the senior team. The team had some apprehensions about the new leader. But BG worked hard on his relationships, and within the first few weeks he had transitioned into the new role well, both from a people and a business perspective.

In his first meeting, he greeted the team and expressed sadness for his predecessor leaving. He was also careful in acknowledging the good work done by the team even though many expected BG, as the new leader, to say negative things about the past. BG's employees noted that 'he also displayed a high level of personal integrity' and 'spent time with his predecessor in the first week'. Importantly, BG's first week was focussed on relationships, and his people marvelled at how he 'got to know the team socially and did not discuss work'.

After the second week, BG spent time learning more about the team from a professional perspective. His predecessor walked him through data but BG wanted more information on the people. The team assumed he would bring his own people in but in the second week in a formal work-related meeting he said, 'We have an outstanding team, I am not going to change the team and structure.' His support of the existing team reassured them, especially because he had done it after speaking to each one of them from both a professional and a personal standpoint. BG followed the same approach of focusing on relationships with clients and other stakeholders as well, early in his tenure. (The chapter on operational leadership highlights the science behind why BG's emphasis on relationships is absolutely essential for leaders to be effective at leading change.)

BG worked with his team on the clear goal 'to get Europe back to twice the company growth rate path'. BG's employees note that his 'ability to communicate what he wanted the team to achieve is very good'. They add that he doesn't create an unrealistic ideal world, and the clear goals tell people where to place their emphasis. They also note that he follows his vision through persistently and tenaciously.

By the third week of BG's tenure, simple growth plans were made and he spent a lot of time with each of the team members. He pushed them to do things they would think were extraordinary. He de-emphasized operational details in favour of more strategic approaches; for example, when the agenda of a meeting was to discuss growth plans for accounts, many would bring up operational issues like the transfer of an individual. Such operational issues would be pushed out to other meetings, and the real growth-related issues such as strategies of positioning vis-à-vis competitors or increasing market share would be discussed. BG's questions stimulated the team to think at higher levels. His compliments helped them have the self-confidence to pursue change processes within their own teams.

When the time came for Europe to be split into a vertical organizational structure, BG got everyone involved and then announced the split. After the announcement, he knew there was still a lot of confusion and uncertainty in the minds of many and went to each and every person, checking the new perspective of the person post the reorganization—even of those who used to be in his team but were no longer with him. The mindset of keeping the organization's needs above others is important; in all reorganizations, BG never fought to keep his team intact and he always let his senior people go for a larger purpose.

One thing BG does well in leading change is that he 'has a good ability to focus on the positives and make them better'. He keeps people involved in all parts of the process, for example when 'the team said local Client Sales Group (CSG) hiring should increase, we should allow people to choose their vertical, local leadership, and we will not touch the HBU (Horizontal Business Unit) business, BG agreed and made it that way.' While Infosys Chief Operating Officer Shibulal's timeline was six months for the change, BG's team 'had an internal deadline and did it faster. This helped since by the new financial year the team members were aware of their individual roles and responsibilities and ready to go.'

BG also focussed on change communications. He held phone calls that he led, where everyone asked questions. Every question was answered; unanswered questions were listed and he made sure that he responded to every question eventually. Incidentally the first call occurred when a lot of rumours were 'flying around'. Knowing that negative rumours were being spread, BG said on the call that 'he wanted this group to feel proud of what we had done. He said he wanted to celebrate this.' Subsequently, he followed through on his vision of influencing a bigger budget and travelled to all the locations he looked after, to personally address the team. This increased people's confidence and comfort. He calmed people's anxieties by forming a committee where he said he 'would make sure every employee is taken care of'. One day before the reorganization, there was an 'all hands meet' where the transition team was announced. His team reports that these were key events that helped reduce anxieties of the team about the changes that were underway.

In the case of China, Sury's experiences were similar to BG's, even though the culture was unique. Sury began by clarifying his purpose. 'Why does my team exist apart from de-risking Infosys operations?' was an important question he worked on. He also realized that to lead the change, he had to be at the location. His first move was to physically relocate to China, a place where, he quickly realized, he had no control. 'Most of the days, I would just about accost every Indian I met to ask them simple questions I would have never bothered to ask in India—where did they live, where and what did they eat, how did they commute?' he reminisces.

He realized that change leadership involves going into details, especially when there are no precedents to follow. He had to understand the legal rules of China and when he did, he realized that there were opportunities to change small things that made a big impact. For example the insurance structure Infosys adopted for the employees could be legally reduced from 40 per cent to 19 per cent. Not only did this change save money for the organization but it dramatically improved his ability to hire less experienced people.

Sury's ability to secure the support of the next level of leaders was the most difficult, given the general belief and respect for hierarchy in China. Sury had to move the team's culture away from people doing work for Sury as the boss to doing it for the customer. This meant he needed to forge closer relationships with more than just his direct reports. So he began meetings with employees two levels below him using dashboards and consistent reviews. Knowing everyone by their Chinese names also helped.

Just as BG spent his early days building new relationships, after Sury built up a personal rapport, he launched new improvement initiatives such as the Capability Maturity Model (CMM). The fact that Sury went out of his way to be approachable for people to discuss their concerns and communicated announcements of changes well in advance of their implementation made them less resistant.

Understanding his boundaries in a new geography was a challenge for Sury. In many cases, he would make a decision and then would learn whether or not it was within his powers of authority to decide. Sriram V., to whom Sury then reported, was also proactive in supporting Sury's efforts to convert China into a destination for growth and systemically influenced IBU (Infosys Business Units) to do business in China.

*

Practice and theory must be used together for effective change leadership. The themes from across the Infosys change leaders suggest that establishing authentic, personal relationships before making changes is paramount, and being personally convinced of the need to change, persistence and patience in dealing with resistance, and appealing to the hearts and minds of those who may resist change are extremely important as well. In successfully deploying change the leaders noted the importance of having a clear message, of a strong business rationale, of role modelling, and of relentlessly monitoring and then celebrating small and ultimate victories. At a systemic level, it emerges that keeping relationships with all the stakeholders is vital for the change to succeed. Leaders who were able to influence different (but interdependent) constituents of an organization's system to lead to making the change succeeded. The models and the experience underlie the need for a leader who aspires to manage change successfully to be ever vigilant. As the second century AD Tamil text the *Naaladiyar* says, the wise one is one who 'realizes that tomorrow will be different from today and therefore does today what they would normally do tomorrow'. The mandate is not an easy one but the rewards are great; as Charles Darwin noted, it is not the intelligent or the strong that survive but those that adapt to change easily and quickly.

Bibliography

Alimo-Metcalf, Beverly and Alban-Metcalfe, John (2005). 'The Crucial Role of Leadership in Meeting the Challenges of Change', *Vision: The Journal of Business Perspective*, 9 (2), April–June, 27–39.

Bordia, Prashant (2004). 'Uncertainty During Organizational Change Types, Consequences and Management Strategies', *Journal of Business and Psychology*, 18 (4), Summer, 507–29.

Conner, Daryl R. (1993). *Managing at the Speed of Change: How Resilient Managers Succeed and Prosper Where Others Fail*, New York: Villard.

The Free Dictionary (2010). Downloaded 14 May 2010 from http://www.thefreedictionary.com.

Hambrick, Donald C. (1998). *Navigating Change: How CEOs, Top Teams and Boards Steer Transformation*, Boston: Harvard Business School Press.

Hoopes, Linda and Kelly, Mark (2004). *Managing Change with Personal Resilience*, Raleigh: MK Books.

Kotter, John P. and Cohen, Dan S. (2002). *The Heart of Change: Real-life Stories of How People Change Their Organizations*, Boston: Harvard Business School Press.

Lucey, John J. (2008). 'Why Is the Failure Rate for Organizational Change So High?' *Management Services*, Winter, 10–18.

Mason, Roger B. (2008). 'Management Actions, Attitudes to Change and Perceptions of the External Environment: A Complexity Theory Approach', *Journal of General Management*, 34 (1), Autumn, 37–53.

Oreg, Shaul (2003). 'Resistance to Change: Developing an Individual Differences Measure', *Journal of Applied Psychology*, 88 (4), 680–93.

Peus, Claudia, Frey, Dieter, Gerkhardt, Marit, Fischer, Peter and Traut-Mattausch, Eva (2009). 'Leading and Managing Organizational Change Initiatives', *Management Revue*, 20 (2), 158–75.

Toffler, Alvin (1970). *Future Shock*, New York: Random House.

Van De Ven, Andrew H. and Poole, Scott M. (1995). 'Explaining Development and Change in Organizations', *Academy of Management Review*, July, 2–34.

ZDnet (2010). Downloaded 14 May 2010 from http://www.zdnet.com/blog/projectfailures/business-change-failures-9-success-tips/1080?p=1080.

CHAPTER 5

OPERATIONAL LEADERSHIP

SATYENDRA KUMAR AND MATT BARNEY, PHD

'A few years ago, I outsourced a development job to Infosys, India and I have to say I was very positively surprised. The big difference is that they actually deliver on time and with quality. We have tried quite a few of the larger international mega vendors with results substantially weaker than what we received from Infosys.'

—*Lennart Åström, CIO, Alfa Laval, Infosys customer*

From its very inception as a company, Infosys has always stood for excellence. Our founders decided that we would be a company that strove to earn respect from all stakeholders. In part, they worked extremely hard to gain respect by consistently delivering significant value to these stakeholders. For us, operational leadership is about achieving goals as a matter of relationship integrity—to fulfil commitments that nurture long-term relationships with all stakeholders. As the chapter on strategic leadership outlined, flawless execution has always been central to our business strategy.

Infosys's results speak for themselves. If we didn't deliver consistently on our promises to customers, employees, shareholders and suppliers, we could never have survived, let alone thrived. As of 2010, more than

98 per cent of our customers renew their contracts with us. Investors have honoured us with a favourable price-to-earnings ratio. Infosys has won numerous global awards for transparency, governance and for being a great place to work for employees. In 2010, our Quality department won the prestigious IEEE Computer Society/Software Engineering Institute's Software Process Achievement Award, withheld for the previous four years.

We could not have achieved these results without a deep commitment to flawless execution. Operational leadership, in many ways, is a dominant attribute of leadership at Infosys because it is central to both our business strategy and our value system that revolves around Customers, Leadership by Example, Integrity and Transparency, Fairness, and Excellence (C-LIFE). Table 1 shows the relationships between Infosys values and operational leadership.

Table 1: C-LIFE and Operational Leadership

Value	Leadership Implication
Customer Delight A commitment to surpass our customers' expectations	Operationally excellent leaders direct operations toward consistently delighting customers
Leadership by Example A commitment to set standards in and be an exemplar for the industry and our own teams	Operationally excellent leaders role model operational performance to teach other leaders to be a beacon of light for performance and virtue
Integrity and Transparency A commitment to be ethical, sincere and open in our dealings	Operationally excellent leaders secure long-term relationships by being straightforward and by following through on our commitments to engender trust
Fairness A commitment to be objective and transaction-oriented, thereby earning trust and respect	Operationally excellent leaders do not hold on to past baggage, but rather objectively evaluate data and make balanced decisions
Pursuit of Excellence A commitment to strive relentlessly to improve ourselves, our teams, our services and products so as to become the best	Operationally excellent leaders are passionate about rejecting the status quo and achieving victories that others believe impossible

While operational leadership begins with relationships and values for Infosys, it ends in consistently realizing all of our business goals. These include consistently delighting customers, delighting shareholders, delighting employees and fulfilling promises to other stakeholders. The Infosys approach to operational leadership builds on the quality sciences from both academia—industrial/systems engineering, operations research and management science—as well as industry—Total Quality Management, Six Sigma, Toyota Production System (Lean) and Total Productive Maintenance (TPM). We have adapted, evolved and innovated beyond these classics with a wide variety of operational excellence practices, methods, toolsets and procedures. This chapter will review a full range of operational leadership methods from an Infosys point of view.

Senior Leadership and Operational Excellence

The Infosys board of directors (IBOD) is deeply committed to sustaining our culture of operational excellence. This kind of passion is perhaps the most important factor in sustaining our perpetual dissatisfaction with the status quo and our commitment to continual improvement. It's the source of our culture that pervades everything from the systematic use of quality tools to our employee performance management system that has 50 per cent of the leadership's pay at risk. As Table 1 notes, our company values devised by our Board strongly support operational excellence as our core business 'operating system' at Infosys.

The values of senior leaders set an example that drives actions in the rest of the firm, thereby creating culture. The scientific literature on organizational culture suggests that senior leaders are fundamental to creating shared values and beliefs that result in their individual behaviours creating organizational norms or ways of working (e.g. Ng and Sorensen, 2005). At Infosys, we believe that we have been able to scale our business globally with performance excellence over the last thirty years because of our founders' early culture of the relentless pursuit of increasing performance. While the vast majority of culture change efforts fail, Burke (2008) notes that those which succeed share the following characteristics:

(i) Top leadership support—including a commitment to change their own behaviour

(ii) Change built upon the natural strengths and values of the organization

(iii) Involvement of all levels of employees in changes

(iv) Holistic integration of processes: pay, training, hiring, information access, structure, everything is adjusted to support the new culture

(v) Planned actions, including involvement, education and detailed work plans

(vi) Stakeholder perspective, especially that of the customer, is paramount in directing the changes

(vii) Never-ending: the key factor for long-term survival is adaptability and change on an ongoing basis

Reflecting on Infosys's history outlined in a previous chapter, you can see major elements of Infosys's operational leadership culture that evolved from our origins. First, our founding CEO, Narayana Murthy, was successful at getting a group of people with complementary skills to subordinate individual preferences for the shared vision of a global multinational software firm. This rock-solid foundation of top management support for operational excellence has been extremely important to Infosys's success.

Second, Infosys's evolution with forays into software, hardware, services (BPO) and products (Finacle) has always been done in a planned fashion, especially since Infosys innovated the Profitability, Sustainability, Predictability and De-risking (PSPD) operating philosophy described in detail in the chapter on strategic leadership.

Goal-setting

For PSPD to work, it is essential for us to clarify our objectives to paint a picture of what success looks like before we begin. Once the goals are set, we use a myriad of ways to track our progress and make appropriate course corrections.

At the beginning of each year, our strategies are formulated and parallely, our goals are set. First, a balanced set of organizational goals are identified by the Infosys Board of Directors and unit Heads. Once finalized at the seniormost levels, the goals are cascaded down through all layers of Infosys globally, including the subsidiaries for each and every employee. These goals explicitly include operational performance improvement aspects such as resource utilization, work productivity enhancement and cycle time improvement.

One major practice for goal-setting is that they are done in a harmonized manner; the goals for productivity improvement are jointly driven by the business units and their respective 'business enabling functions', especially the Quality department. In effect, this provides a 'push–pull' effect to realize objectives.

Business Process Management

Many of the quality tools used today are designed to ensure flawless programme and project management, such that deliverables to customers are predictable, consistent and profitable. Also, Infosys's thirst for improvements has driven us to synthesize a wide variety of process excellence procedures and methods.

The ILI Leadership Journey Series of assessments includes a scale on operational leadership that defines successful operational leaders as those who:

(a) receive numerous compliments from customers
(b) exceed operational parameter targets
(c) demand the systematic use of improvement methods to drive improvements, and
(d) consistently execute new initiatives flawlessly.

This annual leadership assessment process is just one way that we consistently ensure a culture that nurtures operational leadership skills and encourages innovative new methods to continuously improve. In 2010, ILI in collaboration with the Quality department devised a set of 'road maps' that built upon our longstanding set of training and development options for leaders at all levels. Designed to help leaders continue to take their operational leadership to the next level, these are intended to help leaders, especially senior leaders, continuously improve their operational leadership skills.

Business Process Management: Alignment, Integration and Scalability

Infosys uses a wide variety of process design and improvement methods to increase the chance of realizing our goals. PRiDE is the platform we use to provide an integrated process framework that covers procedures, guidelines, standards, tools, benchmarks, systems and 'best practice' experiences that can be shared across the enterprise. This toolset facilitates easy access for every employee in the company to use standardized methodologies, processes and tools needed to execute their work effectively. Importantly, PRiDE and associated tools help Infosys employees focus on enhancing value to the client through a wide variety of quality standards (e.g. ISO 9000, AS 9100, TL 9K, ISO 14K, CMMI, eSCM, MBNQA, ISO 20K, ISO 27K, BS 25999) and toolsets modified from Lean and Six Sigma.

Key Roles and Structures

An important component to our approach has been the use of multiple functions and roles to ensure consistency, predictability, operational efficiency and effectiveness throughout our operations. Quality roles and structures are well established, from a basic infrastructure developed between 1993 and 1995, to better measurements connected to business processes from 1995 to 2000, culminating in the current focus on business value articulation, improvement in estimation processes and revenue productivity improvements in 2010.

Infosys's programme for systematic improvement, Infosys Scaling of Outstanding Performance (ISOP) was instituted in 2000 to promote excellence across all functional areas—from leadership to marketing in the service of customers. Every unit and function is encouraged to evaluate itself annually and high performers win prestigious awards given by Infosys Chairman and Chief Mentor, Narayana Murthy.

In addition to widespread and holistic structures, the quality function has additional specialized roles. Some look at the creation of new process solutions, process institutionalization (change), alignment and analytics of measurements with a clear eye toward business improvement. One special role is that of a Software Quality Advisor (SQA) that brings institutionalized focus in specific projects behind the scenes from a customer's point of view. Similarly, an Account Quality Manager (AQM) ensures that project execution delivers the value promised to clients. Figure 1 depicts the interrelationship between structural roles we believe are required to achieve operational excellence.

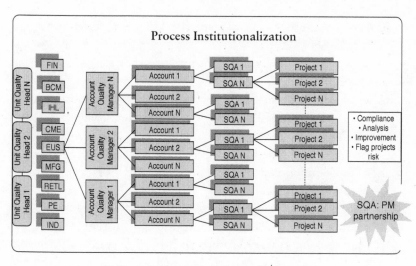

Figure 1: Infosys Process Institutionalization

Risk Identification and Management Focus

You will recall from the chapter on strategic leadership that Infosys's strategy evolved to leverage a variety of operational risk-mitigating mechanisms. De-risking is so important to Infosys—consistent with our core values around fulfilling promises—that we have two different functions addressing different aspects of risk. Whereas the quality function ensures that execution risks are identified across projects and programmes such that they are flagged for appropriate action, there is a separate Chief Risk Officer function that looks more broadly at organization-level risks.

This portfolio-based approach to risk identification and management is consistent with those approaches recommended by financial professionals around diversification. It brings a high level of visibility to contingency planning, especially for high risks that are highly probable to avoid any large-scale failures and mishaps that could affect a client.

Institutionalizing a Continuous Improvement Culture

A major thrust of Infosys's approach to operational leadership is investing heavily to ensure that the culture of continuous improvement is sustained. To achieve this we have six major thrusts:

(i) Improvement goals are set for all units, functions and employees.

(ii) Goals are aligned and harmonized so that support functions share line targets.

(iii) Frameworks from academia and industry have been adapted to Infosys including BRITE for resource and margin optimization, IMM rating of projects for high maturity execution, PROSO for optimized scheduling, ISOP for alignment and integration of cross-functional areas and lastly PRIDE for business process access and management.

(iv) Integrated workflow systems for end-to-end execution of various service offerings. For example Infosys's integrated project management systems ensure all aspects such as engineering, tools, financials, resource allocation and measurement systems are fully integrated, providing a seamless development environment.

(v) Clear methodology for improvement programmes. We have a formal change programme that includes an initiating sponsor, a lead, an anchor, and an appropriate selection of cross-functional experts. After the rollout of a change, sustaining leaders ensure that remedies are permanent.

(vi) Infosys strongly believes in the use of measurement and metrics for decision-making, organizational planning and performance improvement towards the achievement of key organizational results and strategic objectives. There is even a dedicated Measurement and Analytics team in the Quality department that ensures strategic and operational metrics are aligned, insights are provided to the session management for strategic decision-making and online measurement accessiblity is ensured for smooth process control on projects.

Figure 2 depicts both academic and industry methods that inspired the Infosys framework for operational excellence.

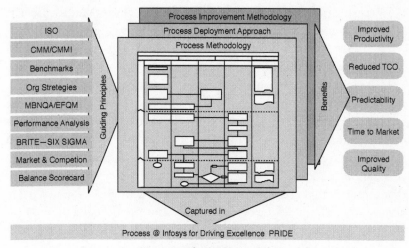

Figure 2: Infosys Frameworks

Research on Operational Leadership at Infosys

One of the areas the Infosys Leadership Institute is currently studying is continuing to improve the way the seniormost leaders make decisions about operational improvements. We're doing this both with research that examines the variables within leaders that predict operational excellence as well as with our own model of organizational effectiveness.

In 2010, ILI completed a global study of effective leadership that found that the biggest factor that predicted effective operational leadership is the leader's drive for excellence; similarly their high moral values, valuing time as a scarce asset and excellent decision-making skills were significantly predictive, accounting for 11 to 21 per cent of the total variability in operational leadership performance (Barney, 2009c; Barney, Shyamsunder and Patnaik, 2010).

Another area of inquiry for ILI is evidence for the usefulness of a new interdisciplinary model of organizational effectiveness called the Cue See model (Barney, 2009a, 2009b). The model tries to build on earlier work in industrial/systems engineering, organizational psychology, economics and finance to:

- improve the effective 'cascade' or 'flow down' of requirements from the ultimate Infosys, unit and operational goals into operational targets

- ensure that the portfolio of improvement efforts the leader selects are necessary and sufficient to realize Infosys-level goals

Based on work in a variety of goal-setting approaches including the Balanced Scorecard, Hoshin Kanri and Quality Function Deployment, ILI's research examines an interdisciplinary approach to help the seniormost leaders realize ultimate firm-level goals. Our premise is that operational risks are one subset of enterprise-level risks that threaten leaders' ability to realize Infosys-level goals. We suggest methods such that senior leaders are able to understand the sources of variation that threaten goal attainment and invest appropriately in remediating actions. In this way, leaders may be able to improve the likelihood that they achieve what the strategy requires.

ILI's approach suggests that the flow-down of requirements from strategy to processes is fundamentally a critical senior leadership task when setting organizational goals. Similarly, when planning quality improvement efforts, it is important for senior leaders to ensure that the entire portfolio of actions is likely to make appropriate improvements across the first six factors of ISOP such that the seventh—results—is highly likely at the level and in the timeframe desired by the strategy.

ILI's Cue See model (Barney, 2009) posits that all processes in a firm should be specified with four variables:

1. **Quality**: Ultimately, this is the degree to which the firm's offering in the marketplace delights the customers, shareholders and other stakeholders. At each process step inside the organization, however, process capability must 'add up' to this ultimate marketplace perception.
2. **Cost**: For the customer, this is the price paid. For Infosys, it is the combined total set of costs incurred to deliver the quality in the volumes and timeframe the customer desires. The price for the customer must be attractive to them; and the costs incurred must be small enough to realize ultimate margin goals.
3. **Quantity**: This is the volume of services, products or customers served as desired by strategy such that ultimate stakeholder goals are realized.

4. **Cycle Time**: This is the timeframe around which the other goals must be realized, in order to execute the firm's strategy on the desired schedule.

Together, QCQC is intended to be an easy acronym to remember (Cue See, QC), so that targets can be set and quality improvement actions taken across the organization to ensure that the strategy is realized. One preliminary success of the model was in 2010 when ILI used the Cue See model with the seniormost leaders of Infosys's Energy and Utilities Services unit (EUS) to help them identify the operational bottlenecks to realizing their goal of $1 billion in revenue. After some initial self-paced eLearning, the senior leaders collaborated in a workshop to identify the bottlenecks and plan actions to focus their attention, time and resources on the sales process that would need to improve to realize their aggressive goals.

Lessons Learned from Infosys Leaders

Consistent with the other chapters, we used ILI's Leadership Journey Series to identify leaders who were identified as exceptionally effective at operational leadership. The leaders included Ashok Vemuri, Yoganand T.D., U.B. Pravin, Sangamesh Bagali, N.R.A. Prasad and Srikantan Moorthy. As they reflected on their approach to operational leadership, they identified four key themes:

1. Attention to detail
2. Empowerment
3. Leading by example
4. Humility

Attention to Detail

If you reflect upon all the quality improvement methods, they all require the leader to understand goals, and the various operational improvement approaches that must be deployed to achieve them. A consistent theme that came across from all the leaders was that they really had to understand their business in all their dimensions to be effective. They had, over the years, built up sophisticated mental models of how their business works, so they can focus their valuable time and scarce resources on the actions that will make the most difference.

In Ashok Vemuri's case, he actually ended up creating new metrics to help him track key bottlenecks to achieving his goals, when the old metrics weren't sufficient. One example of this was his creating an account portfolio review down from the unit level to the account level to better track each account. He went out of his way to automate as much of the reporting as possible so he and his team could spend time on evaluation and interpretation rather than data collection. Ashok says, 'Every morning, I look at six to seven metrics,' and everyone in his unit knows this. He looks for the root causes of metrics that are unfavourable. For example, he notes that when he is worried about low utilization, he checks the 'pulse'—not just at the overall figure, but at visa utilization, skill set utilization, role utilization, country-level utilization and development centre-level utilization. All of Ashok's metrics are tracked in dashboards that are visible to everyone in the team, so everyone can have an appropriate level of detail. Ashok feels that 'information is a commodity' and that everyone should have the information—but that 'insight is sacrosanct'. He keeps the interpretation of the data closely held as a competitive asset, but empowers his team to leverage the same details he looks at to the benefit of the unit.

One way that all the leaders noted they keep their attention to detail is through the use of regularly scheduled reviews. Ashok notes that he has worked hard to 'create a culture that allows people to boldly make statements and take decisions'. He strongly values a diverse team contributing unique, and sometimes contradictory, perspectives so that he can step back and make the best decision possible. He recalls that 'surrounding yourself with different kinds of people is extremely important to be effective, but I didn't always do that. You'll be surprised where you get your next nugget for your business. I have found deep insights and thinking from people I least expected it from . . . there's a lot of intellect at the bottom of the hierarchy that should be utilized.' As an example, Ashok recalls that during a meeting a junior person suggested looking at a new ratio as part of the team's regular portfolio review. Ashok says it was 'absolutely fascinating' how this new metric had a mine of information about why the utilizations were so low.

U.B. Pravin, like Ashok, also works with his team to look at the 'leading and lagging indicators' before he takes action. He focuses on what he calls the 'critical parameters' of the systems and processes that drive his goals. Like Ashok, he goes out of his way to involve his team to drive operational process improvement. He emphasizes his role is to help his people 'have a good appreciation for how things work in the company' and why 'it's important to do things in a consistent and predictable way'.

Pravin also works with his team to make sure there are 'checks and balances' in the system. He notes, 'For instance, to make sure we track receivables well, I assign that to a team member and explain how the whole cycle works—the systems and processes. I coach them to see the importance of continually tracking these to make sure they're on track on all parameters.' Pravin points out that he has periodic monthly leadership meetings where the team comes up with action plans for improvement areas. His systematic review process ensures that they take action based on leading and lagging indicators. Part of his commitment to this level of attention to detail and measurement comes from an earlier role where he says he 'didn't do a good job of introducing metrics and measures to track the value of the solution to the client'.

Srikantan ('Tan') Moorthy emphasizes the similar themes of getting the entire team to understand the context first, and then break the vision down into pieces that can be accomplished by smaller groups, teams or individuals. Similar to Ashok and Pravin, Tan notes that he has a 'mental map' on the things that are happening all the time. Also, like the other effective operational leaders, Tan has regular, systematic reviews of his operations 'calendarized', where everything that was planned must get accomplished or else it gets escalated. He also notes the importance of a dashboard as part of these regular reviews.

N.R.A. Prasad and Yoganand T.D. ('Yogi') both echo the importance of attention to detail. Yogi notes that in his organization, 'we use a lot of data . . . we get data monthly . . . and I ask my team to analyze it and come up with their inferences'. Like Ashok and Pravin, he notes the importance of having the team members have a sense of ownership and self-insight into the operational gaps with their recommended solutions. Yogi further recommends the tool of 'mind mapping' when the team is unsure about how to approach a problem.

N.R.A. Prasad also emphasizes understanding how Infosys systems and processes work as a starting point to operational excellence, because they're 'quite well established' and worthwhile to leverage. He pays close attention to the actual people at the other end of the systems and processes, including customers. Importantly, he highlights the importance of the attention to operational detail of his customers, recalling that 'getting paid by the customer isn't always straightforward—their actual requirements aren't the same priorities as what may be initially stated'. He notes that you have to manage the operational priorities of critical versus non-critical customer requirements. At the same time, he finds that 'it's rare to find a client who knows all their systems'. His approach is to make sure he understands the operations of the customer, and maintains good relationships with them to finesse appropriate and timely payment in the context of the customer's own bottlenecks and relationships. Prasad recalls the importance of attention to detail when a large European customer moved their billing operations to Germany, 'All invoices had to be posted in Germany, regardless of what country we are in and where we do the work. When they changed the process, we promptly posted all our invoices but things weren't running well. We checked with the UK clients and discovered that all they do in Germany is scan the invoice and input it into the accounting system.' Prasad discovered that local people still had the final authorization to pay, so he took his electronic Infosys system and posted both to Germany and to the local country to get fast payment. Going out of his way to understand the customer's process in detail was key to getting paid in a timely fashion.

Similarly, Sangamesh Bagali has his operational aspects running so well on the account he manages that he says it's 'on auto pilot'. He notes that each team member contributes to billing, accounts receivable, revenue opportunities and tracking the resource schedule of projects. He says these are 'so religiously tracked that as a leader I don't need to follow up at all. Over the last four or five years, I've been fortunate that the team has helped me evolve the process to a certain extent so that any leader can get visibility to the team and operational aspects of the account well.'

Empowerment

All the leaders noted the importance of both delegating and energizing their teams to take operational decisions and have a healthy sense of debate. Pravin role models both the delegation and the enablement of his people as part of his approach to operational leadership. He says, 'I try to create a team that can help me execute . . . and give responsibility to drive processes and systems.' He adds that he looks at the enablement component as part of his approach to mentoring. To give his team members the appropriate perspective on operations before they make important decisions, Pravin says, 'I sit with them, I explain how things work, or I bring other experts to help them learn. I try to make sure people have a good understanding how these processes and systems are to be used.' He notes that he spends a significant amount of time coaching his people to 'see the importance of continually tracking . . . make sure they're on track on the parameters'. He notes that the vast majority of the time, this coaching happens in regular end-of-the-month leadership meetings.

Sangamesh's approach is similar to Pravin's; he 'entrusts and charges his team with operational responsibilities'. Sangamesh's approach to the development of his employees' abilities to make good operational choices involves rotating their responsibilities on a regular basis. This way, they have opportunities to learn and gain multiple perspectives—mental models—on different lead and lag indicators of operations. As a result, he says, 'They feel empowered that they have responsibility for the operational aspects'. But Sangamesh notes that in his earlier years, he 'had a habit of trying to do it all myself'. He notes that while he personally felt accomplishment from doing operations on his own, and felt things sometimes went more quickly, 'it was never as effective as entrusting my team'. Once he started delegating and helping each employee make better operational decisions, as the group grew he noted that 'the continuous improvement came as a by-product when we worked together as a team'. He worked to make sure the repetitive tasks were automated so that the team could focus on the more important parts of operational improvements.

Ashok's approach to empowerment is similar, and includes a proactive design of a team that will have diverse perspectives. He says, 'I surround myself with three kinds of people, so I get a balanced view.' He strives to bring in people who 'won't defend me if I say the sun rises in the west, but will support anything logical I say, and who have a balanced view'. He actually seeks people with extremely opposing views on topics, but who are 'smart enough to converge' into a final team decision.

After selecting diverse teams, Ashok works to create an environment within his leadership team for a 'free and open exchange of ideas'. With a diverse set of perspectives and the supportive collegial debate environment that Ashok provides, he is able to 'stand back and evaluate all the options' before making operational improvements.

Leading by Example

Yogi's approach to role modelling came from his very first job as an elevator service engineer. He worked with people with very basic skills, and they would jointly ride a bicycle together to the job sites where they would repair broken elevators. He remembers, 'The first two days it was pretty scary to get into the shaft. I let the helper do it on his own at first. But while he was cleaning, I wouldn't have a clear view of the work, so I climbed in. Once I got in, I could see that my helper was in tears. He said that he had seen a lot of people come into that role, but no one had tried to understand it.' Yogi could appreciate first hand that, 'If it [the shaft] is not well ventilated, people's eyes will start burning from the kerosene and chemical grease.' He began to help the team member greasing the right and left sides of the shaft, which improved their relationship. Even today, he uses this approach with his direct reports, so he's role modelling the very things he wants his employees to do, and makes sure his leadership respects their perspective.

Ashok is also a strong practitioner of leading by example. He looks at the root causes of gaps, such as low utilization, by looking into deeper levels of detail. Understanding his operations in detail every morning enables him to 'send an e-mail by 8.30 to a delivery head asking why a particular set of resources were not used in Bhubaneswar,' he says. He also gets a daily report on new sales acquisitions—'what we are getting from existing clients and new clients'—and uses the customer relationship management software system to understand the key conversations the sales force is having with customers. He helps people follow his lead by making dashboards of performance widely available. For his direct reports, he role models how to cull out the relevant parts of operational details, including changing the metrics when that is required.

Prasad role models leadership by doing the hardest things himself, to encourage subordinates to also work on the toughest tasks so as not to set up direct reports to fail. He shares the fact that he has 'butterflies in his stomach' if he fears an invoice isn't going to be paid on time, so that the entire team shares the anxiety.

Humility

Every leader also noted that they made mistakes, and made sure they learned from them. Ashok, for example, noted an early lesson he took away from when he first became the unit Head for Banking and Capital Markets. He told his people they needed to go from 75 to 90 per cent fully utilized, and 'it brought the unit to its knees'. He recounts, 'I didn't realize the remaining 25 per cent have a job to do when they're not being billed.' He came to the realization that there needed to be time allocated for training and other value-added work that wouldn't be billed in the current period, but was needed to sustain operations. He notes that the lesson he learnt is the reason why he surrounds himself with people who will have different perspectives and might not always agree with him.

Pravin also displayed humility when he describes an earlier role where he led a consulting unit at Infosys. He says that one of the reasons it eventually got merged with the current Infosys consulting unit was that 'we weren't able to adequately show the value this group was bringing to the company'. In reflecting upon his work, he notes that he did a good job leading processes and systems for solutions but didn't feel he did a 'good job of introducing metrics and measures to track the value of the solution to the client organization . . . we didn't do a good job controlling it, killing poor solutions early.' He points out that there is now a group that looks after intellectual property, and the metrics that enable the killing of poor operational initiatives. Pravin strongly advocates junior leaders to:

(a) identify the critical goals of the unit
(b) understand lead indicators that will forecast successful goal attainment
(c) put a process in place where you can measure things
(d) periodically review progress and perform corrective actions based on gaps, and
(e) constantly refresh the process, making sure all factors are considered.

Tan's humility was displayed in relation to leading communications around operations. He notes that previously he sometimes made the 'assumption that you say something to one person and it would flow down or up to others'. Now, he proactively has periodic, calendarized interactions with all key stakeholders. Today, in his current role as head of education and research for Infosys, he conducts these meetings less formally, talking about other things to make sure communications flow effectively.

Bibliography

Barney, M.F. (2009a). 'Leading Scientifically: Introducing the Cue-See Model for Evidence-based Leadership', invited address, Society of Psychologists in Management (SPIM), San Diego, California, February.

Barney, M.F. (2009b). 'Enhancing Utility Analysis to Influence Your CFO with the Cue See Model', Poster at the 2009 Annual Society for Industrial–Organizational Psychology (SIOP) Conference, New Orleans, LA, April.

Barney, M.F. (2009c). 'Innovations in Global Leader Selection at Infosys', in Delany, T. (Chair), Showcase of Successful Global Selection Systems, SIOP Leading Edge Conference, Denver, CO, 16 October.

Barney, M.F., Shyamsunder, A. and Patnaik, S. (2010). *Leadership Journey Series Validation Technical Report: A Test of Evidence-based Leadership Hypotheses in a Global Infosys Sample*, Mysore: Infosys Leadership Institute.

Burke, W.W. (2008). 'Organizational Culture Change is NOT About Changing People's Mental Sets', Presentation for Distinguished Professional Contributions Award (2007), Society for Industrial and Organizational Psychology Annual Conference, San Francisco, CA, 12 April.

Detert, J.R., Schroeder, R.G. and Mauriel, J.J. (2000). 'A Framework for Linking Culture and Improvement Initiatives in Organizations', *Academy of Management Review*, 25, 850–63.

Ng, T.W.H. and Sorensen, K.L. (2005). 'Linking Organizational Culture and Performance: Creation of Employees' Social Capital', presented at the Twentieth Annual Meeting of the Society for Industrial and Organizational Psychology, Los Angeles, CA.

CHAPTER 6

TALENT LEADERSHIP

ASHOK KACKER

As trade barriers have been removed and transparent global communications have become fast and inexpensive, most products and service offerings have become commoditized. As the chapter on strategic leadership suggests, the elusive sustainable competitive advantage in most cases does not come through differentiated products and services but rather from unique resources in the firm (Barney, Wright and Ketchen, 1991). In many cases, the only assets to meet such a standard are employees (Wright, Dunford and Snell, 2001). Each person is unique, and cannot be commoditized. Based on the firm's founding talent, each enterprise develops its own unique character. We typically call this character 'organizational culture' which is a manifestation of the talent of the senior leaders that is used to connect all employees toward the firm's mission and vision. But in the end, the building blocks for advantage are the individuals who work for a company. How we manage them is a key driver in securing a competitive advantage.

There is a large body of research showing a significant relationship between employee attitudes, customer attitudes and profitability (Heskett, Jones, Loveman, Sasser and Schlesinger, 2008). The lesson from the research on the service–profit chain is that we cannot expect disengaged employees to satisfy our stakeholders. Employees who are disengaged are a symptom of a leader who needs to change the way they work. All leaders are required to lead teams. This can be an aggregation of people or true followers who chose to be led outside of the lines of formal reporting relationships. The true mark of a leader is when he/she has followers. For this, it is important how he/she inspires his/her people.

This chapter deals with how we lead people. There are six distinct steps in the life cycle of talent leadership:

- Selection
- Induction
- Goal-setting
- Feedback
- Developing people
- Employee engagement

As noted earlier, the Infosys Leadership Institute conducts a multi-source, 360 degree assessment called the Leadership Journey Series for its senior and high-potential leaders. In the November 2009 study, the following leaders scored among the highest among their peers on talent leadership: U.B. Pravin, K. Murali Krishna, K. Suryaprakash (Sury) and Ramesh Chogule. For this chapter we interviewed each of these four leaders for their views on what they believe they do today that is so effective in leading their talent, and lessons learned from their younger days when they weren't as effective as they are today. While a full excerpt of these interviews is given at the end of the chapter, some salient points have been mentioned in the relevant sections earlier.

The chapter starts by reviewing several methods for assessing people and psychometric tools that can be used as predictors for success. Next, it will cover effective methods for inducting new recruits. However, it could be argued that the most difficult kinds of talent leadership are situations where a leader inherits an existing team of people to lead. Because of the importance and difficulty of this task, the bulk of the chapter will focus on leading teams a leader inherits.

Selection

Most leaders spend a great amount of time and effort in evaluating investments in physical assets. But the very best know that leaders' careers are made or broken based on the team they select. What should we be looking for when choosing a team? The most important questions to answer while selecting employees is: What work is required? Do I understand what job tasks and good 'citizenship' behaviours I need in order for my team, process or firm to successfully realize its strategic objectives?

At the Infosys Leadership Institute, we have devised our selection procedures for leaders based on our own internal models of what predicts successful leadership. While education may be necessary as a precursor to being able to have the skills and knowledge required to perform, in the end there is a lot of variability in leadership performance of even educated people.

To successfully measure the likelihood of successful performance, a significant amount of research points to the following predictors that are best measured in work samples, structured behavioural interviews, or other psychometrically validated instruments. Eminent industrial–organizational psychologists Frank Schmidt and John Hunter did a seminal study that summarized eighty-five years of science to understand what factors best predict employee job performance. Their findings are summarized in Table 1. The column labelled Validity summarizes the ability of a predictor to account for job performance, independent of any other factor being used, and is a correlation coefficient ranging from -1.0 (strongest negative, or inverse relationship) to zero (no relationship) to 1.0 (the strongest relationship possible). Schmidt and Hunter note that many of the lower-validity methods such as experience do not add incremental information that isn't already explained by cognitive ability or integrity-test variance.

Table 1: Selection Procedure Validity Summary
(from Schmidt and Hunter, 1998)

Predictor	Validity
Work samples	.54
General mental ability (intelligence)	.51
Employment interviews (structured)	.51
Integrity tests	.41
Peer ratings	.49
Job knowledge tests	.48

Predictor	Validity
Training and experience (behavioural consistency method)	.45
Job tryout procedure	.44
Employment interviews (unstructured)	.38
Biographical data measures	.35
Conscientiousness tests	.31
Reference checks	.26
Job experience (years)	.18
Training and experience point method	.11
Years of education	.10
Interests	.10
Graphology	.02
Age	-.01

By far, the best two methods to select talent are the cognitive ability test and the work sample at entry level. However, once we are looking for people who are at middle or senior levels, general mental ability may be necessary but is certainly not sufficient. One important meta-analysis of leadership that summarized data from 40,000 leaders in 150 studies suggests that follower perceptions are more than two times better at predicting leader effectiveness than actual objective measures of intelligence (Judge, Colbert and Ilies, 2004). Deep domain expertise that may only come from experience in performing similar job tasks in prior roles is likely to be more important. Similarly, a middle or senior leader's learning orientation, his/her ability to learn, team playing attributes and initiative are important.

At Infosys Leadership Institute, we have devised a variety of these methods as part of our Leadership Journey Series, with advanced computer-adaptive multi-source assessments to gauge likelihood of effective performance. Our 360 degree surveys use the advanced Rasch Measurement technique that removes the leniency and severity bias of raters, to make sure all ratings are fair, accurate and sufficiently precise. We are in the process of using these for both selection and for development, but typically look at different factors for each application.

In recruiting and selection, leaders have to make trade-offs between the different things they want in their team—skills and traits, knowledge and experience. Different prospective employees have different strengths and weaknesses. People effective at talent leadership weigh their selection procedure to focus on attributes that aren't trainable, such as cognitive ability, values and personality traits. What some people call 'proactivity' has sometimes been considered a trait (e.g. conscientiousness) or value (e.g. the need for achievement). Importantly, a significant amount of research suggests that leaders with an orientation towards becoming a master will be more proactive than those who learn only enough to perform or avoid punishments (DeShon and Gillespie, 2005; Day, Harrison and Halpin, 2009). Similarly, effective leaders have to work collaboratively with peers and customers in teams. Many jobs require knowledge and skills, but some skills can or should be developed once the employee is hired. This is an important strategy especially when there is a scarcity of talent with the technical knowledge and skills required by the job specification.

U.B. Pravin recognizes that individuals have different capabilities. He spends a considerable amount of effort in identifying what his people are good at doing and then creating opportunities for them to show their talent. In one case, he recognized the passion of an individual to work in innovative domain areas and assigned him the task of creating intellectual property (IP), and succeeded. If he had ignored this person's interests, and put him in, say, project management, Pravin suspects that the employee may not have succeeded.

Sury also believes choice of people is important and it is better to spend time in choosing the right person or identifying the leaders to invest in if you inherit a team. Once the team is chosen, he firmly believes in backing them up. One of the things he learnt from his superiors is to have people align to the big picture of what is important for the group or unit.

Induction

Once selected, it is important to make sure the employee smoothly transitions into the new environment, ramping up performance to the full level required. ILI recommends several leadership actions to help employees launch their careers into new roles successfully:

(i) Spend time not only in familiarizing the new employee with company operations but also the key aspects of the company's values and working culture. While formal induction programmes are helpful, full socialization is best done by the person's manager and mentor.

(ii) Assigning a 'buddy'—someone with significant experience but at a peer level to the employee—can give the employee additional insight from someone who is like himself/herself.

(iii) Create an environment where the employee feels comfortable expressing ideas. One of the key benefits of bringing in experienced hires is that they come with fresh perspectives on things that worked in other workplaces. If we wish to benefit from new ideas it is important that we listen to ideas with an open mind and acknowledge these contributions. Any attempt to evaluate him/her at this stage or shooting down new ideas ('We have tried it before, but . . .') will lead him/her to withhold good ideas in the future.

Finally, once fully on board, the key challenge for the leader is keeping the employee fully engaged. The remainder of this chapter focuses on this phase of the employee's career, because the key challenge for the leader is mostly about keeping the team fully engaged throughout their life cycle.

Employee Engagement

Goals are the reason for organizations existing. Leaders clearly play a role in goal-setting, and at the same time, the individual needs to work with the leader to ensure alignment. Nevertheless, misalignments do occur. When they do, it is the leader's responsibility to make course corrections, or else he/she will fail as the leader of his/her team. But all relationships are two-way—this chapter therefore does not presume that an individual has no role to play in this alignment; rather the chapter's focus is on what leaders must do.

What Should a Leader Do?

A key factor in employee engagement is the organization's culture—the supporting ecosystem with its policies, systems, ways of working and processes. However, as Marcus Buckingham (1999), after reviewing a

Gallup study of over 80,000 managers, suggests, 'The talented employee may join a company because of its charismatic leaders, its generous benefits and its world class training programmes, but how long that employee stays and how productive he is while he is there is determined by his relationship with his immediate supervisor. People leave their immediate managers, not the companies they work for.'

A good culture and climate is only as good as the experiences that an employee has with his/her manager. Conversely even when the ecosystem is not supportive, the manager can through his/her interactions minimize the impact.

Employee engagement is about how well the employee feels connected to the mission of the organization at the macro level. Similarly, at a micro level, engagement involves feelings about the goals/purpose of the immediate team. At a personal level the question is: is an employee proud of being part of the team/organization? This connection is strongest with immediate supervisors and therefore every individual manager has a role to play in keeping the team engaged. Finally, the creation of the organization culture itself is a function of how leaders engage with their teams. The aggregation of these individual behaviours of each leader is what forms the organization's culture.

As leaders, our role is to create such a culture by first role modelling the desired behaviours ourselves with our direct reports. This will have a cascading effect within the larger team. Because of this important, waterfall-creating effect that leaders have on their teams, this section focuses on developing employee engagement from the point of view of what each individual leader can do to enhance it. To help each leader improve their skills in engaging your team, the remainder of the chapter will share:

- Perspectives of leading thinkers on employee engagement. A common theme is employees will be engaged if they have some control over their destiny.
- One way to do this is to empower people. We therefore look at experiences on empowerment in different organizations.
- Processes to distribute decision-making in the organization are traditionally the focus of empowerment, but this chapter offers a different perspective that goes beyond decision-making.

- Prerequisites for empowerment and related areas like performance management.
- Beliefs leaders hold that can get in the way of empowerment.

Why Are People Not Engaged?

A wide variety of writers have considered numerous perspectives on motivation, from intrinsic to extrinsic perspectives. Herzberg (1987) argues that motivation comes from job enrichment. Argyris (1998) argues that it comes from internal commitment which is closely linked to empowerment. Manville and Ober (2003), building on the Athens model of democracy, argue that commitment comes from shared values, one of which is moral reciprocity (e.g. 'What's in it for me and what's in it for us?'). The importance of this concept of reciprocity for all relationships including talent is covered more extensively in the subsequent chapter on relationship and networking leadership.

Henry Mintzberg (2001) argues that 'beneath the current economic crisis lies another crisis of far greater proportions: the depreciation in companies of community—people's sense of belonging to and caring for something larger than themselves'. He further suggests, 'Communityship requires a more modest form of leadership that might be called engaged and distributed. Community leaders see themselves as being in the centre, reaching out rather than down' (142). Central to this perspective on engagement is Argyris's (1998) argument that when people are in control of their destinies they are motivated. In order to align individual destinies to that of the organization, a leader's style needs to be participative. Participative leadership suggests that people are included as an important part of the decision-making process. Many people call this empowerment—giving people the opportunity to participate in deciding the course of action.

But do people actually take charge of their destinies? Do they actually take ownership of both the process of decision-making and the decisions?

Significant evidence supports the idea that self-efficacy—having the confidence to make these choices and trade-offs—is central to the ability to feel empowered and perform. A seminal meta-analysis that summarizes other research examined 114 studies including 21,616 employees and found a correlation that self-efficacy accounts for around 28 per cent of the variability in job performance—more than goal-setting (10 per cent), feedback (14 per cent) or behaviour modification (17 per cent) (Stajkovic and Luthans, 1998, 252). This research suggests strongly that if people have the confidence to make the choices and trade-offs, they will; but when they lack that self-confidence they will not.

Consider one real world example. Almost sixteen years ago Robert Frey and a partner bought a small, troubled company in Cincinnati that made mailing tubes and composite cans (sturdy paper containers with metal ends). The product line had not changed in twenty years. Profits were marginal. Labour costs were out of control, job definitions were rigid and union relations were poor.

But as of 2003, they started making a new mix of highly differentiated, specially protected, environmentally responsible composite cans. Their work force became flexible and deeply involved in their success; strict job descriptions were a thing of the past; they have not raised the contract wage for eight years; and their relations with the union are excellent. What's more, the company is doing well in a demanding market and making a lot of money. How did they achieve this startling turnaround? According to Robert Frey employee empowerment is one part of the answer. Profit-sharing was another.

Frey describes how instead of making decisions on his own, he posed the issues to his team and asked them to consider the trade-offs. His rationale was that, 'There are no concessions you can squeeze from me. Or, to put it another way, there are no concessions I won't make.' He cites the example of the vacation policy. He told the group, 'There's only one pot of money, and that's profits. You can use your share any way you like. You can have them in cash or in vacations.' The team decided they would rather have the money.

Reflecting upon this successful transformation, Frey concludes, 'No company can change any faster than it can change the hearts and minds of its people, and the people who change fastest and best are the people who have no choice. No choice pushes people to change. Empowerment has meant asking them to share the profits and the responsibility. They like the profits but not the responsibility. Empowerment is only possible when workers and managers are capable of taking the power offered.'

A question is why people are not capable of taking the power offered? Is it possible that they do not have the self-confidence to go down that path? Is that lack of confidence coming from lack of procedural knowledge to pull it off? What stops them from taking charge? This chapter suggests two perspectives. First is the issue of creating an environment within the organization that promotes empowerment. Second, is each individual leader supporting the individuals he/she looks after?

Empowerment at the Organization Level

Many studies have looked at why empowerment has succeeded and why it has not across a wide variety of firms. Butler and Waldroop (1999) suggest that it is lack of 'matching people to jobs that allow their deeply embedded life interests to be expressed'. Similarly, Lee (2010) found that 'individuals were more willing to experiment with the new system—to try out something different—when their department managers consistently did two things: explicitly stated that making mistakes would be okay, and refrained from punishing employees for errors'.

One researcher who studied failed empowerment efforts, Fonestei Russ (2000), says 'empowerment is a tantalizing notion that seems to offer organizations the promise of more focussed, energetic and creative work from employees. But after years of trying, many organizations have not realized the promise the idea held.' Russ presents some reasons why: precipitous empowerment mandates, overreliance on a narrow psychological concept of empowerment, a one-size-fits-all approach to empowerment, neglecting the needs of power sharers, deployment in a piecemeal approach and a distortion of accountability. Russ suggests, 'The shortfalls in empowerment that many organizations have experienced are more about flawed implementation than flawed conception . . . there are ways to correct what has been limiting the success of organizations that truly want to empower employees.'

Argyris (1998) argues that, 'CEOs subtly undermine empowerment. Managers love empowerment in theory, but the command-and-control model is what they trust and know best. For their part, employees are often ambivalent about empowerment—it is great as long as they are not held personally accountable. Thus, despite all the best efforts that have gone into fostering empowerment, it remains very much like the emperor's new clothes: we praise it loudly in public and ask ourselves privately why we can't see it. There has been no transformation in the work force, and there has been no sweeping metamorphosis.'

Empowerment versus Delegation

Most studies have looked at empowerment from the point of giving people the right to make decisions. But there are many situations when leaders have given this authority and told people to decide, and they still have not. The question is why? I strongly suggest that giving people decision-making rights is delegation of authority, not empowerment. Giving people the authority to make decisions may be necessary for empowerment, but it is not sufficient.

In our day-to-day lives there are many situations where we ask someone to do a job. Many a times we realize that he/she could be constrained by the fact that he/she does not have the authority to decide a course of action or choose between two alternatives. In many such situations we correct this by giving him/her the relevant authority to decide. Our diagnosis is that we have given him/her a responsibility but not the adequate authority to discharge his/her functions. Once we give the person the authority we expect him/her to now do the job. Have we in such situations seen that despite giving him/her the authority he/she continues to not exercise it or come back to us to cross-check? To understand empowerment we need to understand what causes this kind of behaviour.

One possible scenario could be that though we have given the person formal authority we still expect him/her to check with us before taking the final step. Could it be that our words convey granting of authority but our actions suggest to him/her that we are expecting him/her to consult us?

Let us now assume that we have indeed both by our words and by our actions conveyed in no uncertain terms that we are vesting authority in him/her. In such cases if he/she does not exercise this authority why does he/she not do so? The research suggests that in some cases a lack of self-efficacy or self-confidence in exercising this authority may be the root cause. This lack of self-confidence can come from many factors:

- We have not explained the big picture. There are facts about the context in which a decision has to be taken. These facts have not been communicated to him/her.

- We have not armed him/her with the skills that are required to perform the job.
- We have not involved him/her in the goal-setting process.
- We have not provided him/her with the resources required to perform the job. Such resources include inputs required from or influencing others on whom he/she has little control.
- We have not created in him/her the belief and confidence to overcome his/her fears about making mistakes.
- We have punished him/her in the past for making wrong decisions.

Whatever the reasons for the lack of self-confidence, unless it increases the person is unlikely to act independently in a manner which is consistent with the overall business objective.

Empowerment is all about creating such self-confidence in people we work with. Empowerment is not about giving them the power to decide or the authority to act but enabling them to act self-confidently towards reaching a shared objective. True power does not come from formal vesting of power. True power is the power of knowledge, influence and confidence.

Empowerment at the Individual Level

When we look at empowerment from this wider perspective, we need to examine what we need to do as leaders to empower people. These include:

- Getting employees to see the big picture—getting them to understand how their contribution fits into the overall objective
- Creating ownership of the goals they manage
- Providing the necessary resources and support they need from you and from others
- Enabling them to acquire the skills and knowledge required
- Supporting their learning when they make mistakes, to help them be resilient in the face of their own decision-making

If we are convinced that our role as leaders is to empower others, there are some important prerequisites.

Prerequisites for Empowerment

Shared objectives

When objectives are shared, people work in one direction. Their energies are not diluted by pulling in different directions. The most desirable scenario is when people are involved in formulating the objective. For them to do so, we need to share information that we have on the environment and other relevant facts that must be considered in arriving at a choice they make.

When people are part of the process of decision-making they take ownership of the decision. This is not an exercise in using as many techniques as possible that will cajole people to see the leader's point of view. Approaching a discussion in such a manner requires us to keep an open mind on all alternatives, and more importantly keeping an open mind on ideas that might come from others even though they are radically different from ours.

When objectives are shared each person takes ownership. Ownership is not mutely accepting a decision that must be carried out but genuinely believing it is the right one. Does this mean that decisions must be arrived at by consensus? Not necessarily. What is important is not whose conviction prevails but that whichever has the most merit prevails.

The alternative is to decree a goal for the team. There are times when this might be necessary as the formulation of a strategy and direction is based on information that may for strategic reasons be restricted to a few. In some cases we have a vision and we do not see others fully comprehending it or buying into it. Even in such cases explaining to an appropriate degree the broad parameters under which the direction is arrived at helps people see why we are moving in the direction we have chosen. Within the broad directions we could brainstorm specific shared objectives to be reached. In these cases, however, there is a greater responsibility on the leader to drive the team and demonstrate that the choices made indeed do succeed.

Regardless of what method we use, for an objective to be shared, the solutions must proceed from the basis of mutual gain, known as a 'win–win' situation.

We can see these general themes play out when we examine the successful strategies of Infosys leaders identified as effective talent leaders. While assigning responsibilities, Pravin agrees on some core values and outcomes. Once agreement is reached, he gives his team members absolute freedom and supports them as required by providing mentorship, investments, creating an environment to perform etc. Similarly, Murali spends a lot of time in communicating with his team. He has regular weekly meetings with his leadership group. This serves as a platform for collaboration, exchanging happenings and seeking support and guidance. Murali has regular meetings with his larger group too as he travels globally to locations where his team is present. Yet another technique he uses is 'corridor management' (managing by walking around).

Just like Murali, for Sury, communication is the key. Sury spends time with his immediate team in agreeing on the strategy and purpose. Once this is done, the clarity of purpose and direction is reinforced in group meetings that he has with the larger team. Sury believes you cannot sit in a room and run the organization based on what comes to the table. You have to know the pulse on the ground and deal with it proactively.

When groups are large (say 4,000+ people in a unit), written communication is important. People look to the leader to have clarity, vision and purpose. Actions through the year should align to the stated purpose. Sury sends out not more than two or three communications to the larger team every quarter, but spends time to formulate them, and yet keeps them informal so that they are conversational in style and that the conversation can be continued in face-to-face meetings with groups of people.

Adequate resources

While empowering people we need to ensure that we have given them all the resources they need to meet the shared objective. Similarly when we want to empower people, before they can assume new roles they may need to acquire the necessary attitudes and skills.

The cornerstone of Ramesh Chogule's approach to talent leadership has been developing his team's effectiveness as consultants in their practice. His belief is that in a knowledge industry helping employees grow in their knowledge and skills adds significantly to their long-term career goals. This is a key factor for them when choosing between career options.

Performance Management

Leading the team's performance could be argued to be the reason for having a leader in the context of executing strategy. One aspect of performance management is helping employees understand why certain performance measures are set for him/her in the context of goals the organization wants to achieve, ideally in a participatory manner as described earlier.

However, it is important that the goals are clear to him/her. In workshops I have conducted I often ask people, 'Why do people not do what we ask them to do?' I have found that in most groups the top reason given by leaders, on introspection, is that they had not clearly communicated what they wanted. There are two variations to this that I have normally found.

1. Expectations have not been clearly defined.
2. Expectations are articulated but they are at variance with what the performance measures are.

In one case, the CEO complained that people were not delivering. The performance measures set for them were on sales volume and they were meeting them. His disappointment was that while they had met sales volumes the margins were not adequate. The CEO admitted that he had never set down margins as an expectation, let alone a key expectation.

Yet another factor that comes into play is the balance between the short term and the long term. If current performance is limited to short-term number achievements, this is what people will focus on, to the detriment of long-term objectives that are vital to the company. Sometimes long-term objectives can be measured through milestones. In other cases there is no objective mid-course measurement and the results come in one spike. Worse, the effort may not get any tangible results but provides learning on what does not work.

Finally, the key question is: Does the performance management system encourage individual performance over team performance? Most endeavours today require team effort. It is therefore necessary that performance measures are such that reward team performance and do not set up individuals in competition at the cost of teamwork. One can argue that in a competitive world it is a reality that individuals compete and those who do not contribute to team goals do not get the benefit of others' work. It is, however, equally a reality that to succeed in the outside world it is the team effort that counts, and not individual effort. So it is important to set some goals that are dependent on team achievement.

There are three levels at which this can be done:

1. Performance measures should balance individual, team, short-term and long-term goals.
2. At the time of annual performance rate most of the individuals based on their absolute performance as poor, fair, good, very good. For a limited number, say 5 per cent, rate them as outstanding. For these people who are rated as outstanding, the leader must give a justification on why they are considered outstanding. The recommendations should be ratified through a panel. These 5 per cent are the people who are the high potentials.
3. Payouts relating to performance must emphasize team achievements, particularly at senior levels.

Goal-setting

While setting targets, Pravin does it from the bottom up, seeking inputs from the team. He finds that people do not low-ball targets, since you trust them, and they do take stretch targets. When the bottom-up approach on target-setting does not add up to what the organization expects, Pravin explains to the group and marks up the targets. He believes that setting unreasonable targets does not work. In such cases people already believe the targets are not achievable and therefore do not even try to achieve them; obviously, this is counterproductive. A large amount of research by Ed Locke has supported the use of difficult but achievable goals as central to effective goal-setting (Locke, Shaw, Saari and Latham, 1981).

Feedback

Finally, it is important to give feedback as part of the process of empowerment. In many cases I have found that people are not clear about what they want to communicate. Two common mistakes leaders make are:

1. Reaching a judgement without really listening to the other person.
2. Hesitating to give negative feedback as it might hurt the other person.

In both cases, we are viewing our responses from what it does to me, the leader, rather than how it will help the person who is getting the feedback. If we are sincere in our effort to improve the person's performance so that he/she grows, eventually they will appreciate our feedback. Part of the feedback will be positive and, where sincerely given, this boosts motivation. But if the compliments are not well deserved, they can do more harm than good.

Pitfalls

Even though some leaders provide all the prerequisites for empowerment and an effective performance management system, empowerment fails at times. Here are some possible pitfalls to keep in mind:

- Pain vs gain
- Belief in people
- Fear of redundancy
- Fear of mistakes
- Creating a win–win situation
- Walking the Talk

Pain vs gain: Is it worth it?

Empowerment requires the investment of our time, money and energy now, while often the results come in much later. In such a situation there is sometimes a temptation to do the job yourself rather than invest time in equipping another to do it. The pitfall is that if you continue to do the job yourself, every time the job needs to be done you will be forced to do it yourself. When we spend effort in empowering others we are preparing them to take care of the situation for all times to come. Temptations to give up on empowering can be very strong. The more pressing the need for a response the more tempted we are to abandon empowerment. Such responses are natural because they meet the requirements of the moment. The only way we can decide on staying with empowerment is first deciding whether the gain is more than the pain. The gains are not just the tangible ones. They could also be the increased involvement of the individual, the creative inputs that he/she could bring to the job, the new ideas that could be generated, the satisfaction that he/she would gain when he/she overcomes a new challenge etc.

Pravin finds that micro-management does not add value in most cases. He also finds that when he does not micro-manage he is emotionally detached and can take objective decisions where required. Similarly, Sury experimented with micro-management early in his career. The project went into turbulence, recovered and delivered to great customer delight. He was rated a high performer. But in the process his team was exhausted. He felt like he was running all the time. Sury realized there was no delegation, no sharing of the big picture. It took him a lot of time to move from micro-management to outcome-based management, and that helped him grow in the organization as he provided space for his next level to take responsibility.

Belief in people: How do we view people?

Through our past experiences we have come to hold certain beliefs about others. These beliefs dictate how we respond to people. Belief in others determines how far you are willing to go in taking the effort required to empower them. In order to invest time and effort in empowering people we need to first believe that they have the ability to:

- Comprehend the big picture
- The motivation and maturity to decide appropriate goals
- The inclination to acquire the needed skills and knowledge

Our belief starts with first believing in people as individuals. When we believe that they are, just like us, eager to take on challenges, they are, just like us, wanting to raise their self-esteem, we are likely to then view whatever limitations they have at this point as part of a natural process of evolution and development of an individual. After all, many of us did not start our lives with all the knowledge, skills and wisdom in the world. We acquired them as we went along, and so can our people. We acquired expertise because we had a purpose in life; so can they. We acquired them because we wanted to grow as individuals; so can they.

Belief also determines how you respond to people. Many times our responses tend to reinforce our beliefs. When we expect positive contributions from a person our response encourages him/her to take actions that reinforce our positive beliefs. When we expect negatives from a person our responses lead him/her to take actions that only reinforce our negative image of him/her. This is the power of self-fulfilling prophecies. What we fail to recognize is that the results are not just the results of actions he/she takes. His/her actions are determined by how we respond to him/her.

Our beliefs about others are also dictated by what we believe about ourselves. If we feel that we work when we are pushed, we are likely to believe that others also work only when they are pushed. If we are hesitant to take decisions, we believe others are also likely to be hesitant to take decisions.

Pravin says fundamental to his leadership approach is belief in people. Sury also says that while one is required to be firm and professional on the outcomes, it is very important to build personal bridges with the next level, as you need to understand and relate to them as people. You also have to actively show interest in their careers.

As Murali worked on the challenges in his unit, there were times initially when he felt he was going nowhere. He persisted. One of the things that helped him was the realizations about the capability of this team. Since everyone was going through a lot of change, he focussed on giving more support, time and space.

Fear of redundancy

Often a consideration is whether in the process of empowering others we are moving to a position where we as the leader are rendered redundant. This is correct: we are indeed moving to a position where we become redundant. The redundancy, however, does not have to do with us as individuals or as leaders but is in relation to our present role.

When we empower others it allows us to get the time and energy to strengthen the abilities and attributes that are uniquely ours. It also allows us the time and energy to develop abilities and attributes that are necessary to assume a higher role. It affords us the bandwidth to consider the strategic competitive landscape rather than consume ourselves with work our team members can perform successfully without us. How can your boss give you higher responsibilities if you're still needed to do your old job because you grew no one else to take your place?

Fear of mistakes

A crippling fear is that those we empower would make mistakes. They will. What is important is how we view mistakes. You make mistakes when you try something new. It is a part of learning. In travelling that road, mistakes would teach us what does not work. The expertise literature suggests that it takes 10,000 hours of concerted practice to work at the highest levels of performance (Day, 2010; Ericsson, 2009). The first few thousand hours will certainly be less effective than the ten thousandth.

Creating a win–win situation

Empowerment in the long run will succeed when everyone sees a win for themselves. The win for you as the leader may be the ability to get more done. The key for you as a leader is to understand your people well enough to know what they care about and help them see how achieving the goals and making decisions on their own toward the goals helps them achieve their personal goals.

Walking the Talk

When we empower people they also look to us for direction. Their own belief in what we are asking them to do is strengthened when they see that our actions are consistent with what we say. This is particularly true in situations where difficult choices have to be made. The choices we make are far more powerful than empty slogans, plastic cards or banners. The key to empowerment at an individual leader level is evaluating our own beliefs that promote or hinder empowerment and working on them.

Successful Talent Leaders at Infosys

In this section we summarize what each leader told us of their approach to talent leadership. While all four examples of effective talent leaders in Infosys had, on the surface, different approaches, there were eight themes in common:

1. They all held belief in the ability of people to be responsible and take ownership.
2. They spent time in understanding their people and what interest them.
3. Their role was to match these interests with the organizational goals.
4. They spent time in giving their teams the big picture and how their efforts fitted in.
5. Theirs was not a 'soft mollycoddling' approach; they reached clear understanding on approaches and objectives.
6. Once these agreements were reached they left it to their people to deliver; they did micro-manage when required but not as a rule.
7. They ensured visibility and recognition for their people.
8. They acknowledged mistakes and learned from them.

U.B. *Pravin Rao*

There are fundamentally three aspects that Pravin has used in dealing with people:

(i) Recognizing that individuals have different capabilities: His effort has been to identify what they are good at and then creating opportunities for them to show their talent.
(ii) Listening to people: He found that even in cases where he has not been able to fully solve their problems, by listening his people felt they have been heard.

(iii) Being transparent: Transparency creates belief in people about your intent.

As a consequence Pravin finds that even when they are personally not in agreement with his decisions, his team members recognize that he is fair and will not compromise with the unit's objectives.

RECOGNIZING CAPABILITIES

Pravin recognizes every individual is different. He spends time in discussing with individuals what their interests are, what they have done in the past that corroborates their interest and based on intuition decides what kind of a job would interest them. In creating a sales group Pravin did not limit himself to people with a sales background. He looked around in all streams and was able to leverage the varied experiences and capability to create a strong foundation for the unit.

When assigning responsibilities, Pravin agrees on some core values and outcomes. Once agreement is reached, he gives his team members absolute freedom and supports them as required by providing mentorship, investments, creating an environment to perform etc.

Pravin believes that he should surround himself with people who are more capable than him. He also believes in letting people go in deference to their career aspirations, preferably to other parts of Infosys.

LISTENING

Pravin finds listening to be beneficial because people felt he was being non-judgmental. 'When you listen to them, they are more receptive to listen to you. Of course, there are times when despite long discussions, they continue to persist with an approach that is not acceptable. At such times, I finally tell them to either accept the reality, or work to change it.'

MICRO-MANAGEMENT

Praveen is against micro-management. He has found that in the past when he made the mistake of micro-managing all he was doing was spending time reviewing with no significant value addition from his end. 'There is no need to micro-manage when things are going well,' he says. However, he does hold periodic reviews to keep himself abreast of the progress. 'When things are not going well, I do micro-manage to see where I can support them,' he concludes.

TARGET-SETTING

While setting targets, Pravin seeks inputs from the team. When the bottom-up approach on target-setting does not add up to what the organization expects, he explains to the group and marks up the targets. He does this because fundamentally, he has a strong belief in his people.

When people request additional responsibilities, Pravin gives it to them. When they succeed, they come back and ask for more. Normally, these additional responsibilities are either a small part of their goals or do not figure on their goal sheet at all. However, Pravin has never found this to limit their enthusiasm. 'In my view they also see this as a development initiative which will pay off in the medium to long term. But when you force something on them, I have found that they come back to ask you why they should do it and where does it add up in their goals.' Because Pravin's individual and organizational performance has continued to be good, these results 'have reinforced [his] belief in [his] approach to target-setting'.

Pravin adds, 'Of course there are people who are contented and do not want to stretch. I understand this. With such people I do have career conversations where I clearly lay out the implications of their choices.'

HOW DID PRAVIN DEVELOP HIS APPROACH TO PEOPLE MANAGEMENT?

At the start of his career Pravin had only a one- or two-man team. In those days he interacted with the founders and saw them practicing what he has talked about above, and saw what it did to him. Pravin says, 'I guess I picked it up from them.'

He also had a leader who was aggressive but loved people too. People normally saw only one side of him—he was demanding and pushy. Pravin saw the other side—his genuine care for people. Even in his pushing, he wanted people to push the envelope in order to grow.

'I saw how people who accepted his intentions grew,' Pravin says. Pravin also had a micro-manager and he picked up from him what he should not do.

K. Murali Krishna

Murali moved into a role running a business-enabling function (BEF) in October 2007. This group has a track record of successfully aligning with the business demands to continuously deliver even when Infosys was growing at 60 per cent each year. When he took over, he noticed:

(i)   His new team worked in silos.
(ii) Each person had his/her own domain focus.
(iii) Collaboration was low, which in some cases led to longer project timelines.
(iv) There was a vast untapped capability and potential to fit into the larger company landscape.

His new employees naturally had concerns. They carried a stigma that since they were a BEF and not a line function, they weren't important. They were unclear about how decisions got made, and just knew when they were handed down to them. They had no opportunities to learn and, consequently, there was frustration. Murali notes, 'They felt it was nice to be in a revenue generating unit; in a BEF people are not considered an integral part of the business model and therefore their value is perceived as less.'

MURALI'S APPROACH

Murali did a variety of things that had worked well for him previously. First, he initiated weekly meetings with the leadership team. This improved communication and collaboration at senior levels. Second, he took steps to break through the silos of the past. He ensured that all projects or initiatives had a primary and secondary anchor from the leadership team. Murali required every project/initiative team to have a cross-section of team members to form a core team with members coming from the technology group and the operations group. This helped ensure participation from all groups within the unit and also provided more learning opportunities.

Next, he introduced innovations to further improve the engagement of his team. He started brown bag lunches where people would communicate with each other and learn. He launched new awards. He empowered the leadership teams and held them accountable for evaluating and rewarding their teams. He initiated new efforts to drive skill development with various forms of training. His introduction of monthly managers' meets covering all the centres globally, including subsidiaries, was a big hit.

Part of Murali'ss strategy was to give his senior leaders more visibility and better branding inside Infosys. He established an anchor for the unit's skill development through both internal and external training based on the unit's strategic direction and career growth. Every quarter he scheduled two meetings with internal Board members, one to showcase the unit's performance in delivering services and the other to review the top projects. He also promoted the team externally, for example, at the Confederation of Indian Industries (CII) where he served as co-chair, and at other high-profile governing councils in India that he served on.

MURALI'S ATTRIBUTES

Murali feels that his persistence was a key factor in his success. Since everyone was going through a lot of change, he focussed on giving more support, time and space to his team members. Teams were aware that changing was the only option. He sustained the changes with a strong willingness to listen to his team, remaining open to their ideas, recognizing strengths and achievements, collaborating on projects and initiatives and finally with humour—he tried hard to make work more fun. He acknowledges some downsides to his approach, though: people tended to come to him more for everything, and by coming directly to him rather than to one of his leaders, decisions could potentially disempower them.

WHY DID PEOPLE ENGAGE?

Murali feels several factors were paramount in the successful transformation of his group. First, he lightened tension with humour.

He often talked about non-work things to keep things fun. Second, they could see progress in the way the unit was positioned inside and outside Infosys. Team members were more involved in unit-level initiatives which would not have happened previously. They also saw considerable recognition from inside the company and outside.

HOW DID MURALI DEVELOP THESE ATTRIBUTES?

Like Pravin, Murali is one of the select few who have worked with all the founder members of Infosys and grown with the company. He says, 'I learned a lot watching the leaders in action, which I leverage effectively in dealing with my day-to-day work in one form or the other. Also, I have learnt a lot from customers with whom I worked for twenty years.'

K. Suryaprakash (Sury)

According to Sury a leader has to engage with several people and do so effectively. There are at least three groups of 'reporting level' people one has to engage with—direct reports, skip level and the rest of the team—and the approaches will vary for each.

REST OF THE TEAM

According to Sury, people at all levels, but more so the larger team (who do not have a lot of day-to-day interactions with him) expect clarity of purpose and direction and a genuine interest in what matters to them as individuals. Since he feels 'a unit leader is often a representative figurehead for the team', he feels it is important that he demonstrate knowledge on things that matter to them. Sury also tries to genuinely connect with people so that they feel listened to and well represented. He works hard to keep an open, non-threatening environment where people feel comfortable speaking in meetings.

Sury says one way in which he connects with each individual, even junior people, is that, 'When I do meet people in person as I walk past them or in other situations, it is important that you remember their names, smile and greet them. With the help of my human resource business partner, I am very focussed on completing the actions I have promised.'

SKIP LEVEL

The skip level is an important level for Sury. He normally keeps talking to his direct reports on a daily basis about their strategy and purpose and they communicate the same things to their skip level. When he reinforces it, the job of his immediate next level becomes easier, as emphasis is provided.

The skip level can play a role in critiquing the strategy/purpose and also give feedback on the pulse of the people. Sury's relationship with his skip level also allows him to redress any issues that arise. He says, 'I encourage every leader to connect on direct work with their direct reports and on an informal basis with their skip level. With skip levels, I will not talk on work specifics but only as a friend and colleague.'

DIRECT REPORTS

Sury's work with his direct reports is 'more intense as they will discuss various transactions, strategy and alignment to strategy regularly'. He includes them as part of the discussions on the strategy so that they co-own it. Once there is alignment on outcomes, Sury assigns appropriate responsibility with the authority. 'I never superimpose or impede on that authority on a daily basis,' he says.

Finally, Sury notes that 'while one is required to be firm and professional on the outcomes, it is also very important to build personal bridges with the next level, as you need to understand and relate to them as people.'

MICRO-MANAGEMENT

Sury learned about micro-management 'the hard way', as we have seen before, with the warehouse management solution that he micro-managed in the 1990s. In 2003, by the time he was starting up Infosys's business unit in China, he had become much more collaborative. He notes, 'I had progressed to asking for outcomes from people instead of micro-managing. I laid out specific problem statements to various senior individuals. Over time, I found that some of them performed well, some did not.'

Over the years Sury has realized that: 'Selecting the right people is important; once chosen, back them—you need to have confidence in yourself and must not be perturbed by loss of control.' One of the things he learnt from his superiors was to have people align to the big picture of what is important for the group or unit.

Today, Sury normally does not micro-manage. But if there is a crisis, he says, 'I do tend to slip into micro-management, particularly where there are not enough process and governance mechanisms in place. However, these are rare and do not lead to burnout.'

HOW DID SURY DEVELOP?

Sury has used his 360 degree feedback survey to get patterns of effective and ineffective behaviour. He also openly solicits feedback from his direct reports. 'I ensure that there are some "nay-sayers" as well in the 360 feedback to ensure the feedback is balanced,' he says. 'My view is that 360 feedback is for you and your development and therefore it is most important.'

Ramesh Chogule

Ramesh heads the delivery of Life Sciences in Infosys's Enterprise Solutions unit. He has grown the unit from $17 million in 2007 to $58 million in 2009—a 40 per cent growth rate despite the global economic downturn of 2008–09.

Ramesh has consistently communicated the importance of domain competence, and that for growth it 'is essential that we continuously upgrade our knowledge'. He says, 'As we executed our efforts, the results on the ground were evident to the team. This created a willingness in the team to continue with the practice as they saw opportunities to learn and grow as professional consultants. This also helped in retention.'

To keep his team engaged, Ramesh meets with 600–700 people in groups of 50–150 for quarterly skip level meetings. He discusses growth, new wins, 'go lives' and marketing activities to create a positive environment about the team's work. To reinforce his message around development, in all informal discussions he asks his team members what they have learned in the last quarter.

Ramesh feels strongly that by upgrading his team's knowledge, he is enabling them to grow in their career. 'If they see the practice as one that supports their personal development, they will want to be a part of it,' he notes.

In the discussions regarding concerns and issues, the practice that Ramesh has always followed is to be upfront about a situation and be direct in his discussions. He says, 'When I look back I ask myself why I was enthusiastic to learn. The answer is: the eagerness to learn something new is at the very core of my personality. My belief about talent leadership is based on what drove me. I am assuming this holds good for others in Infosys too, looking at the more or less similar educational accomplishments.'

*

At the heart of all what successful leaders at Infosys told us are two overarching points:

- They treated people as people and not resources to carry out the job.
- All of them did not learn this from formal interventions but by observing how they were led by other effective leaders. Further, they reflected on their own successes and failures and learned from their experience.

The last point is extremely important. Developing employee engagement is typically not about developing a large-scale initiative and rolling it out organization-wide. Formal initiatives are useful as a point of reinforcement and will be required. However, true learning comes from what people experience in the work day. If this has to become part of the DNA of an organization, it must start at the top. When direct reports experience the benefit of such an approach they will exhibit similar behaviours and over time it will become part of the DNA of the organization.

If the top management embodies engagement and empowerment in its true sense as well as intent, the ecosystem will change to one where this is the culture. This will also spearhead the systemic changes that are required to support such a culture. Big change initiatives are not required. Changes at the top will snowball into this becoming an organizational culture. The important thing is to get started—a few people at a time.

Bibliography

Argyris, Chris (1998). 'Empowerment: The Emperor's New Clothes', *Harvard Business Review*, May/June, 98–105.

Barney, Jay, Wright, Mike and Ketchen, David J. (2001). 'The Resource-based View of the Firm: Ten Years after 1991', *Journal of Management*, 27, 625–41.

Buckingham, Marcus and Coffman, Curt (1999). *First Break All the Rules*, New York: Simon and Schuster.

Buckingham, Marcus (2005). 'What Great Managers Do', an interview, *Computer World*, 28 March.

Butler, Timothy and Waldroop, James. 'Job Sculpting: The Art of Retaining Your Best People', *Harvard Business Review*, September/October, 144–52.

Day, D.V., Harrison, M.M. and Halpin, S.M. (2009). *An Integrative Approach to Leader Development: Connecting Adult Development, Identity and Expertise*, New York: Routledge.

Day, D.V. (2010). 'The Difficulties of Learning from Experience and the Need for Deliberate Practice', *Industrial and Organizational Psychology: Perspectives on Science and Practice*, 3, 41–44.

DeShon, R.P. and Gillespie, J.Z. (2005). 'A Motivated Action Theory Account of Goal Orientation', *Journal of Applied Psychology*, 90, 1096–1127.

Ericsson, K.A. (2009). 'Enhancing the Development of Professional Performance: Implications from the Study of Deliberate Practice', in K.A. Ericsson (ed.), *Development of Professional Expertise: Toward Measurement of Expert Performance and Design of Optimal Learning*, Cambridge, UK: Cambridge University Press, 405–31.

Frey, Robert (1993). 'Empowerment or Else', *Harvard Business Review*, September/October, 80–94.

Herzberg, Fredrick (1987). 'One More Time: How Do You Motivate Employees?' *Harvard Business Review*, September/October, 109–20.

Heskett, James L., Jones, Thomas O., Loveman, Gary W., Sasser, W., Schlesinger, Earl, Jr., Judge, T.A. and Piccolo, R.F. (2004). 'Transformational and Transactional Leadership: A Meta-analytic Test of Their Relative Validity', *Journal of Applied Psychology*, 89 (5), 755–68.

Judge, Timothy A., Colbert, Amy E. and Ilies, Remus (2004). 'Intelligence and Leadership: A Quantitative Review and Test of Theoretical Propositions', *Journal of Applied Psychology*, 89 (3), 542–52.

Lee, Fiona (2001). 'The Fear Factor', *Harvard Business Review*, January, 29–30.

Locke, Edwin A., Shaw, Karyll N., Saari, Lise M. and Lathaom, Gary P. (1981). 'Goal Setting and Task Performance: 1969–1981', *Psychological Bulletin*, 90 (1), 125–52.

Manville, Brook and Ober, Josiah (2003). 'Beyond Empowerment: Building a Company of Citizens', *Harvard Business Review*, January, 48–53.

Mintzberg, Henry (2009). 'Rebuilding Companies as Communities', *Harvard Business Review*, July/August, 140–43.

Russ, Fonestei (2000). 'Empowerment: Rejuvenating a Potent Idea', *Academy of Management Executive*, 14 (3), 67–80.

Schmidt, Frank L. and Hunter, John E. (1998). 'The Validity and Utility of Selection Methods in Personnel Psychology: Practical and Theoretical Implications of Eighty-five Years of Research Findings', *Psychological Bulletin*, 124 (2), 262–74.

Stajkovic, Alexander D. and Luthans, Fred (1998). 'Self-efficacy and Work-related Performance: A Meta-analysis', *Psychological Bulletin*, 124 (2), 240–61.

Wetlaufer, Suzy (1999). 'Organizing for Empowerment: An Interview with AES's Roger Sant and Dennis Bakke', *Harvard Business Review*, January/February, 110–23.

Wright, Patrick M., Dunford, Benjamin B. and Snell, Scott A. (2001). 'Human Resources and the Resource-based View of the Firm', *Journal of Management*, 27, 701–21.

CHAPTER 7

RELATIONSHIP AND NETWORKING LEADERSHIP
AARTI SHYAMSUNDER, PhD AND JEFF KAVANAUGH

'We are caught in an inescapable network of mutuality, tied in a single garment of destiny. Whatever affects one directly, affects all indirectly.'

—*Martin Luther King Jr.*

Consider this for a minute. Where did you first hear about your favourite restaurant? How did you find that mechanic or hairdresser you swear by? Where did you find your best employee? How did you decide to stay in that great hotel on your favourite vacation? They probably were all results of a coincidence, a chance conversation with a friend or colleague, which snowballed into these wonderful outcomes. What we do not often realize, though, is that these coincidences and chance happenings are all the results of the relationships and networks in our lives.

The quote by Martin Luther King Jr. above captures what has become a widely accepted truth in business. Even so-called 'individual contributors' no longer have the luxury of doing completely independent work. In today's flat world national boundaries, time zones and even lines of authority are quickly becoming meaningless. Thus, it has become not just possible, but imperative to build relationships and to network, to weave our threads into a 'single garment of destiny'.

An online search for relationship and networking leadership yields thousands of hits. There are books, brochures and seminar programmes around the world filled with 'experts' who promise fame and riches based on their respective formulas for success in using networking strategies. So what, indeed, does it take to become an authentic leader who is great at relationship and networking leadership? Is it as simple as using the most popular social networking site or the best voice conferencing tool? Or is it something more fundamental—a skill that requires a lifetime of developing patience, understanding and appreciation of people and how we all impact each other? At Infosys, the focus is on developing and using such skills, with a simultaneous appreciation of the tools and techniques required.

Defining Relationship and Networking Leadership

Although we do have a sense of what relationship and networking leadership means intuitively, for the sake of creating a common understanding, we will first explore a few ways in which we might define it. To start with, we will look at a few definitions from the research on leadership. Then we will review the Infosys model of leadership behaviour that describes the specific meaning of this dimension for all Infosys leaders. Finally we will consider the working definition—a simple commonplace understanding of relationship and networking leadership.

The technical definition

In organizational science, most definitions of the word 'leadership' include the concept of influence over others. For instance, according to Katz and Kahn (1978), leadership is 'the exertion of influence on organizationally relevant matters by any member of the organization'. Beyond influence though, relational leadership is seen as a contrast to what Murrell (1997) calls the 'hero myth', that is, earlier views of leadership where the leader was the centre of the 'leadership relationship'. In contrast, relational leadership may be seen as 'a social act, a construction of a "ship" as a collective vehicle to help take us where we as a group, organization or society desire to go' (Murrell, 1997, 35). Mary Uhl-Bien, in her treatment of relational leadership theory, merges the influence view and the social construction view, and defines relational leadership as 'a social influence process through which emergent coordination (i.e. the evolving social order) and change (i.e. new values, attitudes, approaches, behaviours, ideologies etc.) are constructed and produced' (Uhl-Bien, 2006, 655). Thus, relationship and networking leadership is not about the leader alone—it is about the process he/she engages in with others to influence change.

The Infosys definition

In the Infosys leadership model, 'relationship/networking leadership is about developing, maintaining and leveraging long-term internal and external relationships and networks'. Growth in this area at Infosys means moving beyond using existing networks and relationships for attaining tactical wants. It implies building and strategically leveraging networks in order to realize business and career objectives. Ultimately Infosys leaders strive to become recognized as an expert and a trusted advisor to multiple stakeholders at multiple levels. Echoing the description of ethical influence, relationship and networking leadership at Infosys is about mutually beneficial relationships for short-term as well as long-term gain.

The layperson's definition

The essence of this facet of leadership may simply boil down to this: 'relationship and networking leadership is about influencing action through people'. Leaders with the best networks are actually friends with the people with whom they work.

In the end, leaders learn that their legacy will endure based on the capital they build and grow. Social capital arguably is as important a resource to build in organizations as financial capital (i.e. raising monetary resources) and human capital (i.e. developing individual knowledge, skills and abilities). With social capital, the focus is on building networked relationships which enhance cooperation and resource exchange to create organizational value (Tsai and Ghoshal, 1998). Social capital is based on relationships created through interpersonal exchange, and is therefore defined more by function than structure (Coleman, 1988). That is, it is not just who you are, but what you do that creates social capital. Cashing in this social capital for mutual social incomes is what exercising ethical influence is about.

While all leadership seems to be about influence, not all exercises in influence necessarily are about leadership. Influence is a key element about relational leadership, the means by which leaders achieve their ends. Ethical influence is about achieving those ends in ways that enhance the long-term well-being of all people involved. It is important to note that authentic leaders and change agents do not abuse power or influence, do not manipulate and trick others into action for one-sided gain or become 'smugglers of influence' (Cialdini, 2001). On the contrary, they use their networks, built using trust and charisma, in genuine ways that are satisfying to both parties. The most effective networker is one who builds relationships with no agenda or vested interests, but is merely powered by the joy of making a genuine connection with people (Darling, 2002). Don't you trust your friends— people who like you and whom you like as well—for good advice?

THE EVOLVING NATURE OF NETWORKING AND RELATIONSHIP BUILDING

Historically, the act of influencing action through people has been evolving along with human society itself. Whether it is about influencing your fellow caveman to use fire and hunt wild boar along with you, or negotiating a tough acquisition of an former business rival, leaders have always relied on their relationships. There are several levels at which networking and relationship-building has worked and continues to work:

- **Physical networks:** Meeting in person. The first epoch of networking involved meeting face-to-face. Relationships were built in people's homes, at social gatherings and marketplaces. Travellers were held in awe for the tales they brought from distant lands about people who looked different, ate different foods and spoke in strange languages.
- **Telephone calls/Letters:** Bridging distances. The second wave of networking came with advances in the means of communication. With the postal system, the telegraph and telephone lines, entire continents were being connected in new and exciting ways. Townships developed around telegraph roads, diplomacy and romance found new ways of expression and distances were being closed.

- **Electronic:** Staying connected. The advent of computers, television, fax/copy machines and more than all of these the Internet, changed the way people connected and communicated. Whether it is automated billing, online shopping, electronic news publishing, social networking or blogging, the name of the game currently is convenience and connectivity.
- **Electronic/Virtual spaces:** Making an impact. The next epoch of relationship-building will also largely be mediated using electronic means. The world arguably is already flat, however. Moving beyond the need to communicate and stay connected using electronic media, future generations will find new ways of making an impact using these and currently unknown future means of networking. Economies will increasingly revolve around these means of making an impact possibly without ever even actually speaking to those we are impacting in person.

Infosys Leaders and Clients Who Have Ethically Influenced Action through People

Consistent with the other chapters in this book, we used the Leadership Journey Series assessments to identify Infosys leaders who were rated by a sample of stakeholders as exceptionally high in their effectiveness at relationship and networking leadership. The Infosys leaders who shared their insights with us for this chapter are Satyendra Kumar, Sridhar Marri, Srikantan ('Tan') Moorthy, Rishi Raj Paul, Anand Swaminathan and V. Sriram. We have also included the views of an executive client of Infosys who is strong in this area: Michel Langlois, Senior Vice President of Junos Software at Juniper Networks, a leading telecom network equipment provider.

Evidence-based Model of Relationship and Networking Leadership: The Science of Influence

Distilling over six decades of research in social psychology, Robert Cialdini (2001) has developed a model of the six principles of persuasion. Because of its roots in science, the model is robust with a substantial amount of support for the practical utility of its methods. Leaders can learn to use these six principles of ethical influence to improve their relationship and networking skills, helping their teams buy into organizational goals and becoming trusted advisors to their clients or prospects and achieving mutually satisfying goals.

THE SIX PRINCIPLES OF ETHICAL INFLUENCE

1. **Reciprocity:** We give back to those who have given to us
2. **Liking:** We are more easily influenced by people we like
3. **Authority:** We follow those who we trust with unique expertise
4. **Consensus:** We decide what to do by looking at what similar others have done
5. **Consistency:** We have a strong urge to remain consistent with our prior beliefs and behaviours
6. **Scarcity:** We want more of that which is less available

---

The simplicity of these principles belies a long-standing and still ongoing programme of research to establish the relationship between the use of these principles and positive practical consequences. Each of these principles involves initiation and also certain elements which augment the effect of that principle or increase the power of the influence. These principles are described briefly below, with a few examples from Infosys and client leaders as applicable.

Reciprocity

The principle of reciprocity shows consistently that across all cultures, people feel obliged to give back to others who have given to them. Gifts and concessions set the principle of reciprocity in motion. Reciprocity is made more powerful when the gifts are meaningful, personal and unexpected and concessions are made at the appropriate moment.

Anand Swaminathan describes how focusing on the relationship with a team member helped drive excellence and improve overall team morale. At the time Anand took over the Microsoft account as Group Engagement Manager (GEM) about three years ago, he had an employee who was extremely smart but somehow not living up to his potential at work. Moreover, he was occasionally abrasive, even to the point of undermining Anand's authority at times. Through the first few months, Anand treated him patiently. However, when the person lost a $50 million contract because of a misguided risk, Anand needed to take action. Anand decided to make a magnanimous and surprising gesture—not only did he not fire the person, but he recommended him for a promotion based on his untapped potential. With this gift of forgiveness and a second chance, things turned around for the team member; his negative attitude disappeared and his performance improved rapidly. Today he has contributed to over $400 million of business for Infosys. Not only did Anand trust his relationship and networking leadership radar on this, but he also demonstrated great talent leadership, the attributes of which you will remember from the previous chapter.

Satyendra Kumar describes an instance when the generosity of his time and expertise brought in very real rewards for both Infosys and his client. In describing how Kumar moved his 'relationship index' with this client from about a 2 (out of 5, on a hypothetical scale) all the way to 5, he mentions that the client relationship began when he was brought in to consult as a credible expert in Quality. As a vendor, all he needed to do was consult for the specific problem and walk away with his fees. Instead, Kumar went beyond the call of duty to spend sufficient time needed to provide an excellent solution and conducted regular check-ins until the solution was working well. This specific project helped propel the executive in the client organization into the CIO role. This CIO now maintains regular contact with Kumar, even insisting on taking Kumar out to lunch or dinner whenever he is in the same city. Further, the CIO has video conferences with Kumar, calls him regularly to keep in touch and proactively recognizes all he did for the organization. Moreover, the quality consulting contract itself was significant (worth $2 million), and it was by no means a conventional Infosys engagement. This, in turn, will help Kumar expand the Infosys footprint using this client as a reference or even further within this one organization itself. Kumar's willingness to give the client the gift of his time and advice made him reciprocate with good will, support and a lot of business for Infosys.

Another important element of reciprocity is making appropriate concessions. This can take the form of retreating from a large request to a smaller one, showing the other party that you are willing to sacrifice some of your needs in the interest of the relationship. Sridhar Marri describes an instance where passion and commitment to an idea allowed him to make such a concession, which eventually paid off in a big way. He was the one who conceived and launched a new innovation called InfyTV. This first-of-its-kind corporate TV channel delivered programming directly to the laptops of thousands of employees across the world through four channels: news, learning, entertainment and special features. Within a span of twelve months, InfyTV became an integral part of the Infosys culture and radically changed the way the organization viewed communication, the way people could share knowledge and learn in short learning modules across the organization. It also entertained, enthralled and brought in experts in various fields across industries.

When Sridhar first shared his vision with senior management, they were very excited but there were no budgets. He decided to not give up, and instead produced a proof of concept and presented a shoestring budget. Even then, there was no money due to severe cost control across the organization. Finally, Sridhar decided to make a radical concession and do this without any new money, using existing infrastructure and bandwidth. This implied several changes in the design and compromises on some of the 'cool' features of the solution. But it also allowed him to launch it at a very influential forum, the leadership strategy planning event. At the meeting, the innovativeness and power of this medium was made evident by the very style of its unveiling. Following presentations by the company's CEO (Kris Gopalakrishnan) and COO (S. Shibulal), InfyTV came on, featuring a news anchor who covered those very presentations that had occurred less than fifteen minutes ago! This made for a huge impact and garnered tremendous support from the attendees of this meeting. Realizing the immense potential of the channel, the company finally made the required investments to take it to the next level. Today, InfyTV is the only powerful rich media on-demand communication channel at Infosys. Leaders today address employees across the world using InfyTV. Considered one of the top innovations at Infosys, InfyTV in used by several units for their global communication rollouts and has reduced global air travel, saving costs and the environment. The way people learn in future is being shaped by InfyTV right now, in a large part because of Sridhar's willingness to retreat from his major request in the interest of the project.

V. Sriram talks about reciprocity as 'unconditional giving first'. To him, doing something because it is the right thing to do, or because it will help someone, is the only reason to do it—not because you expect something in return. For instance, in a conversation with someone from a security organization, he learned that they were looking into entering the Indian market. Soon afterwards, on a personal visit to India, Sriram made time to take this organization's representatives on a tour of various houses and shopping complexes in Bangalore, talking to owners of these establishments on the organization's behalf to help them understand the infrastructure security market in India. He did not have any business need to do this; they were not even a client. However, soon after his gesture of help, the organization approached Infosys for some SAP implementation work they were planning, thus paying off in an unexpected but pleasant way.

Whether it is with clients or with peers, subordinates or supervisors, leaders who remember and use the principle of reciprocity well understand the nuanced nature of building good, long-lasting relationships and networks. Making investments of gifts (even intangible, inexpensive gifts like praise or personal time) or concessions (like forgiveness or lower expectations) should be with no immediate expectation of those investments being returned, or else the other person may see reciprocity as manipulative and even unethical. It is important to continually work on relationships, instead of waiting until you need to. Initiating the principle of reciprocity with no hidden agenda or vested interests is a great way to build long-term relationships.

Liking

People respond positively to requests made by those they know and like. Similarity, praise and cooperation are three ways to trigger liking. What makes this principle even more powerful is appreciating others first instead of waiting for them to like you.

Satyendra Kumar admits to doing this unconsciously in all his relationships. He says, 'I don't know why, but I always assume that people are good and I give them a chance.' When people like Kumar start all relationships with this basic assumption, they are harnessing this powerful enhancer of the liking principle—the fact that the liking is real and genuine rather than contrived.

Similarity in values, preferences, dress, lifestyles and attitudes all influence liking. As leaders, emphasizing what team members have in common, or what the organization shares with its clients or prospects, why the organization is similar to the people it serves and other such reminders are likely to result in positive results, especially if done proactively. In cases where we don't know enough about the other party to like them, it helps to invest time and effort in finding similarities or engaging in activities that result in positive outcomes that enhance feelings of unity and similarity.

For Srikantan ('Tan') Moorthy, making a connection in order to persuade someone always starts with listening. Even if he is selling a solution or looking for others to agree with him on something, he starts by listening to their views and then offers a solution based on data and logic. Listening helps him find points of intersection between what he has to offer and the other person's needs and wants. At that point, the other party is more receptive to Tan offering data on why his recommendation makes sense in that specific situation.

Anand Swaminathan notes that there are several things that he does unknowingly that have helped him practice the liking principle. Triggering liking using similarity with others can occur at a superficial level or at a deep level. Living in the Pacific northwest, with its great outdoors and fitness fanatics, Anand finds it easy to make friends and meet business acquaintances at the gym, while training for a bike ride or marathon, or playing golf. He has even got business relationships with the parents of his children's classmates in their school. Talking about the weather, sports or your children is a safe way to build liking based on surface similarity. For deeper similarity, he relies on striking a chord even with senior leaders by first confessing to some personal vulnerabilities, like a problem he's faced with or something that he's afraid of. He finds that when he does this the other person often warms up to him, since they've also invariably had a similar experience. Sharing concerns over team-building and delegation without losing authority over them, the problems of work–life balance (or 'work–life integration' as Anand likes to call it) and de-risking one's own organizational goals, he finds, are universal issues to which nearly everyone can relate.

Rishi Raj Paul acknowledges the difficulty and importance in making those initial connections with possible strangers. In his career, he has worked in multiple cultures including Japan, Germany, Spain and now America. The initial difficulties he faced while dealing with people from cultures different from his own included issues like the different terminology or jargon used, the way of life, and even topics of everyday discussion like local politics. These things are only learned over time after being embedded in a particular culture. In Rishi's perspective, there needs to be some investment in learning these things in a new culture to help make connections with those who may be superficially dissimilar, in an effort to get them to relate to you better. Over time, these skills become practiced and he is now comfortable building new relationships.

Michel Langlois notes that when joining an organization as an executive, it is important to develop the relationship strength that enables credibility and the social capital to actively lead transformative efforts. It is a delicate balance, because you must deliver results scoped within the time period of your mandate, yet you must also allow time to develop the relationships before having the understanding to make significant change or launching initiatives. This was evident at Juniper, when he was brought on board to transform its software development capability, but first he had to understand his peers and develop the relationships that would withstand the stresses of complex transformative change over the duration of a long-term initiative.

Consensus

In deciding what is appropriate behaviour in a situation, people examine what others are doing, thinking or feeling. Consensus is made more powerful by evidence from a majority or many others, or from similar others, in times of uncertainty. Leaders can benefit greatly by using consensus information in the form of benchmarking studies, survey results, competitive market analyses and similar data for gaining clients' trust and influencing their decisions. Similarly, knowledge of how other leaders especially in similar roles or contexts influence their followers helps inform the relationship with their team members. Influencing others to adopt your recommendation comes much easier when you can point to evidence that several similar others are doing the same, especially in times of crisis or uncertainty.

In using the principle of consensus, Rishi leverages his experiences and past successes with clients to influence future business development efforts. He finds a success story in a given vertical (e.g. high-tech), connects people from that vertical to other verticals (e.g. services or utilities) within Infosys, focusing on getting those of similar roles or designations to talk with each other, and has them discuss the successful implementation that he enabled. Specifically, he typically uses three types of social proof or consensus information: testimonials and case studies; getting clients to talk about successful implementations directly to decision-makers in the potential new vertical; and sharing with the potential new vertical the monetary value of previous contracts to provide concrete proof of the opportunity. He feels that the last kind is the most compelling, because it provides immediate and tangible numbers derived from client representatives similar to the ones he is trying to influence, of possible revenues for those verticals.

In making client presentations about user interface designs for software applications, Sridhar likes to open with an innovative, cutting-edge presentation. He uses his experience and knowledge about the domain to find examples of how other organizations in the same industry as the client have bungled design. In an interesting twist to the social proof or consensus principle, instead of showcasing how similar others have succeeded by using what he is suggesting, Sridhar shows clients how similar others have failed because they used something else. This is a great example of the 'contrast phenomenon'. Contrast is the unseen principle that binds all six principles of persuasion together—it can serve to enhance the effects of all six principles by focusing attention on how something is unique. Thus, harnessing the power of the contrast phenomenon within consensus, Sridhar immediately establishes credibility in the client's mind, because he clearly seems to know something they don't about companies very similar to them. This immediately draws the client in and motivates them to sit up and take notice of what he has to offer.

Sridhar also describes an effort he led where he used the principle of consensus in increments over time. 'User experience' today has become one of the hottest service offerings at Infosys. Sridhar pioneered user experience (UX) as a service at Infosys and today this service caters to over 165 clients globally with about 700 UX projects per annum. User experience for most of Infosys's internal innovative technology solutions also comes from Sridhar's group. All this was achieved through sheer 'intrapreneurship' without a mandate from the top. What this means to Sridhar is first spotting an opportunity, then convincing others about his team's capability to deliver, showing commitment over time, creating a critical mass of demand, demonstrating business value around the offering and finally scaling it. Since this project started out with Sridhar proactively identifying a need, top management needed a proof of concept before committing to it financially. Sridhar thus first approached early adopters of user experience solutions by identifying industry sectors/verticals who would be interested in it. He first contacted finance, health care and a few other units within Infosys who may like to pilot this initiative. Once he got one of the units to agree, the relevant clients came back with very positive feedback. Sridhar took this to senior management as social proof of the utility of the UX idea. Instead of stopping there, he took it back to the field and tested it with several more units, building upon past proof points to make the case for future opportunities. Simultaneously, he worked on building capability and recruited three or four new employees who had expertise in this specific field. This focus on talent leadership along with socializing the idea using the principle of consensus has led to one of the great success stories of Infosys and for Sridhar, personally. Today, twelve years since the inception of this idea, Sridhar's CDG team has the largest UX group in the industry and the user experience ecosystem at Infosys is probably the strongest among all the software services players in India. This makes it one of the key differentiators for Infosys in its portfolio today.

Authority

People are guided by others who have superior knowledge or wisdom compared to their own. While credibility—demonstrating expertise and trustworthiness—improves the effect of authority, in the absence of such information, even mere trappings or external cues of authority are sufficient in initiating this principle of influence. Such cues include dress, credentials or titles, status symbols such as size and location of office, awards and certifications on display etc. Leaders will do well to remind people of their own credibility, when genuine and appropriate, in ways that don't seem vain.

Satyendra Kumar describes a few ways in which he gains respect in the eyes of others as a person of authority. Before he goes into client meetings, especially if he is meeting them for the first time, he encourages his contact to share information that builds his image as an expert in the domain. Perhaps he served as a judge in the panel for the

Wisconsin State Award the previous day, or was in a Board meeting for the Quest Forum or in an advisory council meeting for the Underwriter Laboratories or the Confederation of Indian Industries earlier that day. By gently reminding the contact to mention this in a subtle way to his clients or prospects before his meeting them, his credibility in their eyes is established. During the meeting, he consciously steers away from any devices or behaviour that might appear to be a sales pitch. Instead of a pre-packaged PowerPoint presentation, Kumar prefers to think on his feet and use the whiteboard or flipcharts extensively while interacting with his audience. This refusal to use conventional 'crutches' for his presentations and relying instead on his obvious expertise and presence of mind enhances his image as a credible expert, so much so that he has earned the nickname of 'the professor' with a few clients. His obvious passion for his subject combined with his ability to come across as honest and sincere (rather than an aggressive salesperson) has helped neutralize the defences of audiences who are wary of being sold against their will. As one of his clients marvels, 'I always thought Quality was a dull subject until I saw the passion Kumar brings to it.'

Tan has another approach to building his authority and credibility. True to the spirit of authentic leadership, he believes in making a personal connection to build credibility. In doing this, of course, Tan is harnessing the principle of liking as well. He is open to discussing examples from his own life, especially examples of how he is not infallible. For example while talking about the need for good communication skills Tan would talk about how he failed in winning a proposal even when the solution was right because he did not understand the power of communication at that stage in his career. By owning up to his weaknesses up front, he disarms the other person into believing what follows—at which point he can then focus on his strengths or where his conversation is leading up to.

Rishi brings up an interesting point about authority. Sometimes, like in his current role as Global Alliance Manager, the way to influence others may not lie in flaunting one's own authority. Instead, an authentic leader might be a facilitator and bring together various credible experts to influence action. For instance, Rishi serves as a mediator and brings together experts from Oracle and from Infosys in helping solve a client need. In order to do this successfully he has built a reliable network of trustworthy experts whom he can rely on. The eventual success of such business efforts in turn enhances Rishi's own credibility as a business leader (even though he may not be the domain expert or 'thought leader').

Consistency and commitment

People are motivated by personal and interpersonal pressure to behave consistently with what they have previously said, done or committed to, especially if these commitments were active, public and voluntary. Leaders who practice what they teach are able to command respect instead of merely demanding it. Moreover, obtaining small initial commitments from followers, clients or other peers whose support you need for a cause improves the chance of gaining their cooperation for larger commitments. This is because something changes in the way they view themselves by committing first to the small request, thereby allowing them to commit to larger changes that may even require persistent effort (e.g. Sensenig and Cialdini, 1984).

As any leader knows, one of the biggest challenges is to get others to buy into goals that may not come from them. Anand encountered one such situation some time ago. When Infosys Consulting (IC) was launched four years ago, Anand wanted his client to take advantage of IC's offerings and become one of their top accounts. To this end, he worked with IC's CEO Steve Pratt to send a consulting partner to engage with the client and sure enough, they were awarded an engagement worth $11 million per quarter. This not only served the clients more effectively than the competition, but Anand's proactive approach also helped accelerate growth for an important Infosys subsidiary early in its existence. While this early success was noteworthy on its own, Anand and his consulting colleagues wanted to further expand the consulting footprint at the client's, and for that, they needed others to share his vision. Anand used a couple of influence techniques before he used the principle of consistency. He highlighted that current revenue at IC was only 25 per cent of its biggest competitor on the account. He also asked Infosys stakeholders on the account to change focus from current revenue levels (which were substantial) to what they were possibly losing to the competition (which was an even larger amount). These two aspects of persuasion are called the 'contrast principle'—discussed earlier—and 'loss framing' respectively. Loss framing actually is an enhance for another principle—scarcity—wherein focusing on what's to be lost motivates action more than emphasizing gains. Finally, when Anand got to the goal-setting piece, the ambitious goals of having 50 per cent of the client's consulting and transformation work go to IC were adopted by everyone. Today, they check each other's progress towards these goals and motivate action based on them.

Scarcity

Opportunities, goods and services appear more valuable and desirable when they are less available. Knowledge of scarcity i.e. information that something is rare or dwindling is amplified by the way the information is framed such that we are motivated to avoid losses more than gain something. Exclusivity of such information enhances the efficacy of the principle of scarcity as does the knowledge of competition to obtain that scarce resource.

Kumar describes a recent case where he leveraged the scarcity principle to great advantage. Infosys is currently a CMM Level 5 company, and its certification expiration date is approaching. In order to maintain it, Kumar and his team need all units to cooperate in the upcoming assessment. This time, the assessment is not routine because if it doesn't occur in the time and manner required, there is a risk of a second (more stringent) evaluation by another external agency. When he approached some Board members for their support in his efforts to prepare for this assessment, Kumar used a loss-framing approach whereby he alerted them to the fact that if the first assessment failed for CMM, the second one would be more risky and more effortful. They immediately approved funding for Kumar to prepare for both eventualities—a task which might otherwise have taken several more attempts to pull through.

As head of the Communication Design Group (CDG), Sridhar has a constant battle—CDG is an internal support unit (a 'business enabling function' or BEF) and as such, is constantly being approached for client resources. As a BEF, it also has limited resources and in Sridhar's words, 'minuscule budgets'. After several years of persistently asking for increased resources and budgets, Sridhar decided to change tactics. He turned client requests from the delivery functions into projects that would be mostly funded by those functions themselves.

In this manner, he highlighted the scarcity of CDG talent and resources and got other organizational functions to become more discerning in their requests. Moreover, he created the concept of a 'mini-CDG'—a group of CDG team members fully dedicated to specific projects, like five people for SI, ten for Finacle etc. Again, this highlighted the scarcity of available CDG resources, so much so that over time, he has been able to open up more and more positions to support internal demand. Even in a down economy, CDG was recruiting talent.

*

Relationship and networking leadership is more than merely applying the principles of influence. After all, 'no one can hope to lead any organization by standing outside or ignoring the web of relationships through which all work is accomplished' (Wheatly, 1999, 165). At the heart of such a relational model of leadership are three elements: commitments in the form of mutual obligations, supported by reciprocated trust and respect (Brower, Schoorman and Tan, 2000). Of late, relationship-based leadership theory has begun to move beyond a focus on leader–follower exchanges to consider other types of leadership relationships that can occur in the broader context (Balkundi and Kilduff, 2005). The next section considers this broader context: the 'web of influence' of relationship and networking leadership.

Web of Influence

Recall that we described relationship and networking leadership as 'influencing actions through people'. This influence can take on many forms, depending on the action and the people in question. We discussed the various actions one can take seen through the six principles of the persuasion lens. Here we have used a simple classification based on the people: the focus or target of influence. For each category, we highlight important research findings as relevant.

Employees

The most important stakeholder group for leaders in a work context is their employees. This group includes direct reports, subordinates, people lower in the organizational chain than the leader who report up to him/her directly or indirectly—the 'followers' in classic leadership literature. Some leadership theories such as leader–member exchange (LMX) and vertical dyad linkage (VDL) have explored leadership relationships with subordinates. LMX/VDL research has shown that over the short term the model relies on skillful correction of deficiencies of intervening variables in the work unit; for instance, followers from the leader's 'in-group' are motivated to contribute towards the leader's agenda (e.g. Graen and Uhl-Biehn, 1995). Over a long term, the model relies on the leader changing situational variables to be more favourable (e.g. strategic planning, policy formation, programme development, organizational change, political activity etc.) (Yukl, 1994).

In a different view of leadership which focuses more on the power of the leader to influence the followers' self-identity and motivate action, a transformational leader is someone who articulates a shared vision of the future, intellectually stimulates followers, providing support to individuals and recognizing individual differences, and sets high expectations (Bass, 1985). In fact, transformational leadership is at the very top end of a spectrum called the 'full range leadership model' (Avolio, 1999). Around the middle of the full range is transactional leadership, which is demonstrated in effective ways by setting goals and objectives and providing feedback, recognition and rewards with one's followers to achieve expected performance. Slightly lower on the range is the more corrective transactional style where leaders focus on finding what might go wrong, or did go wrong, and correcting it. At the very bottom of the full range and the least effective style is passive–avoidant leadership.

In the workplace, the 'leader as role model' is a compelling construct, and it focuses on the attributes most likely to be imitated by followers. Results from the research on this model suggest that highly recognized charismatic leaders are often ignored in favour of leaders who are more proximal to the individual. This means that the leaders must connect with and influence the employee base through other managers, not just a broadcast, one-to-many projection.

What are the predictors of successful leadership, especially relational leadership? This question has been asked by many, in different ways, and there have been many answers throughout history. As far back as the sixth century, Lao-Tzu (regarded as the founder of Taoism) described the qualities of a wise leader: selfless, hardworking, honest, able to time the appropriateness of actions, fair in handling conflict, and able to 'empower' others (Heider, 1985). Modern science has similar findings. In a meta-analysis of seventy-eight studies of leadership, Tim Judge and his colleagues (Judge, Bono, Ilies and Gerhardt, 2002) concluded that the 'Big Five' personality traits—emotional stability, extraversion, openness to experience, agreeableness and conscientiousness—are all related to leader effectiveness and all but agreeableness are related to leader emergence. Extraversion was most strongly related to leadership, followed by conscientiousness, neuroticism and openness. In our own research at Infosys, we used the Zaccaro, Kemp and Bader (2004) model of leadership, which describes the distal attributes (e.g. personality, cognitive abilities, motives and values) and proximal attributes (social appraisal skills, problem solving skills and tacit knowledge/expertise) which predict leader emergence, effectiveness and advancement/promotion via several processes. From the data we collected on Infosys leaders, there is evidence that openness to experience, being a team player and agreeableness emerge as strong predictors of relationship and networking leadership. Thus, being selfless and fair, being open to sharing power with others, as Lao-Tzu had proposed, does seem to be a critical component of relational leadership.

Change leadership is also important for an authentic leader who uses relationships and networks to lead more effectively. Leaders need to successfully architect and implement change while understanding there will be resistance, and that they will need to develop champions for the cause. The larger and more mature the organization, the more the leader will have to use guiding principles to communicate their message, not just a sophisticated organization design or transformation road map. Talent leadership, applied to relationships and networks, means knowing how to lead authentically while understanding when to stop and let someone else lead. In other words, consistent development of others is one of the most powerful means to become successful at relationship and networking leadership.

Peers

Senior leaders almost by definition have few true peers within an organization. As such, this constituent of the 'web of influence' includes internal and external peers at the same or similar level and scope of responsibility. Today's matrix organizations require executives to lead others not in their reporting structure. Further, senior managers need to be able to lead their peers across the organization, at least for the initiatives for which they are responsible. Michel Langlois states that to reach the next level of performance, leaders need to become like founders: they need to passionately embrace guiding principles and make them real for their colleagues. The hard part is that they have to embrace the guiding principles—the 'constitution'—of something that they did not create.

Leaders work with their internal peers to develop the organizational structure and culture by influencing the way decisions are made and interactions take place in the organization. Teamwork is a useful lens through which to study how relationship and network leaders connect with their peers in a meaningful way. Councils, boards, senior executive staff meetings, offsite events and transformational initiatives all offer opportunities for teaming and leadership. Research by Janis Cannon-Bowers suggests that shared mental models (SMM) among team members may help them to make successful decisions (Cannon-Bowers, 1999). The way decision-making occurs in teams especially is often understood in terms of the SMMs of the tasks and team, i.e. the common or overlapping mental representations of task requirements, procedures and role responsibilities (Cannon-Bowers, Salas and Converse, 1993, 221). This shared understanding, when transmitted throughout the organization, strengthens the organizational culture. Langlois reinforces this point, stating that employees can lose sight of what is required of them, and to what they can aspire. They are 'citizens' of a country that is their ecosystem, not just their company organizational structure. Each citizen carries certain obligations to live in the country—and the leader must communicate and reinforce these obligations through relationships and networks.

Networking and building relationships within the professional community or other communities of interest has become more important as the percentage of knowledge workers has increased. This aspect of networking based on mutual respect and credibility is related to the dimension of content leadership (discussed in the next chapter). Content is important to peer leadership, but it can also become a trap.

Content enables someone to be respected amongst peers, which leads to trust, which is the foundation for leadership among equals. However, leaders must not rely only on content, because the more senior they become, the less likely they are to be the most knowledgeable on a particular topic. Effective leaders don't try to be the smartest person in the room. They develop the network of relationships to bring people with content who are respected by peers to address problems. The more effective the relationship and network, the more successful the result—which over time does more for a leader's reputation than trying to convince others that that he/she is the smartest person in the room.

Partners

Partners have a special place in the corporate landscape. They are neither employees (which means you can't hire or fire them) nor are they customers (which means they do not directly keep you in business by purchasing your products and services). However, business partners are vital to the success of many companies, especially those with heavy channel sales and those that require alliances to make complex sales—and when marketing, design, the supply chain or distribution have joint responsibilities.

Often, certain partner relationships favour one party, such as a dominant manufacturer or software provider who distributes through channel partners. Even so, given the enabling role partners play, treating them more like customers and less like employees is a better way to drive long-term success. In the increasingly interconnected web of relationships, a partner today could easily become a customer or owner tomorrow. Truly successful alliances are those in which the whole is larger than the sum of its parts: where partners cooperate to create something bigger than what either could have done separately.

Since partners can align with multiple organizations over time, it is important for leaders to develop relationships with partners that make them more hesitant to ally with competitors. This stickiness is directly attributable to the degree of authentic leadership demonstrated and to the strength of the relationship leaders develop over time with partners.

External customers/clients

This node of the web of influence consists of the people who use the products/services the leader's organization develops. Successful executives understand the importance of relationship and networking leadership in developing strong customer connection and influence. After all, these are the very people who use the company's products and services, and the source of the revenue lifeblood to the company. In corporate leadership, there is plenty of evidence to show that not only are authentic and effective leaders respected in the eyes of their followers and customers, but they also very really impact the financial bottomline; in fact, up to 45 per cent of an organization's performance (in economic terms) may be explained by its executive leadership (Day and Lord, 1988). This makes good leadership nothing short of a competitive advantage, as the chapter on strategic leadership shows. Leadership can be a source of competitive advantage, one of those lynchpins of a successful firm's corporate strategy. A firm's effort to dominate competitors requires a well-crafted strategy executed effectively, and leadership is critical both in formulating strategy and during the execution stage. Relationship leadership that enables customer acquisition, retention and development intersects two levers of competitive advantage: leadership and customer experience. While some companies have used senior management as sales closers and marketing figureheads, there is also value in developing long-term relationships with influential customers to drive product roadmaps, provide references, and to be dependable in tougher times.

One model by which leaders use their relationship and networking skills combined with their content leadership skills and other strengths to positively impact customer or client relationships is by becoming what David Maister calls a 'trusted advisor' (Maister, Green and Galford, 2000).

The relationship and networking leadership grid

The 'web of influence' framework is a useful way of classifying influence stakeholder types, and to organize thinking to consider how leadership is exercised through each type. The framework also shows the relative applicability of the six principles of influence to each type. Finally, it highlights areas to emphasize and pitfalls to avoid.

WEB OF INFLUENCE

	Employees	Peers	Customers	Partners
Common scenarios	•Business transformation •Crisis management •Operational workflow •Addressing performance problems	•Annual planning •Business transformation •Post-merger integration •Cross-functional projects	•Product road map definition •Master service agreement •Expanding market footprint	•Co-branding •Design collaboration •Distribution channels •Competitive advantage

Relevance of influence principles

○ ◔ ◑ ◕ ●
0 1 2 3 4

	Employees	Peers	Customers	Partners
Reciprocity	◔	●	◑	●
Liking	◕	●	●	●
Consensus	◑	◕	◕	●
Authority	●	◑	◕	◑
Consistency and Commitment	●	◕	●	◕
Scarcity	◕	◕	◑	◕
Good practices	•Motivate beyond immediate self-interests •Project inspiration, intellectual stimulation, individualized consideration	•Be seen as equal and contributing member of the relationship •Be visible •Communicate guiding principles	•Earn the right to be a trusted advisor •Develop vocal advocates for your products and services	•Invest time to develop deep relationships with primary partners •Build web with ultimate customers
Common pitfalls	•Avoid command and control, yet be assertive	•While content promotes respect, don't try to be smartest person in the room	•Distorted view of voice of customer, not incorporating relationship inputs	•Reliance on channel strength in lieu of strong relationships

What Infosys Leaders Say About Building Strong Client Relationships

For clients, one way in which relationship and networking leadership is manifested is in the development of a relationship that ultimately leads to becoming a trusted advisor. That is, in moving from a mere vendor or supplier to a consultant and, even better, to a concerned friend and trusted advisor, leaders can change the very nature of the way business is done with customers.

Satyendra Kumar

Satyendra Kumar shares his thoughts on what makes a leader a trusted advisor to a client. According to him, being a trusted advisor results from a number of things:

- First, it requires having credibility resulting from a proven track record of delivering results.
- Second, there needs to be genuine concern about the client's risks and problems. A trusted advisor understands his/her clients' business thoroughly, having done the homework to understand it and also having the expertise and thought process required to analyse it. What is required is the ability to meet the clients' needs and not focus on your own.
- It is very important to avoid being perceived as someone who is trying to sell all the time. The trusted advisor is seen as someone who looks at mutual interest and always articulates and follows a win–win strategy.
- Finally, becoming a trusted advisor means being seen as a peer. The fundamental constraint in any client relationship is that the supplier or vendor by definition is the one providing the service. But once someone earns the right for the client to also see them as a peer, as an equal, it is so much easier to gain their trust and convert it into a long-term relationship.

Rishi Raj Paul

In Rishi's model of becoming a trusted advisor, the following steps are critical:

- **Understand:** Identify the goals of the other party. Sometimes when dealing with alliance partners this may even involve asking pointed questions about what's in it for them, how will their performance be measured or how will they be compensated for the project in question. This helps Rishi understand what the other party is looking to get out of this.
- **Align:** Next, assess what you can do to help as well as what goals of yours will be met. Goal alignment, according to Rishi, is one of the most important prerequisites of a successful relationship. This assessment phase involves a great deal of due diligence and objective evaluation.
- **Leverage:** If there is goal alignment, moving towards goal achievement can be initiated. If, however, after the assessment step, there seems to be an imbalance, Rishi identifies other people who might better serve the needs of the other party by leveraging his networks, and identifies other areas in which Rishi and Infosys might contribute.
- **Celebrate:** It is important to showcase successes so that the loop of credibility is closed and feeds future efforts at becoming a trusted advisor.

Rishi is one of the top revenue generators in the Infosys–Oracle alliance, and this reputation itself opens doors at several client organizations and helps him get other business for Infosys. This kind of success does not happen overnight. Rishi's journey of becoming a trusted advisor has been one of discovery and learning from mistakes. For instance, earlier, when someone would approach him with a request, he would always agree to follow it up. Sometimes, though, it was not a good fit if Infosys happened to have a less mature solution in the area. Over time, Rishi learned that to be a true trusted advisor, it was important to do the necessary homework in investigating if each opportunity is truly worth following through. If he found that it is not, it may be best not to follow it through. Saying 'no' in such cases, or even better, finding better alternatives for the requestor, builds trust more than recklessly acquiescing and then falling short of expectations. Now, Rishi is in a better place to showcase true successes because the

projects he takes up have been thoroughly vetted for their potential
for mutual benefit.

V. Sriram

One of Sriram's favourite quotations is, 'Other things being equal,
people will buy from a friend; other things not being equal, people
will still buy from a friend.' To Sriram, the essence of developing a
relationship of trust with a client is to establish mutual professional
respect. One of the signs that this has happened is when a client is
not merely tolerant of meeting with you, but in fact looks forward to
meeting with you. There are several ways Sriram thinks one can develop
into a trusted advisor:

- Establishing your subject matter expertise; allowing the other
  person to realize that there are insights and knowledge you have
  to offer that he/she does not have.
- Always follow through on commitments made, even if—especially
  if—they are trivial, because these are signs of how well you will
  stick to larger commitments.
- In keeping with the signs of being an authentic leader, Sriram
  believes in being upfront and honest about what you can and
  cannot do. Blaming the 'system' or the 'company' as if it were
  an entity foreign to you destroys credibility, as does promising
  a great deal and not delivering on it. He describes an example
  of how he laid all the cards on the table with a client who
  wanted a deal in a country that is new to Infosys. With the tax
  laws, visa issues and other challenges in setting up an entirely
  new foreign operation, Sriram was justifiably guarded in his
  promises, although he did vow to do the best he could. At the
  time of writing, this contract (initiated recently) is still a definite
  possibility, thanks to the candid approach Sriram took.
- Sriram talks about the need to give to the client in every
  interaction. Consistent with the spirit of reciprocity, a true
  authentic leader tries to bring something to every meeting—and
  it's not necessarily a gift or a discount either; it can be a key

insight to a business problem, news about a product launch, a story about how another industry deals with an issue they are facing or an introduction to someone who may be of mutual benefit.

- Repeatedly demonstrating that you can help with the client's issues over time strengthens and enhances the relationship.

In maintaining the trusted advisor relationship over time, though, Sriram offers a caution: never take it for granted. He refuses to share what has been told to him in confidence, works very hard to earn the respect especially of peers and direct reports and often consciously maintains a professional distance. He has learned some of these lessons from a mistake he once made with a Japanese client. About four or five years into their relationship, over dinner one day, Sriram had made a comment teasing this person. He said nothing offensive, just engaged in some friendly banter that is routine in most Indian friendships. Being from a more formal cultural background, however, this client reminded Sriram, 'No matter what, I am still your client.' This immediately caused Sriram to realize that he had overstepped his boundaries, and he apologized. Due to his humility and willingness to accept blame for a mistake, the relationship was not damaged; in fact, today the person still comes to Sriram for career advice and they are in regular touch.

Sridhar Marri

Sridhar describes his mental model of what makes someone a trusted advisor. In approaching a client with a solution, he believes in doing the following things:

- First, Sridhar brings examples of mistakes done by similar others in the client's industry. This establishes that (a) Sridhar has sufficient knowledge about the client's industry, (b) he knows the domain well enough to point out the mistakes made by others, and (c) he has knowledge and expertise that the client does not.
- Having established his authority thus, Sridhar thinks of innovative features and possibilities, demonstrating thinking

that's 'ahead of the curve' in contrast to the mistakes he showcased earlier. This stage is about out-of-the-box creative thinking and presenting possibilities, not feasibilities.

- Next, Sridhar evaluates these creative ideas for relative merit and presents a careful analysis to the client for implementation.
- Once the client buys into this, he/she has established a relationship with Sridhar. It is now up to him to nurture and continue this relationship. Like Sriram, Sridhar reiterates the importance of not jeopardizing such a precious relationship.

Thus, knowing the business, the domain and the client help establish initial credibility. Then, in proposing creative solutions but following these up with practical solutions establishes that the leader is not merely all talk and no action, thus setting the trusted advisor relationship up for continued success.

Anand Swaminathan

A few signs, according to Anand, that one is a trusted advisor include:

- The other party is comfortable opening up in any conversation (personal or professional) and is willing to share anything with the leader.
- Just because a solution is suggested by the leader, it carries enough weight and credibility to be accepted. The other person recognizes that the leader, as a trusted advisor, will help navigate any challenges on their behalf. The solution is accepted because it came from him/her, not because of its inherent qualities alone.
- Some of the strongest relationships are the ones that have gone through the deepest crises. Without such a test, relationships are not deep or intense enough to turn into those enjoyed by trusted advisors.

Anand allows the trusted advisor relationship to naturally develop and doesn't force it. He creates opportunities and leverages crises to obtain a client's trust and confidence by being honest, committed and authentic about their options.

He narrates an interesting story about moving from a relative stranger to a trusted advisor for one of his clients at Microsoft. In early 2009, he started talking to a General Manager (GM) about a $200 million outsourcing contract done jointly with another organization. During one meeting, a disturbing fact emerged: it appeared that a very large cost was entirely missed from the estimate provided during the RFP (request for proposals) process. The GM was livid and declared that Infosys had lost her trust by not disclosing this cost. Anand immediately asked for some time, spoke with the partner and found out that they had failed to account for this cost, and somehow both Infosys and Microsoft had overlooked it until that point. He went back to the GM, apologized and took accountability for this oversight, instead of blaming the partner entirely. He probed deeper to understand what would break this deal for her, and promised to help her resolve this. He got the partner (privately) to find a solution, helped the GM position the issue internally and also positioned it with Infosys and finally got the deal rolling again. It turned out that the GM was aware of the fact that it wasn't Infosys's fault but was impressed that Anand didn't throw the partner under the bus or blame them exclusively. By focusing on the solution (instead of the problem), damage control and forward thinking, he earned her trust. Today, she regularly talks to him two or three times a week, sharing her own internal issues but also continuously engaging him on Infosys-specific issues.

*

Throughout this chapter, a few threads have bound together the research and practice on authentic relationship and networking leadership: trust, credibility, ethical influence and the desire to ultimately work towards mutually beneficial goals of all the parties in a relationship. Whether it is in initiating relationships of trust and candour with employees, or taking client relationships to the level of becoming trusted advisors to them, or treading carefully to avoid some of the pitfalls in misusing authority or manipulating influence principles—it is clear that authentic relationship and networking leadership does not come easily. However, whether one is naturally inclined towards building relationships or not, it is our belief that this aspect of leadership can be learned and developed in everyone. The stories and research contained in this chapter comprise our attempt at propelling you on your personal journey into the next step of relationship and networking leadership.

Bibliography

Avolio, B.J. (1999). *Full-range Leadership: Building the Vital Forces in Organizations*, Thousand Oaks, CA: Sage.

Bass, B.M. (1985). *Leadership and Performance Beyond Expectation*, New York: Free Press.

Brower, H.H., Schoorman, F.D. and Tan, H.H. (2000). 'A Model of Relational Leadership: The Integration of Trust and Leader–Member Exchange', *Leadership Quarterly*, 11, 227–50.

Balkundi, P. and Kilduff, M. (2005). 'The Ties That Lead: A Social Network Approach to Leadership', *Leadership Quarterly*, 16 (6), 941–61.

Cannon-Bowers, J.E., Salas, E. and Converse, S. (1993). 'Shared Mental Models in Expert Team Decision-making', in J. Castellan (ed.), *Individual and Group Decision-making: Current Issues*, Mahwah, NJ: Lawrence Earlbaum and Associates.

Cialdini, R. (2001). *Influence: Science and Practice*, 4th edn, Boston: Allyn and Bacon.

Coleman, J. (1988). 'Social Capital in the Creation of Human Capital', *American Journal of Sociology* Supplement, (94), 95–120.

Darling, D. (2002). *The Networking Survival Guide*, New York: McGraw-Hill.

Graen, G.B. and Uhl-Biehn, M. (1995). Relationship-based Approach to Leadership: Development of a Leader–Member Exchange (LMX) Theory of Leadership Over Twenty-five Years: Applying a Multi-level Multi-domain Perspective', *Leadership Quarterly*, 6, 219–47.

Heider, J. (1985). *The Tao of Leadership: Lao Tzu's Tao Te Ching Adapted for a New Age*, Atlanta, GA: Humanics New Age.

Judge, T.A., Bono, J.E., Ilies, R. and Gerhardt, M. (2002). 'Personality and Leadership: A Qualitative and Quantitative Review', *Journal of Applied Psychology*, 87, 765–80.

Katz, D. and Kahn, R.L. (1978). *The Social Psychology of Organizations*, New York: Wiley.

King, Martin Luther, Jr., Letter from Birmingham Jail (n.d.), The Martin Luther King, Jr. Research and Education Institute at Stanford University, retrieved 30 April 2010 from http://www.stanford.edu/group/King/frequentdocs/birmingham.pdf.

Maister, D.H., Green, C.H. and Galford, R.M. (2000). *The Trusted Advisor*, New York: Free Press.

Murrell, K.L. (1997). 'Emergent Theories of Leadership for the Next Century: Towards Relational Concepts', *Organization Development Journal*, 15 (3), 35–42.

Sensenig, P.E. and Cialdini, R.B. (1984). 'Social Psychological Influences on the Compliance Process: Implications for Behavioral Health', in J. Matarazzo, N.E. Miller, S.M. Weiss and J.A. Herd (eds.), *Behavioral Health: A Handbook of Health Enhancement and Disease Prevention*, New York: Wiley, 384–92.

Tsai, W. and Ghoshal, S. (1998). 'Social Capital and Value Creation: The Role of Intra-firm Networks', *Academy of Management Journal*, 41 (4), 464–76.

Uhl-Bien, M. (2006). 'Relational Leadership Theory: Exploring the Social Processes of Leadership and Organizing', *Leadership Quarterly*, 17 (6), 654–76.

Wheatley, M.J. (1999). *Leadership and the New Science*, 2nd edn, San Francisco: Berrett-Koehler.

Zaccaro, S.J., Kemp, C. and Bader, P. (2004). 'Leader Traits and Attributes', in J. Antonacis, A.T. Cianciolo and R.J. Stemberg (eds.), *The Nature of Leadership*, Thousand Oaks: Sage.

CHAPTER 8

CONTENT LEADERSHIP

CHITRA SARMMA

'If I have seen farther than other men, it is because I stood on the shoulders of giants.'

—*Sir Isaac Newton*

A martial arts student was in a hurry to achieve distinction in the field. He approached his teacher and asked how long it would take him to reach his goal. The teacher's reply was a casual, 'Ten years.' Now, this was quite unacceptable to the student. He now promised the teacher that he would put in many more hours, and repeated his question. The teacher responded, 'Twenty years' (Davenport, 2010).

What did the teacher mean? That hard work actually slows development? Or could it be that the teacher wanted the student to think very differently about the ways in which he could achieve distinction and not merely believe that investment of more time automatically ensures mastery? Like all instructional stories this one too is meant to encourage reflection. The answer of the teacher sounds quite illogical at first, but it can make us question some of our assumptions related to gaining expertise in a particular area of interest and moving towards creating thought leadership. Is visionary content leadership an outcome of many years of hard work? Or can it be achieved with a few instances of inspired creativity? How do you know whether you have the potential of becoming a thought leader?

This chapter is about content leadership—or, in the currently popular business vernacular, 'thought leadership'—at Infosys. It is about how leaders can influence the direction of the organization, their team and possibly their very profession by means of their expertise and unique conceptual contributions in the area in which they work.

First, the chapter will look at the term 'thought leadership' as writers in the popular business press have conceptualized it. Second, we will review the academic literature dealing with content leadership, mental models and the development of expertise. Lastly, we will review the techniques thought leaders at Infosys use to grow and apply their thought leadership. The purpose is to highlight points of view, practices and experiences that have helped people become content leaders. A second purpose is to note that the path to becoming a thought leader isn't always easy—the chapter will also highlight some of the challenges faced by Infosys leaders.

Thought Leadership

Wikipedia (2010) suggests that thought leadership is 'an increasingly vital driver of business success'. The term thought leadership was coined in 1994 by Joel Kurtzman, editor-in-chief of the magazine *Strategy & Business* (Wikipedia, 2010). Kurtzman used the term to refer to people he interviewed who had contributed new ideas to business.

Wikipedia provides another perspective: 'Thought leadership is a buzz word . . . used to describe a futurist or person who is recognized among their peer mentors for innovative ideas and demonstrates the confidence to promote or share those ideas as actionable, distilled insights . . . [it] has come to mean someone who enlivens old processes with new workable ideas.' They argue that when a firm is labelled a thought leader, 'It is the recognition from the outside world that the company deeply understands its business, the needs of its customers, and the broader marketplace in which it operates' (Wikipedia, 2010).

Consolidating these perspectives, thought leadership may be seen as a significant factor in creating value that is differentiated from competitors, from a combination of both insight and foresight.

Innovative ideas can win over clients, taking them to a point they didn't know existed, or propel employees to novel ways of thinking that add unimaginable value to their lives.

Examples of thought leaders throughout history include British economist Adam Smith, Stanford economist Paul M. Romer, Apple CEO Steve Jobs, Mitsubishi president Minoru Makihara, University of Michigan strategist C.K. Prahalad and his co-author Gary Hamel, a professor at the London Business School. But since the term was first used, it has extended from business to other disciplines and has come to mean someone who enlivens old processes with new ideas. As a result, there are thought leaders today in several fields: in the sciences, humanities, arts, consulting, IT companies and even in government. This broader definition has given rise to the idea that Nobel Prize winners too should be considered thought leaders. Another common theme among thought leaders is that the leaders' original ideas became the source of their company's competitive advantage. Thought leadership thus is actually a component of strategic leadership. The contemporary enthusiasm about thought leadership is perhaps largely due to the belief that it has the potential to open new markets and create enormous growth options for companies.

The Essence of Content Leadership

But yield who will to their separation,
My object in living is to unite
My avocation and vocation
As my two eyes make one in sight.
Only where love and need are one,
And the work is play for mortal stakes,
Is the deed ever really done
For Heaven and the future's sakes.

This great poem by the poet Robert Frost suggests that thought leadership is the realm where our avocation and vocation converge. When our passion—the source of our energy—and work come together it is possible that work is play and endless possibilities for making novel contributions are opened up. One of many perspectives on thought leaders is provided by the business magazine *Leadership*

Excellence which has rated the top thought leaders in management and leadership; according to their website, 'the gurus who make our Excellence 100 list today possess a rare combination of traits and abilities'. The factors the magazine's editors consider when evaluating thought leaders include:

- **Preparation:** academic and professional
- **Character:** values, ethics, beliefs, purpose, mission, integrity, walking the talk
- **Principles:** big message, point of view, tenets, main points
- **Personality:** charisma, style, originality, authenticity, one of a kind
- **Performance:** inspiring action, real-world performance, work ethic
- **Experience:** beyond local and regional, more national and international
- **Expression:** substance and style in writing, speaking, coaching, consulting, mentoring, training or teaching
- **Influence:** difference, results, change, transformation

However, this definition seems to miss something fundamental about the ability to consistently generate original, useful ideas. It is perhaps possible that someone can be high on all the areas mentioned but still not as innovative as Steve Jobs or as creative as Robert Frost. On the other hand, C.K. Prahalad was a thought leader in business strategy who introduced not only the concept of 'core competence' (Prahalad and Hamel, 1990) but several other great ideas including that of 'the fortune at the bottom of the pyramid' (Prahalad, 2004). Prahalad expressed many of the virtues noted by *Leadership Excellence*, but he also possessed the ability to synthesize and go beyond what was dreamed by others before—in other words, 'standing on the shoulders of giants', as Newton put it. So, thought leadership may be a combination of two factors: original ideas as well expertise built upon past knowledge.

Are Decisions Based on Content Leadership?

Consider a scenario where you have to recommend one of two orthopaedic surgeons to your best friend. The first surgeon has written seminal books on the topic but has never operated on even one patient. The other has performed thousands of successful knee surgeries, but hasn't written even one article on the subject. Whom would you recommend? One hypothesis is that the ideal thought leader in applied sciences should have both thorough experience and original ideas. For example, Steve Jobs holds multiple patents and has significant credibility in designing great consumer technology; he also has a proven track record of converting these original ideas to applications that have favourably impacted millions of lives.

Should Every Leader be a Thought Leader?

One question every leader should consider is: should every leader be a thought leader? Kotter's (1990) and other definitions of leadership argue that it involves installing a new order, or bringing the future to the present. Even though Kotter didn't use the term content leadership, he suggests that at least part of leading change includes originality. It might be better to consider that different types of leadership may require varying amounts of thought leadership. Some jobs may not require many original ideas (e.g. transactional government jobs), and consequently, for them, thought leadership may not be very important.

Research on the full range leadership model (e.g. Bass and Avolio, 1999) over the last thirty years with thousands of leaders globally consistently shows that one of the most effective forms of leadership, 'transformational leadership', has elements of thought leadership. In particular, the factors of intellectual stimulation and inspirational motivation have strong components of original ideas threading through them. This research demonstrates convincingly that in the vast majority of leadership positions, a vision that does not inspire others to action definitely is not as effective as having an inspirational vision that stimulates others' hearts and minds.

Becoming a Thought Leader

Scientists recognize that Newton, Feynman, Edison and other high profile scientists are all thought leaders. In the field of consulting, many would identify organizations such as McKinsey and Boston Consulting

Group as content leaders, especially since they have techniques that have been admired and used by many firms globally. However, when examined more closely, other evidence contradicts these assertions. An online article by Elise Bauer (2003) underlines an important aspect of thought leadership: 'Thought leadership is recognition from the outside world that a company deeply understands its business, the needs of its customers, and the broader marketplace in which it operates. Thought leadership is built on what others say about you.'

It seems clear that others' perception of your ideas is central to the idea of thought leadership. One simply cannot anoint oneself a 'thought leader' without others seeing you in this light.

Developing Thought Leadership

There are several options all of us can pursue to improve our thought leadership. First, we can grow our expertise in our particular domain. This would include reading, studying and practicing creating our own original ideas that solve problems in our area of interest. In addition, there are tools from a wide variety of sources—ranging from engineering to biology and social psychology—that you can employ to improve your ability to generate innovative ideas and solutions.

For example, consider TRIZ, one such resource that can help you generate novel ideas. TRIZ, which stands for a Russian acronym for 'the theory of inventive reasoning', is 'a methodology, tool set, knowledge base, and model-based technology for generating innovative ideas and solutions for problem solving. TRIZ provides tools and methods for use in problem formulation, system analysis, failure analysis, and patterns of system evolution (both "as is" and "could be")' (Wikipedia, 2010). TRIZ has traditionally been used in creative engineering applications but has also been adapted to other domains. Current research in TRIZ looks at the science of biomimetics—how biology has solved problems over 3.5 billion years—to identify potential solutions to human problems (Vincent, Bogatryeva, Bogatyrev, Bowyer and Pahl, 2006). Using either physical or biological science analogues have been in use for thousands of years to solve various engineering problems, and increasingly can be used to innovate new solutions to old business problems.

Second, we have to make sure our expertise gets used. A cure for cancer is useless if no one knows about it and is willing to use it. Getting clients to use your thought leadership involves demonstrating supportive and caring behaviour by listening, uncovering needs, crafting a strong solution and delivering value even before starting any intense engagement. It is precisely in this area—getting your expertise used—that Robert B. Cialdini has studied and practiced his entire career. Cialdini is the most cited living social psychologist and has led a forty-year-long programme of research in the social psychology of persuasion and influence. In his book *Influence: Science and Practice* he elaborates on the principle of consistency and authority, among others, as powerful principles of ethical influence (Cialdini, 1993a).

Cialdini's research and business experience suggest that if people commit orally or in writing to an idea or goal, they are more likely to honour that commitment (Cialdini, 1993b). Even if the original incentive or motivation is removed after they have already agreed, they will continue to honour the agreement. This is why many car dealers get you to agree to one price, and then have another salesperson try to sell you many additional products and services. Cialdini's principles suggest that another way to enhance your content or thought leadership is to share case studies and client testimonials that demonstrate your new thinking in the industry. In so far as other leaders perceive this as useful input, they will consider it a gift and be more likely to reciprocate your favour, another Cialdini principle. Leaders who make promises and then follow through completely create the invaluable feeling of trust in clients that the organization delivers on commitments.

Mental Models and Thought Leadership

Brilliant new ideas like Apple's iPhone don't generally come from novices; they come from experts. Here, it is important to remember that while earlier the possibility was considered that expertise is a natural outcome of length of experience, the more recent literature suggests that it takes about ten years or 10,000 hours of deliberate practice in almost any field to become an expert (Ericsson, 1993).

This could explain why even when we have very experienced people nominated as experts by their colleagues, their actual performance is sometimes unremarkable. Individuals who choose to go the way of deliberate practice would focus on extending themselves beyond their current capabilities and are more likely to reach their potential (Ericsson, 2006).

But what is an expert thought leader? One approach to thinking about this is by understanding what happens to the human cognitive system when one learns. Early on, we simply detect and encode information into our short-term memory, which later becomes stored in long-term memory. As we practice and gain mastery, we organize this information in ways that ensure that we are clear how new information is similar and different from old information. Eventually, after roughly ten years of concerted practice, most people acquire models we use in our mind about how our knowledge 'works' in the real world. Mental models are knowledge structures or frameworks for describing the interrelationship between activities, objects and abstract items of knowledge in a person's mind, and can also involve prediction of future events (Johnson-Laird, 1983).

In other words, mental models are representations in our brains about causation. When we know how things cause other things, we can make predictions about what might happen in different scenarios. These 'mental models' become useful to experts who can use their creativity to conduct mental or real-world 'what if' experiments to create new ideas, or combine old ideas into something new. They are an important part of an individual's thought processes because they provide structure to the thinking and increase the efficiency of leadership decision-making.

Lord and Hall (2005) suggest that leadership development may be seen through the lens of such theories of learning and expertise. In this view, as there are changes in the way leaders think and process information, their underlying knowledge structures or mental models change, and this is how leadership skills develop. At each skill level (novice versus intermediate versus expert leader), different knowledge and information processing capabilities exist. In a similar vein, Ford and Kraiger (1995) believe that effective leaders have more efficient thought processes and use appropriate mental models because their decision behaviours 'contain more diagnostic clues for detecting meaningful patterns in the learning or transfer environment'. This research suggests that leaders must understand how complex processes—markets, governments, employees and shareholders, among others—work. By building their mental models about one or more of these areas, they may be able to become an expert and conceive of better ways of realizing their organizational goals.

Building New Mental Models

The term 'mental model' indicates the existence of a paradigm which could be the sum total of a person's ideas, beliefs and practices that helps them understand how the world works. Ultimately, this impacts the way a person interacts with the world. In order to build new mental models or refine existing ones, leaders need multiple options, or 'discovery methods', that make them aware of different possible situations where different factors cause the outcomes of interest in a given domain (Moreno, 2004, 99). In simulation, learners have the opportunity to experiment with different mental models and have the option of a living experience to understand complex systems and realities. Experiential learning has become a powerful possibility through learning games and simulations.

Infosys and Thought Leadership

At Infosys, thought leadership is central to our leadership model. Our definition includes the following behavioural indicators that our leaders are expected to learn and apply. For us, an excellent content leader:

- stimulates the business ideas of his/her team far beyond competitors
- has produced ideas that will redefine the competitive landscape to be favourable for his/her unit for years to come
- is respected globally by experts in his/her field as a successful innovator
- is a highly sought after keynote speaker at major industry conferences.

If we were to derive a few characteristics of a thought leader from the above, we can say that a content leader is someone with original ideas that are highly relevant and significant for solving business problems, and someone who has the persuasive ability to influence others to adopt innovative ideas.

Content Leaders at Infosys

What do real thought leaders do at Infosys? The remainder of this chapter will review both successes and lessons learned from successful Infosys thought leaders—Satyendra Kumar, Valmeeka (Val) Nathan and Girish A.R. Pay careful attention to their passionate combinations of avocation and vocation so that you can emulate their thinking processes in order to derive potential ways to nurture your own thought leadership. These leaders scored highest in thought leadership in the eyes of their stakeholders, as part of Infosys Leadership Institute's Leadership Journey Assessments. Details on each leader's professional background can be found at the back of the book.

Each leader was interviewed for their perspectives on what made them so successful in the area of content leadership as measured by ILI's Leadership Journey Series, and any lessons learned they would share for others striving to grow their thought leadership. Seven themes emerged:

1. Metacognition and Thought Leadership
2. Unconventional Thinking
3. Collective Thought Leadership
4. Building on Existing Thought Leadership
5. Foresight + Insight
6. Focus + Flow
7. Personal Connects, Views and Challenges

Each theme is explored in detail below.

Metacognition and Thought Leadership

Metacognition is defined as 'cognition about cognition' or 'knowing about knowing'. It can take many forms and includes knowledge about when and where to use particular strategies for learning or for problem solving (Metcalfe and Shimamura, 1994).

One USA-based client heard about Kumar's training sessions for Infosys employees and sought a meeting with him. The client shared his problem as one of not being able to deliver on time to his clients—40 per cent of the projects were late. The client had little faith that the projects were predictable, and consequently faced a struggle to secure budgets from superiors. Even worse, the team members themselves had a very low confidence level in their ability to deliver projects effectively. As the client was disclosing his challenges, Kumar's new ideas were coming into focus. What was critical in this case was to arrive at an effective solution that could work in their environment. It struck Kumar that he could not suggest too many drastic changes because there were many senior people in the client system who could feel threatened by the solution being proposed. Consequently, he recommended that the aggregate data related to the solution be shared with the Senior Vice President, but not used for any appraisal process. Kumar's final solution revolved around enabling the client to identify the potential risks and bottlenecks in the projects early on. The shift he attempted was from troubleshooting to 'early warning'. In one year 75 per cent of projects were being delivered on time. After two and a half years more than 90 per cent projects were delivered on time. The client Vice President has now become CIO and is a good friend of Kumar's. Infosys has subsequently done a lot of work with this client and there has been a whole lot of appreciation from them for the value delivered by Infosys.

Consider some insights from Kumar's example. First, he built a new solution only after very carefully listening to the client, understanding the unique political dynamics. Second, he first made new associations, building on the original, and adapted an approach to ensure that his expertise got used. Third, Kumar kept getting new ideas as the conversation evolved. Clearly, Kumar's multi-decade set of experiences allowed him to use his sophisticated mental model together with his client relationship skills to identify a new solution. His example suggests that a thought leader must have the ability to process new data as it emerges and synthesize it with what is already known. This is an essential feature of having and continuously improving a leader's mental model, and it seems to be a winning combination in Kumar's case.

Unconventional thinking

Girish's experiences in the realm of building thought leadership indicate a strong procedural mental model for generating new ideas. In his words, 'You need to have an eye for real good business problems that do not yet have an elegant solution.' This is very different from the conventional approach of asking what a client needs and then working towards a solution. When Infosys restructured itself to focus on industry vertical markets, there was a clear need for developing new service lines that demonstrate the value of its unique combination of technology and deep domain understanding. 'We saw a large market opportunity emerging around radio frequency identification (RFID) technology services, and identified a void in the space of real time event management software for enterprise applications. Joining hands with a colleague with expertise in real time telecom systems, I leveraged my background in warehouse automation applications to develop a unique platform which eventually led to a patent filing,' Girish says. This intellectual property enabled Infosys to acquire business from a number of early adopters of RFID and successfully delivered a much differentiated value proposition in each of those engagements.

In 2002, Kumar demonstrated unconventional thinking in another example. He was asked to resolve the challenge of a sudden increase in customer complaints—they had risen to almost sixty per month. He came up with a new unconventional approach: project level risk monitoring. This was a mechanism for a weekly review of risks to identify potential risk aspects. One of the key challenges was to reposition the mindset such that high risk was not perceived as something negative but merely meant that help was needed. It took six months to ensure the success of this approach. In this example, the key seems to be that instead of taking up each one of the problems individually, the attempt was to put in place a process which would indicate the possibility or likelihood of a problem coming up. It seems to suggest a shift from advocating a solution to following an inquiry process so that the real cause of the problems are anticipated and addressed.

Val's strategy for new ideas comes from challenging assumptions, or the way things have always been done, saying, 'There is one behaviour that I would encourage and many times role model myself—question the status quo.' In fact, Val feels that 'the true human spirit' of innovation and agility comes from questioning the status quo. For example, he notes that Kodak did not survive the early digital cycle since they did not question their analog roots. Val feels, 'I must have a model that will kill my current business model let's say three to five years from now, because by this time others would have already copied it—so what is my differentiator? So, we have to shift the game—can we create stepping stones for others to build on?'

Collective Thought Leadership

Val also notes that, as a leader, 'It is not about my thought leadership, it is about creating an ecosystem around it—creating a team that understands the "complimentarity" and the multiple views.' He views himself like a 'lightning rod' that encourages others to rally round and he helps in creating the value proposition. 'For me this means, even if I get tired, when I drop off, somebody else takes over and vice versa; it is about creating a team—leveraging the outcome of many people's passionate effort. This for me is thought leadership,' he says.

Val's perspective suggests teamwork is central to his own thought leadership. He recalls that when he first joined Infosys, 'I only knew engineering—not much about the processes or alignments required. I was initially scared when people started leaving. Very soon, others joined the team and I found that they were helping me understand system terminologies, processes, the internal workings of Infosys. They helped navigate through this initial stage. I found myself aligning emotionally with some of my team members. Shantanu, for example, brought out some compelling points and his method was to create value and move on. I aligned to his thinking and it worked for us both. I basically trusted my people unless the data proved otherwise. I had people who were different from me, better than me in certain aspects, and this also worked very well.'

Building on existing Thought Leadership

Kumar gives another important example of where his thought leadership was instrumental in solving a major problem. He recollects,

'In 2004, we had delivery and sales units—then the transition took place to industry business units (IBUs), horizontal business units (HBUs) etc. Business planning was always the forte of corporate planning and hence a proposal was put to me by Kris and Dinesh that indicated the need to provide a perspective to the leaders about their business, their customer's challenges, their market segments etc. It was quite clear by then that engineering processes needed to be tuned to the domain they are working in. The challenge was: how do we do this?'

Consequently, Kumar studied the Malcolm Baldridge framework, and tailored it to take the business to a higher level in the area of business planning and customer focus. He further produced a proposal for how this could be used to create the business transformation desired by the Infosys Board of Directors. Kumar outlined a very detailed step-by-step transition plan to deal with the challenges and accentuated the logic and the mechanisms of working out the implementation. The outcome of Kumar's work was the ISOP framework and programme.

In this example, you can see where Kumar built on what others had done and also took it to new levels. He improved and personalized a model of quality in tandem with the unique context at Infosys. Here, his thought leadership combined both his mental model of quality methods with his mental model of Infosys's culture, history and relationships.

Foresight + Insight

Girish notes that he recognized quite early on the need for Infosys to explore new client engagement models. 'While the Global Delivery Model (GDM) was central to our strategy to deliver value to clients and achieve market leadership, our growth had an almost linear relationship with our headcount. That had to change, and there was an opportunity to leverage our intellectual property to create new business models where our success could be based on business value delivered rather than mere effort spent,' he recounts.

Girish conceptualized a RFID-based wireless data acquisition appliance that could be used to track and trace a class of products that are mission critical, perishable and also expensive. He notes that the engineering team was excited about the prospect of the development of such a device that could open up a new market, and successfully created a software and hardware platform notwithstanding resource constraints. 'We secured our first business from a global medical devices company and helped them significantly optimize their consignment inventory business model. The engagement model did not require them to make upfront capital investment in our technology; they just paid us a monthly fee to use our service which was priced based on the business benefits that they achieved.'

But Girish is candid to admit that this was not really a textbook-like process. He notes, 'We entered the health care market not entirely by design, rather we entered with a hypothesis: if a product has high value and there is a need for traceability, then we have a solution for it.' He adds, 'With the intellectual asset paying off, the revenue productivity and profitability was significantly higher than our conventional service delivery model. It also gave us a fantastic opportunity to internally evangelize the value of IP-based technology services.'

Encouraged by the success of the new business model, Girish's team went on to extend and create an IP portfolio based on wireless sensors, real time location systems (RTLS), mobility and pervasive computing. This has been the basis for new business from global clients in the gaming and entertainment, health care, logistics and consumer retail industries. Most of these opportunities were a result of proactive identification of a client need and a compelling business model that enables rapid adoption of new technology.

Val reflects on his foresight and insight at Infosys, 'It has been four years now. When I joined, I did not know this business. People were dismissive about what we did and the team had low morale.' Remarking on the insightful technical knowledge of the group, Val says, 'They are people who had designed aircraft and automobiles, and had spent their young years wanting to be engineers, but something was not working.' Val's work with his team today has changed that. A significant part of his approach relates to the transformation possibilities anticipated. Val had the foresight that 'engineering cannot be a low margin business, rather it is about creating'. He felt the key was 'to enrol people in the journey . . . and have a grand vision'. Val's vision was to grow from $30 million to $1 billion in five years, and eventually to become at least 10 per cent of Infosys's entire business. He comments that today, 'one can see a phenomenal transformation . . . Product Lifecycle and Engineering Solutions (PLES) is now one of the most profitable businesses in all of Infosys'.

Focus + Flow

Kumar reflects on whether he builds his new ideas in the normal flow of work or whether it's a particular focal point that he concentrates on in specific segment of time. He recalls:

> In the late 1990s when I was consulting as an individual, my question to myself was, 'Two years later what am I going to do differently?' I got the answer only when I started working with Tata in their new entity called Tata Quality Management and experienced the excitement of a constant intake of knowledge and applying it in a variety of business scenarios for creating new experiences. So, for me, engaging constantly in gathering new knowledge and experience is part of building thought leadership. I would also concede a large part of my growth and mental abilities to training. Even in Tata, I had facilitated close to 150 workshops. The fact is that I was never trained in the subjects. I would get interested in a subject, find an opportunity for a training programme and sharing it with others, and this has led to my growth. For the last five years I have devoted 25 per cent of my time to developing others. Even now, for my direct reports I set an aspiration for at least ten days in a year to be spent in facilitating a training session. This gets the person to start thinking about what questions could get asked, what new things can emerge. This engaging in developing others builds your content leadership; otherwise you cannot speak in depth in front of other people.

What is emerging from Kumar's experience is that the approach of focusing on one aspect and then immersing oneself in it to the extent that it becomes a natural flow is a way in which one can build and sustain thought leadership.

The concept of 'flow' was developed by Mihaly Csikszentmihalyi, a psychology professor at the University of Chicago, who proposed that 'optimal performance in all of us occurs at a time when we are fully immersed in an activity to the point that we achieve an almost "zen-like" sense of oneness with that activity' (Ryde, 2007, 26). The flow state also implies a kind of focussed attention, and indeed, it has been noted that mindfulness, meditation, yoga and martial arts seem to improve a person's capacity for flow (Wikipedia, 2010).

Building Thought Leadership: personal connects, views and challenges

According to Kumar:

> The two distinct pieces related to content and leadership need to come together. Leadership is required to extract from one's depth knowledge to lead into the future; seeing the big picture is critical. Articulation and content also need to come together. I interpret the term leader to mean somebody who can lead into the future. Regarding content, can you make it mean something significant to the organization and its business? The content could be engineering, it could be people leadership, or it could be domain. In my view, my content leadership is about the larger engineering, big-picture thinking and execution, along with articulation and strategic thinking. One of the biggest challenges I faced was to manage and deal with the politics of the organization. If you are a thought leader you should not indulge in it; you should just focus on value creation: content or thought leadership is predominantly value creation. John has written a book in which the first quote is by Jamshedji, the second quote is mine; I am saying this because I know I have a lot of raw material for a book but have still not got around to writing one. Is this a disadvantage, does this affect my thought leadership? I am not sure. But I do understand that one of my challenges is to write this book which is there in my mind.

Importantly, Val notes that he's human too, saying, 'I am not the most fantastic leader and so people may have had a challenging time [with me]. I managed to recruit some very smart and capable people. I also reached out to junior levels. I looked for people and got people who have the energy and I must say that they have helped a lot. I created an environment that leverages energy. When it is my turn to feel low—I too get tired and so I too need a lift at times—the environment, basically the people, create the energy for me to push ahead.' He draws an analogy with the world of biology, 'It is like the migratory birds; when one bird gets tired of leading and dips, another bird steps in and once again provides the lift. I remember in any conversation I had with my people I would consciously keep in mind that at the end of the conversation we both should feel positive and energized for further creation.'

For Val, part of being a thought leader is acknowledging that not all thoughts can be good ones, and as he tells his son, 'We all are "mistake gods". We make mistakes and learn and there were mistakes that I made and learnt from—also from my team members. In the end, it was the belief, passion and energy for the engineering value we could create that took us on a growth track.'

Kumar's early history indicates that perhaps part of the reason for his content breadth is that he is well read in a variety of domains. He recalls:

One of my early interests in life was reading literature. I was excited to understand how human beings and social structures behave. My struggle was to understand the bigger picture, how the larger society works, so I would read and reflect on elements of it as it came through in literature. The influencers were multiple pieces from different authors. Ayn Rand built in me the belief that it is important to build the self. The self is all about content and conviction. The works of Maxim Gorky, Albert Camus and Jean-Paul Sartre made me aware of different points of view, made me tolerant to understand different points of view and deal with conflicts more easily. They helped in understanding that in corporations there are conflicts—you have to live with realities of the company, be very open-minded, not pass judgments and hence deal with current realities more effectively. This helped me a lot, because later on, I was amazed to see that the discipline of quality management gives an opportunity to observe how a large company functions.

Kumar believes that what makes him successful as a quality professional is his ability to relate the engineering element with the business requirement of the company. The aspect of feeling excited and curious about the big picture, the ability to understand the nuances and connect with senior management gave him the confidence that he could make a difference.

Regarding business relationships, Kumar shares his view that very often people grow hierarchically from doers to managers, but sometimes they don't use best practices because they are not easily available. He could take the route of applying the best practices because they get grouped under the Quality umbrella. The experience of applying all the knowledge pieces and best practices of his consulting days was very exciting for him and shaped his thought leadership.

Reflecting on his own journey to becoming a thought leader, Val suggests, 'Thought leadership is about getting the required results by using wisdom in a natural rhythm.' For Val, working in an effective team environment is essential; 'the effort is proportionate to the outcome required, I am in synch with the ecosystem, working in a team environment in tune with others; the experience is humbling since it is about creating value for others,' he explains. Val considers everyone a thought leader in their own way, but not intellectually. For Val, 'It is more emotional. When you feel passionately about something, it is also related to your views about the subject. The fact that you feel passionately about something, and decide to invest your intellectual bandwidth to engage in it and start socializing it, shows your emotional connection with the domain.' Val is convinced about the avocation component: 'the passion aspect is absolutely key,' he insists.

Girish believes that his thought leadership is shaped primarily by his innate curiosity. Even when he started his career as a developer, he looked for opportunities to gain breadth and depth in both technology and business. Being part of a high growth organization, his exposure in different roles—he has had stints in engineering, pre-sales, client services, consulting and innovation labs—influenced him to a great extent. Girish accepts that while he personally faces the challenge of understanding the organization's network and influencing decisions that imply more risk, he is a firm believer in the process of ideation, exploration and experimentation for enhancing thought leadership.

Despite the challenges they faced, the leaders have been successful in sharing their thought leadership with many others. Kumar with his vast experience in using various quality management models and techniques like ISO9000, MBNQA, EFQM, CMM/CMMI and Six Sigma, is a regular speaker at Software Engineering and Process Group (SEPG), QuEST, Nasscom and CII forums. He has served as a Director on the executive board of the QuEST Forum from 2006 to 2008 and chairs the India hub for the forum. In his own words, 'The ability to use the experience and knowledge to generate and articulate higher value is the essence of being invited to speak at a conference. For example at the level of a keynote speaker one has to abstract the concept at a higher level, lay out the scenarios related to applying of the thought leadership subject, failing or succeeding with the approach—and this sharing leads to discovering new ideas that can be used. Another benefit is that when we disseminate and share our thoughts in larger forums, they start inviting us to more such forums.'

Val has been recognized for his thought leadership in global engineering by a wide variety of international luminaries. He was a speaker at the PLM summit in 2008. He has been interviewed on topics pertaining to green engineering and lean global engineering by media like *CXO* magazine, *eGov, EE Times, Dataquest, Hindu Business Line* and *Deccan Herald*. Val is a member of the Nasscom executive council for engineering services. He has also been an executive council member of Singapore Industrial Automation Association and led a sub-committee with the Singapore government on collaborative PLM initiatives for local small and medium entrepreneurs.

Girish has authored multiple patent filings and several trade, technical and business media have published his business/technology viewpoints. He has been invited as a speaker at key industry and academic events. He has developed and sold multiple non-linear service delivery models like Information as a Service and IP licensing.

*

The conversations with the leaders and the preceding literature seem to suggest that content or thought leadership leads to highly engaged and contributing leaders who are hence able to influence and transform the thinking of people around them too. While the need to gain mastery in the domain aspects of their thought leadership is essential, the greater mastery is perhaps over their thinking habits and having the ability to switch to new and different mental models. In some of the examples, it is clear that when the leader moves towards thought leadership the team too moves towards becoming more innovative. Consequently, thought leadership is most likely to result in building tremendous capabilities in those who work with the thought leader.

Considering the kind of energy that thought leadership can bring about, it almost seems like an antidote to low morale or the disengaged employees syndrome. An aspiring thought leader can aim to first understand the thinking habits and then use some concrete methods to change his or her thinking. Studies suggest that where effective leaders differ is that they are able to move beyond a description of problems they face to the prescription of what should be done, and how to get there. This framework of leadership 'sense making' holds that prescriptive mental models arise from reflection on and analysis of current problems in terms of their personal history and experiences, with particular emphasis on the integrative themes arising from the meanings that leaders extract from them (Strange and Mumford, 2005)

One of the key aspects of content leadership is the development and use of a mental model that helps a leader focus on the quality and not the quantity of time spent on different challenges. The insightful use of past knowledge and experiences in newer and different ways and—most importantly—in a very qualitative, value-adding way, has moved the leaders at Infosys toward ever-better thought leadership. Integrating the leaders' examples, the words of the Zen master and the poet Robert Frost, it seems that by using some of the mental models outlined, by thinking differently and by uniting our vocation and avocation we can embark on the journey of becoming thought leaders.

Bibliography

Adelson B. and Soloway, E. (1985). 'The Role of Domain Experience in Software Design', *IEEE Transactions on Software Engineering*, 11, 1351–60.

Avolio, B.J. and Bass, B.M. (1995). 'Individual Consideration Viewed at Multiple Levels of Analysis: A Multi-level Framework for Examining the Diffusion of Transformational Leadership', *Leadership Quarterly*, 6, 199–218.

Bass, B.M. and Avolio, B.J. (1990). *Transformational Leadership Development: Manual for the Multifactor Leadership Questionnaire*, Palo Alto, CA: Consulting Psychologist Press.

Bauer, Elise (2003). 'Be a Thought Leader', retrieved from http://www.elise.com on 12 May 2010.

Bryman, A. (1992). *Charisma and Leadership in Organizations*, London: Sage.

Canterucci, Jim F. (2005). *Personal Brilliance: Mastering the Everyday Habits That Create a Lifetime of Success*, New York: AMACOM.

Cialdini, R.B. (1993a). *Influence: Science and Practice*, 3rd edn, New York: HarperCollins.

Cialdini, R.B. (1993b). *Influence: The Psychology of Persuasion*, rev. edn, New York: Quill.

Davenport, M. Güne (2010). Zen Stories, 13 May, retrieved from http://goto.bilkent.edu.tr/gunes/ZEN/zenstories.htm.

Ericsson, K.A. (2006). 'The Influence of Experience and Deliberate Practice on the Development of Superior Expert Performance', in K.A. Ericsson, N. Charness, P. Feltovich and R.R. Hoffman (eds.), *Cambridge Handbook of Expertise and Expert Performance*, Cambridge, UK: Cambridge University Press, 685–706.

Ericsson, K.A., Krampe, R.Th. and Tesch-Romer, C. (1993). 'The Role of Deliberate Practice in the Acquisition of Expert Performance', *Psychological Review*, 100, 393–94.

Ford, J.K. and Kraiger, K. (1995). 'The Application of Cognitive Constructs and Principles to the Instructional Systems Model of Training: Implications for Needs Assessment, Design and Transfer', in C.L. Cooper and I.T. Robertson (eds.), *International Review of Industrial and Organisational Psychology*, vol 10, West Sussex: John Wiley.

Johnson-Laird, Philip N. (1983). *Mental Models: Towards a Cognitive Science of Language, Inference and Consciousness*, Cambridge: Harvard University Press.

Kotter, J.P. (1990). *A Force for Change: How Leadership Differs from Management*, New York: Free Press.

Kotter, J.P. (1999) *What Leaders Really Do*, Boston: Harvard Business School Press.

House, R.J., Spangler, W.D. and Woycke, J. (1991). 'Personality and Charisma in the US Presidency: A Psychological Theory of Leader Effectiveness', *Administrative Science Quarterly*, 36, 364–96.

Gladwell, Malcolm (2000). *The Tipping Point: How Little Things Can Make a Big Difference*, London: Abacus.

Gladwell, Malcolm (2005). *Blink: The Power of Thinking without Thinking*, London: Penguin.

Lord, R.G. and Hall, R.J. (2005). 'Deep Structure and the Development of Leadership Skill', *Leadership Quarterly*, 16, 591–615.

Metcalfe, J. and Shimamura, A.P. (1994). *Metacognition: Knowing about Knowing*, Cambridge: MIT Press.

Moreno, R. (2004). 'Decreasing Cognitive Load for Novice Students: Effects of Explanatory versus Corrective Feedback in Discovery-based Multimedia', *Instructional Science*, 32, 99–113.

Prahalad, C.K. (2004). *The Fortune at the Bottom of the Pyramid: Eradicating Poverty through Profits*, Philadelphia: Wharton School Publishing.

Prahalad, C.K. and Hamel, Gary (1990). 'The Core Competence of the Corporation', *Harvard Business Review*, May/June.

Ryde, Robin (2007). *Thought Leadership: Moving Hearts and Minds*, New York: Palgrave Macmillan.

Strange, J.M. and Mumford, M.D. (2005). 'The Origins of Vision: Effects of Reflection, Models and Analysis', *Leadership Quarterly*, 16, 121–48.

Vincent, J.F.V., Bogatyreva, O.A., Bogatyrev, N.R., Bowyer, A. and Pahl, A.K. (2006). 'Biomimetics: Its Practice and Theory', *Journal of the Royal Society Interface*, 3, 471–82.

Wikipedia (2010). TRIZ: http://en.wikipedia.org/wiki/TRIZ, retrieved 13 May.

Wikipedia (2010). Flow: http://en.wikipedia.org/wiki/Mihaly_Csikszentmihalyi, retrieved 19 May.

CHAPTER 9

ENTREPRENEURIAL LEADERSHIP

GAURAV RASTOGI

'As long as Infosys innovates, it will survive and succeed. The day it stops, it will disappear like dew on a sunny morning.'

> —*N.R. Narayana Murthy, Chief Mentor and Chairman,*
> *Infosys* (Raman, 2004)

'In today's world, where there is so much transparency and diffusion of knowledge, I believe our lead in practicing GDM is very small . . . We have to constantly innovate, add new capabilities, and increase the effectiveness of the service we deliver.'

> —*S. (Kris) Gopalakrishnan, CEO, Infosys* (Trimble, 2008)

'Right now Infosys is at the top of its game. But, in five years, you can bet that Infosys will begin to see some maturity in its core business. At that stage, it will want to find another growth business that is becoming very large. If Infosys wants to have such a business five years from now, it has to start it today. If it waits until the numbers look bad, that will be too late.'

> —*Clayton Christiansen, Robert and Jane Cizik Professor of*
> *Business Administration at the Harvard*
> *Business School* (Raman, 2004)

'And it ought to be remembered that there is nothing more difficult to take in hand, more perilous to conduct, or more uncertain in its success, than to take the lead in the introduction of a new order of things. Because the innovator has for enemies all those who have done well under the old conditions and lukewarm defenders in those who may do well under the new. This coolness arises partly from fear of the opponents, who have the laws on their side, and partly from the incredulity of men, who do not readily believe in new things until they have had a long experience of them.'

—*Machiavelli* (1532)

Infosys has built a reputation for its innovative business model, as we have successfully extended our Global Delivery Model (GDM) into newer services. Starting with IT services, the company has expanded into Business Process Outsourcing (BPO), package implementation, independent validation, consulting and learning services; each is built upon the same global delivery model that powered the company in the 1980s and 1990s.

As noted in the chapter on strategic leadership, Infosys's business relies on the operational principal focusing us on predictability, sustainability, profitability and de-risking (PSPD). PSPD is an essential part of the company's DNA, the basis of its culture of paranoid excellence. Maintaining revenue predictability and operational control over profitability is the reason Infosys has been admired by investors for its ability to scale new global heights. Strong operational controls take care of the company's short-term business performance, and allow the company to respond quickly to sharp turns in the market, such as the business downturns in 2001–02 and 2008–09. These controls allow leaders to make big choices quickly and decisively. They also enable us to pursue our dreams with confidence, knowing that the company will be able to execute strategy like a well-oiled machine.

Operational controls, however, are typically designed to avoid or solve familiar problems that the entity has already faced in the past. The higher the historical frequency of a problem, the stronger the instinctive response. This presents firms with a conundrum: how should previously unseen problems and opportunities be handled? How does one anticipate and address capabilities that will enable the firm to be more than just lucky? Solving yesterday's problems mindlessly is hardly useful preparation for addressing tomorrow's opportunities. There is a need to be alert to the future, and be ready for what's next. That's the courage required of a leader, and that's the reason Infosys has nurtured its entrepreneurial leadership carefully.

For Infosys, entrepreneurial leadership is defined in two ways: first, as the enterprising opportunistic leader whose motto might be *carpe diem* ('seize the day'); and second, as the unique ability to be 'intrapreneurs' who take responsibility for business results from new ventures. Intrapreneurs are leaders who go outside the narrow definitions of the company's business and help expand it with new offerings successfully. These are also leaders who, when they see an opportunity in the market, have the courage to take decisions that will write Infosys's future success story. Entrepreneurial leaders at Infosys exist at all levels, and in this chapter we will highlight leaders who have started new businesses and those who have shown their extraordinary entrepreneurial leadership in their operational roles.

Definition of Entrepreneurship

Wikipedia defines entrepreneurship as 'the act of being an entrepreneur, which is a French word meaning "one who undertakes an endeavour"' (Wikipedia, 2010). It further suggests that entrepreneurs assemble resources including new ideas, finance and business acumen in an effort to transform innovations into economic goods. This may result in new organizations or may alternatively revitalize mature organizations in response to a perceived opportunity or necessity (Wikipedia, 2010).

Academic definitions of entrepreneurship tend to focus on both the opportunity and the leader. The definition that is close to Infosys's interpretation is by Shane and Venkataraman (2000): 'We define the field of entrepreneurship as the scholarly examination of how, by whom, and with what effects opportunities to create future goods and services are discovered, evaluated and exploited.' Their definition suggests that entrepreneurship involves the study of sources of opportunities; the processes of discovery, evaluation and exploitation of opportunities; and the set of individuals who discover, evaluate and exploit them.

Is there evidence that some people are just naturally better at leading entrepreneurially? Zhao and Seibert (2006) found that entrepreneurs score lower than managers on neuroticism and agreeableness but score higher than managers on openness to experience and performance orientation. The Five-Factor model is a framework for understanding

normal personality at work that is well established among industrial–
organizational psychologists, the scientists who study people at
work. The model combines forty years of research on the emotional
and interpersonal attributes of an individual. Zhao and Seibert's
research suggests that it also is a useful taxonomy of traits that define
entrepreneurial aptitude. The five factors are:

- **Neuroticism**, which represents individual differences in
  adjustment and emotional stability. People who score low
  on neuroticism can be characterized as self-confident, calm,
  even-tempered and relaxed. Zhao and Seibert's meta-analysis
  concludes that successful entrepreneurs score lower than
  managers on neuroticism.
- **Extraversion** describes the extent to which people are assertive,
  dominant, energetic, active and talkative. Entrepreneurs must
  interact with a diverse range of constituents including venture
  capitalists, partners, employees and customers. They are often
  in the role of a salesperson, whether they are persuading an
  investment banker or venture capitalist to back their idea or a
  client to buy their product or service. In contrast with research
  on other types of leadership that strongly suggest extraversion
  to predict leadership, Zhao and Seibert's meta-analysis was
  inconclusive in establishing any direct relationship between
  extraversion and entrepreneurship.
- **Openness to experience** is a personality dimension that
  characterizes someone who is intellectually curious and tends to
  seek new experiences and explore novel ideas. Someone high on
  openness can be described as creative, innovative, imaginative,
  reflective and untraditional. Zhao and Seibert conclude that
  successful entrepreneurs score higher on openness to experience
  than managers.
- **Agreeableness** assesses one's interpersonal orientation. Individuals
  high on agreeableness tend to be trusting, forgiving, caring,
  altruistic and gullible. Someone at the low end of the dimension
  can be characterized as manipulative, self-centred, suspicious and
  ruthless (Digman, 1990). Zhao and Seibert conclude that effective
  entrepreneurs have to drive hard bargains and, therefore, must
  score lower on agreeableness than managers.

- **Conscientiousness** indicates an individual's degree of organization, persistence, hard work and attention to detail in the pursuit of goal accomplishment. Conscientiousness can be considered as two separate facets: achievement orientation and dependability. Zhao and Seibert conclude that, unlike managers, entrepreneurs choose to operate in a more discretionary and self-directed environment, where personal dependability has a more important role, rather than rely on the organization's controls to mitigate risks. They found that strong entrepreneurs score higher than managers on conscientiousness on account of their significantly higher achievement orientation, but score the same as managers in terms of dependability.

These findings are not surprising as entrepreneurship requires stepping off the beaten path. An individual high on neuroticism (with a lower ability to deal with ambiguity) is unsuited to become an entrepreneur. Similarly, an individual with a high need to be liked by others will make suboptimal choices as his/her affiliation needs may override his/her objectivity. Openness to experience is also an advantageous attribute for an entrepreneur; he/she has to make his own path based on new ideas and pick up the best and most suitable practices. Entrepreneurs value freedom but recognize that focussed self-discipline is essential to achieve their objectives. Learning constantly from all sources is one of the cherished attributes of the successful entrepreneur. Similarly, no entrepreneur will succeed without unrelenting focus on performance. He/she knows that the only way to impress the importance of high performance is by producing high performance himself/herself.

However, all these attributes come into play only if an individual decides to be an entrepreneur. Making this decision of adopting an entrepreneurial mindset and displaying entrepreneurial leadership is the starting point of the journey.

Entrepreneurs as Transformational Leaders

Entrepreneurs help steer the company in times when it is called to both leverage new business models, new product offerings and entirely new value propositions as well as times when firms experience distress and change. In his seminal work on leadership, Burns (1978, 530) describes the concepts of transformational and transactional leadership: 'Whereas transformational leaders uplift the morale, motivation and morals of their followers, transactional leaders cater to their followers' immediate self-interests. The transformational leader emphasizes what you can do for your country; the transactional leader, on what your country can do for you.'

Bass (1985, 256) argues that transformational leadership energizes groups to persist when conditions are unpredictable, difficult and stressful, while transactional leadership is more likely to be observed in a well-ordered society: 'The interests of the organization and its members need to be aligned. Such is a task for the transformational leader. In contrast to the transactional leader who practices contingent reinforcement of followers, the transformational leader inspires, intellectually stimulates, and is individually considerate of them. Transformational leadership may be directive or participative. Requiring higher moral development, transformational leadership is recognized universally as a concept.' Later research further describes the components of transformational leadership, including the following (Bass, Avolio, Jung and Berson, 2003):

- **Idealized influence:** These leaders are admired, respected and trusted. Followers identify with and want to emulate their leaders. Among the things the leader does to earn credit with followers is to consider followers' needs over his/her own needs. The leader shares risks with followers and is consistent in conduct with underlying ethics, principles and values.
- **Inspirational motivation:** Leaders behave in ways that motivate those around them by providing meaning and challenge to their followers' work. Individual and team spirit is aroused. Enthusiasm and optimism are displayed. The leader encourages followers to envision attractive future states which they can ultimately envision for themselves.
- **Intellectual stimulation:** Leaders stimulate their followers' effort to be innovative and creative by questioning assumptions, reframing problems, and approaching old situations in new ways. There is no ridicule or public criticism of individual members' mistakes. New ideas and creative solutions to problems are solicited from

followers, who are included in the process of addressing problems and finding solutions.

- **Individualized consideration:** Leaders pay attention to each individual's need for achievement and growth by acting as a coach or mentor. Followers are developed to successively higher levels of potential. New learning opportunities are created along with a supportive climate in which to grow. Individual differences in terms of needs and desires are recognized.

In contrast, transactional leadership occurs when the leader sets expectations, standards or goals to reward or discipline a follower depending on the adequacy of a follower's performance, in the following ways:

- **Contingent reward** (e.g. 'rewards us when we do what we are supposed to do')
- **Management by exception** (active and passive forms, represented in the items 'directs attention toward failures to meet standards' and 'delays responding to urgent problems' respectively)

The research concluded that the best leaders are both transformational and transactional contingent, being able to positively maintain a high standard of performance while providing their teams with the ability to make sense of the challenges posed before them.

Since the essence of entrepreneurial leadership involves creating a new order of things within an existing successful concern, entrepreneurial leaders at Infosys are transformational leaders, while being simultaneously good at creatively executing existing operations. Instead of being purely transactional leaders, the entrepreneurs act as transformational leaders by setting a high moral standard consistent with Infosys's values and mission, inspiring, creating an environment with high intellectual stimulation and being individually considerate.

So far, we have considered entrepreneurial leadership as a personality trait exhibited by leaders who can find and exploit opportunities for the company while playing traditional roles, and who choose to take charge of their own role definition and outcomes. Now, let us consider the other aspect of entrepreneurial leadership—as an 'intrapreneur' who is tasked with extending the company's business model and business footprint. This requires stepping out from the familiar terrain of what the company is good at and into uncharted waters of creating new offerings, new business models and new clients. The intrapreneurs in Infosys's history have played a key role in extending the company into new businesses which, in time, have become 5–15 per cent of the company's revenues. But intrapreneurs have to act not in the future, when the innovations have become mainstream, but in the present, when the innovation is still new and the jury still out.

Definition of Intrapreneurship

Intrapreneuring is a relatively new word, popularized by Gifford Pinchot's (1985) best-selling book where he describes the phenomenon of executives starting business ventures not on their own but within the confines of a much larger corporate entity. Pinchot (2010) says:

Intrapreneuring means two things to me:

1. A set of business practices that liberates people with entrepreneurial personalities to innovate rapidly inside larger organizations for the benefit of that organization and its customers.
2. The actions of an individual and/or a team that is acting in an entrepreneurial manner to serve the best interests of a larger organization and its supply chain, with or without official support.

Like entrepreneurs, intrapreneurs are the 'dreamers who do', but they innovate inside going concerns rather than in new start-ups. As Pinchot (1987) explains:

In most organizations people are thought to be either dreamers or doers. Both talents are not generally required in one job. But the trouble with telling the doers not to bother about their dreams is that they dream anyway. When they are blocked from implementing dreams of how to help your company they're dreaming dreams of revenge. A mind is meant to imagine and then act. It is a terrible thing to split apart the dreamer and the doer.

Based on his research on intrapreneurs, Pinchot (1985) lays out the Ten Commandments for Intrapreneurs as follows:

1. Build your team, intrapreneuring is not a solo activity
2. Share credit widely
3. Ask for advice before you ask for resources
4. Underpromise and overdeliver—publicity triggers the corporate immune system
5. Do any job needed to make your dream work, regardless of your job description
6. Remember it is easier to ask for forgiveness than for permission
7. Keep the best interests of the company and its customers in mind, especially when you have to bend the rules or circumvent the bureaucracy
8. Come to work each day willing to be fired
9. Be true to your goals, but be realistic about how to achieve them
10. Honour and educate your sponsors

Building on these commandments, the authors of another book (Govindarajan and Trimble, 2005) reflect on the difficulty of maintaining a culture of intrapreneurship and of reaping the rewards of the few intrapreneurs in an established and historically successful company:

> Certain ingenious, creative and highly determined souls can doubtless overcome both the long odds facing any strategic experiment and the organization fighting them at every turn, but these people are rare. Organizations are almost always more powerful than individuals. Corporations that truly want to build the capacity for strategic innovation cannot simply hope for a few good 'intrapreneurs' to save the day on their own initiative.

Infosys's corporate culture has a strong bias in favour of Pinchot's fourth commandment: 'Underpromise and overdeliver'. As we will see in the interviews later, Infosys's intrapreneurs also have a strong hands-on orientation, as written out in the fifth commandment: 'Do any job needed to make your dream work'.

Building on these diverse perspectives, Infosys's own definition of entrepreneurial leadership emphasizes the leader who takes charge, creates a compelling vision, and drives the achievement of a seemingly impossible goal through inspiring team leadership and a strong positive bias for performance.

Infosys's Definition of Entrepreneurial Leadership

Infosys's business context—of seeking high growth in the face of strong global competition—dictates that we pay attention to the facet of leadership that is involved in building new growth engines and in incubating new ideas. In that sense, Infosys's internal definition aligns very closely with Pinchot's definition of the classical intrapreneur.

In addition, Infosys encourages business leaders to continuously innovate around their business portfolio in an effort to expand Infosys's business and relationship footprint. Leaders at Infosys have to drive the market acceptance of their new business ideas, business models and working arrangements in new markets, new product segments and services to drive growth. This means that even outside the context of new business launches (intrapreneuring), Infosys is also expecting its entrepreneurial leaders to be transformational leaders. These are leaders who are encouraged to think and act different in order to help Infosys evolve.

In other words, Infosys deliberately cultivates leaders who tire easily of the status quo, and who are expected to challenge conventional wisdom and question the accepted logic of the prevailing business model and respective products and services. Much like a well-balanced investment portfolio, where low-risk assets are balanced with high-risk and high-return assets, Infosys maintains a leadership portfolio that has operational leadership alongside non-conformists and dreamers—not just ordinary dreamers, but dreamers who, like Pinchot says, do . . . and succeed.

Infosys's Entrepreneurial Leaders

In this chapter, we will review insights from Infosys leaders who created new businesses, launched new services, dreamed up new business models, and took Infosys deeper into pioneering segments than the market had previously thought possible. We identified these leaders through their exceptional scores on the Leaderhip Journey Series. They are people who made a difference and shaped Infosys into the company that it is today; they are Infosys's authentic entrepreneurial leaders.

Infosys tier-leader Nandan Kaluskar is a practice–engagement manager and leads the value council for Infosys's Pune campus. He also presents as a guest speaker at various events and has published in industry forums. Further, he is entrepreneurial in charitable work as well as a trustee of two trusts aimed at building a temple and hospital in rural India.

Nandan's advice is to 'know your blood type', which means that entrepreneurial leaders must know their core competency. His core competency is his ability to communicate and connect with people. In building his team—Pinchot's first commandment—Nandan seeks to reach the 'person within' his teammates. He believes that everyone wants an identity of their own, and it is important to understand what each individual wants to become. Nandan's advice is a good example of Bass and Avolio's 'full range leadership model' that we looked at in an earlier chapter. A very large body of research has supported the fact that transformational leaders outperform others, and they do this by creating a shared vision of the future, stimulating the ideas of followers, supporting each person as a unique individual, and setting high expectations (Bass, 1985; Avolio, 1999). When you consider the task of either an entrepreneur or an intrapreneur, it is inherently obvious that transforming a new offering, start-up or original business model is inherently transformative and requires inspirational and charismatic leadership to persevere in the face of uncertainty and adversity. Understanding of each individual's personal perception of their goals can help the leader connect the team's vision to each individual's personal goal. This makes the team's success possible.

Curious and enthusiastic, Nandan recommends not accepting pre-existing constraints. Here, he echoes Pinchot's definition of 'dreamers that do'. In any project that he undertakes, Nandan approaches the work one thread at a time, breaking down boundaries and challenging constraints as he goes along.

Nandan believes in doing whatever it takes to get the work done, consistent with Pinchot's commandment: 'Do any job needed to make your dream work, regardless of your job description'. He picks up the threads one by one and takes them to completion, worrying little about whether the job is 'officially' part of his responsibilities.

Nandan also inspires his team by practicing his personal credo of leaving a lasting impact on the society beyond his work responsibilities. He does this through his work with the two hospital trusts he created, as well as by being a speaker at local colleges to inspire and educate students. He holds out his own example to his team, and inspires them to go out and contribute to a higher cause than their own personal good. In this, Nandan exemplifies both Bass and Avolio's adage of inspirational motivation and Infosys's value of leading by example, which is consistent with Bass and Avolio's idealized attributes.

Another Infosys Tier-leader who scores exceptionally high on intrapreneurial leadership is Mritunjay (Munjay) Singh, a divisional manager at Infosys and the development centre head for the largest delivery centre in Pune. In his career at Infosys, Munjay has created new solutions for big problems affecting his client's industry (European financial regulations), and also created new products that were launched as an internal start-up within Infosys. An example of new products launched under Munjay is Infosys's multi-lingual and multi-asset class banking portal iTrade, targeted at mid-sized broker dealers and investment banks, which was built on top of a product built by Munjay's team.

Munjay emphasizes the importance of managing relationships above and below you to be successful as an entrepreneurial leader. Where subordinates are concerned, he picks his team carefully. He believes that it is not possible to carry everybody along—it's better to find the ones who are truly excited by the vision and go forward with them. Munjay also believes in managing senior stakeholders in positions of formal authority. Echoing Pinchot's tenth commandment ('Honour and educate your sponsors'), Munjay believes in doing homework and preparation for these interactions. Aware that the sponsors' priorities tend to shift, Munjay makes sure that he only takes practical ideas to them so that these ideas can be executed as soon as he gets approval. Doing this consistently has helped him build trust with the key sponsors over time, which allows him to get quicker approval for his new ideas now.

Consistent with the research cited earlier on entrepreneurs' openness to new experiences, Munjay believes that 'the kick is in doing many things', and not in doing the same thing over and over again. This openness has led him to interpret his roles and organizational mandate in a new light, which allows him to create his own job responsibilities that go beyond the written job description.

Every system has its boundaries, according to Munjay, and his job is to test and stretch the outer limits of these boundaries. He expects to be reprimanded once in a while (low on agreeableness), but has the satisfaction of having pushed the system to its limits and not done something that's merely 'safe'. This is in line with Pinchot's sixth commandment: 'It is easier to ask for forgiveness than for permission'.

Conversely, Munjay says it is important to be organization-savvy, and he has learned to drop some ideas when the resistance to them is high. For example, he devised an idea for a platform-based games business several years ago. Despite his strong advocacy, he found little interest in the idea at the time. Munjay felt it is important to be realistic in a large company, and it is important to let go of ideas that 'don't have legs' and move on to other things.

Munjay counsels others that it is a misconception that one cannot be an innovator in a large company. In fact, he says, large companies need innovation more than the others, and most new ideas will find support. The trick is to be able to sense where, and how, to seek that support.

Another example of considerable success and an exemplary career growth within Infosys is the entrepreneurial leader Subhash Dhar, who is now a member of Infosys's executive council, and also the Global Head of Sales, Marketing and Alliances, as well as the Unit Head for the Communication, Media and Entertainment vertical.

Subhash's entrepreneurial career began before he joined Infosys, when he worked at a start-up in the mid-1990s. When he came to Infosys, a relatively 'large company' with revenues of $36 million, he joined with the mandate of starting Infosys's foray into the Internet e-business. Started by Shibulal, then a returning founder of Infosys, the e-business practice grew at an exceptional level, growing to almost 10 per cent of the company's business within two years. The success, however, was short-lived. In March 2000 the dot-com boom turned into the historic dot-com bust. The company's prudent financial and operational controls ensured that it did not lose too much money as one after another of Infosys's dot-com clients went bankrupt.

Seeing the writing on the wall, Subhash recommended the dissolution of the e-business practice and went on to become the Head of Sales of the Communications and Product Services (CAPS) business that focussed on building custom products for telecom hardware companies. When he inherited the business, it could not have been in worse shape. The sales were declining quarter-on-quarter, and the team had a set of formerly successful sales folk who believed that they needed to continue working on the previous strategy. Subhash believed that the future of the business lay not with the telecom hardware suppliers, but with the telecommunication service companies like AT&T, British Telecom and others. This was considered foolhardy by many in the company, and several people decided to leave the sales team over time. Subhash stayed with his vision and hired more people into the team who could engage with the new kind of clients. Eventually, after facing six quarters of self-doubt and internal questioning, Subhash was relieved to finally see his strategy bear fruit as his team created opening relationships with some worldwide telecom majors like Nextel, British Telecom and SBC Communications (which eventually became AT&T).

Like others highlighted in this chapter, Subhash shows a high openness to new experiences, to the point of 'craving the next challenge' in his work. He advises others to believe that: 'Your responsibilities are unlimited. Don't inherit the goals of your manager—redefine your goals according to whatever the business needs.'

Subhash also believes that it is very important to take personal ownership of the results, echoing Zhao and Seibert's finding on dependability. In his own case, he felt obliged to stick with his strategy for CAPS even though it meant allowing his career to take a backseat. His career eventually recovered the gap, and his success has eventually propelled him into one of the highest executive roles in Infosys.

Subhash's attitude towards building a team is to adopt his personal leadership style to the individuals in his team. Consistent with the research on transformational leadership, Subhash likes to give individualized consideration to his team. His strategy is to alter the relative level of 'guidance' versus 'air cover' for his team as per their individual achievement orientation and skills.

Finally, an example of successful intrapreneuring is the launch of a new business—Learning Services—by the author, Gaurav Rastogi. Started in 2008, at the lowest point in the worldwide recession, the service line has grown rapidly to one of the largest learning services businesses out of India in only two years, having tripled in revenues every year for the first two years, in a time when the learning services industry was declining 10 per cent every year. The business has a strong 'solutions' orientation, and has already achieved one of the highest revenues per employee in Infosys. Built from first principles to represent the future of Infosys, this business has hired and successfully assimilated engineers, creative designers and instructional designers into a single team. Started by Gaurav, this service is only the latest example of Infosys's success with new service introduction. New services, that is services that are outside Infosys's traditional core of 'application development and maintenance', including but not limited to Learning Services, now constitute 53 per cent of Infosys revenues, and continued success in launching new services is important to Infosys's growth and expansion plans.

Like others highlighted in this chapter, I have had a varied career both before Infosys and within my stint here. I have been an equities analyst and an executive search consultant after my MBA. When I joined Infosys in sales in 2000, I had no background in IT other than my years of hobby programming and my love for systems thinking. Then, when I got the chance to lead the global sales transformation programme within Infosys, I saw a role that fit the narrative arc of my career so far: I would get to crunch numbers (from my job as an equities analyst), think about people and teams, and put in systems that would help Infosys's sales team achieve new heights (from my experience as an executive search consultant). After five years in that role, I scanned the environment for the next thing to do, and immediately sensed that the arc of my career was moving inexorably in the direction of creating a new business for Infosys from the ground up. My experience with sales transformation had already alerted me to the gaps in the global learning market. I presented the idea of Learning Services to the Infosys Board who, at the time, were scouting around for new services to fund that would help Infosys expand revenues and relationships within its current global client base, and one that would help Infosys diversify its talent base into non-engineering disciplines.

I attribute Infosys's success in Learning Services to my dedicated core team, each of whom have donned different hats and carried out responsibilities far outside the traditional job description to make the business work. As Pinchot says, intrapreneuring is not a solo activity, and the first priority is to build the core team. As an intrapreneur, I was surprised by the number of people who, like me, 'wanted to try something new' and were willing to risk a few years in their career to learn and grow professionally. Again, as noted in the meta-analytic research on entrepreneurs, openness to experience is a key trait for a successful intrapreneurial team.

Mistakes and mis-hires were made, but the core team has stayed true to its original purpose of creating an exceptional global leader in the learning services business. Like other Infosys entrepreneurial leaders, I believe that it is not possible to carry everyone along, and have been open to relieving team members who did not share the team's vision. As a new service, many of the hires into the team were external laterals. Bringing them into Infosys's global culture has been a challenge, and the team has had to create innovative onboarding practices to ensure that the rapidly expanding team feels connected and stays informed and engaged.

Before starting the business, I reached out to the main board sponsors to seek their advice on what they wanted the new business to achieve. Getting their advice helped secure their commitment to helping later, when the fledgling business needed resources. Echoing Pinchot's tenth commandment—'Honour and educate your sponsors'—the learning services team created deliberate channels of communication with our sponsors in order to share our success and frustrations with them openly. The idea was to create a better understanding and 'pride of ownership' within Infosys's senior management in this fledgling business. Keeping the sponsors and well-wishers informed and excited about this new business has been an important part of the team's challenges. The team has maintained a 'friends of Learning Services' list of people who must be educated about the opportunities and successes of the business.

Launching the business at the deepest part of the global recession has taught me the need to be pragmatic about the business model. Infosys's priorities have shifted in line with the external market conditions, and there is no point in clinging to the original business plan. It is always best to be true to the original intentions, but be ready to improvise.

Entrepreneurial Leaders Are Critical to Infosys's Long-term Success

Infosys's long-term success depends on our ability to identify and innovatively solve new business problems. To solve challenges that customers and Infosys itself has never seen is no small challenge. This long-term need for opportunistic responses and innovation is balanced against the operational leadership noted as a key piece of Infosys strategy in the chapter on strategic leadership, and executed flawlessly in our operational leadership accomplishments noted in another chapter. Infosys has to ensure that the short term does not override the company's need for long-term innovation; we have worked hard to carefully nurture entrepreneurial leadership.

Finally, a successful entrepreneur does what Infosys's original entrepreneurs have turned into a mantra: 'underpromise and overdeliver'. Infosys's success in the market can be directly traced back to Infosys's ability to deliver beyond any hype. Infosys's entrepreneurial leadership allows the company, to paraphrase Steve Jobs, to stay hungry and stay foolish (Jobs, 2005).

Bibliography

Bass, B.M. (1985). *Leadership and Performance Beyond Expectations*, New York: Free Press.

Bass, B.M., Avolio, B.J., Jung, D.I. and Berson, Y. (2003). 'Predicting Unit Performance by Assessing Transformational and Transactional Leadership', *Journal of Applied Psychology*, 207–18.

Burns, J.M. (1978). *Leadership*, New York: Harper and Row.

Digman, J.M. (1990). 'Personality Structure: Emergence of the Five-factor Model', *Annual Review of Psychology*, 417–40.

Govindarajan, V. and Trimble, C. (2005). *Ten Rules for Strategic Innovators: From Idea to Execution*, Boston: Harvard Business School Press.

Jobs, S. (2005). Commencement Address at Stanford University, 14 June, retrieved 18 June from http://news.stanford.edu/news/2005/june15/jobs-061505.html.

Machiavelli, N. (1532). *The Prince*, Florence: Antonio Blado d'Asola.

Pinchot, G. (1985). *Intrapreneuring: Why You Don't Have to Leave the Corporation to Become an Entrepreneur*, New York: Harper and Row.

Pinchot, G. (1987). 'Innovation Through Intrapreneuring', *Research Management*, 30 (2), March–April.

Pinchot, G. (2010). 'Back to Intrapreneuring: The Pinchot Perspective', 21 January, retrieved 15 June from http://www.pinchot.com/2010/01/back-to-intrapreneuring.html.

Pinchot, G. (n.d.). 'The Intrapreneur's Ten Commandments', retrieved 15 June 2010 from http://www.intrapreneur.com/MainPages/History/TenCommandments.html.

Raman, M. (2004). 'Can Infosys be a Disruptive Innovator?' *Business Standard*, 20 January, retrieved 14 June 2010 from http://www.business-standard.com/india/news/can-infosys-bedisruptive-innovator/142819.

Shane, S. and Venkataraman, S. (2000). 'The Promise of Entrepreneurship as a Field of Research', *Academy of Management Review*, January, retrieved 29 August 2008 from JSTOR: http://www.jstor.org/pss/259271.

Trimble, P.C. (2008). *Infosys: Maintaining an Edge*, Dartmouth College, Tuck School of Business: Trustees of Dartmouth College.

Wikipedia (2010). 'Entrepreneurship', retrieved 14 June from Wikipedia.org: http://en.wikipedia.org/wiki/Entrepreneurship.

Zhao, H., and Seibert, S.E. (2006). 'The Big Five Personality Dimensions and Entrepreneurial Status: A Meta-analytical Review', *Journal of Applied Psychology*, 91, 259–71.

THE IMPORTANCE OF LEADERSHIP

T.V. MOHANDAS PAI

It is not an overstatement to say that leaders are perhaps the most important drivers in the progress of humankind. Leaders transform the lives of other people by the power of their ideas, by their ability to communicate and enthuse people, by bringing in social change and giving a voice to neglected sections of society, by creating wealth, winning battles, overcoming crises and thrusting nations toward a better future. The history of progress is the story of leaders who have made a difference. Leadership is a unique attribute—and that is why there are so few leaders! Making a better life on this planet requires vision, influence and values that inspire others to follow.

One timeless question is whether leaders are born or made. Some people feel that great leaders are made, naturally; this is called the 'trait theory'. Others note that certain situations—crises or important events—may cause a person to rise to the occasion, bringing out extraordinary leadership qualities in an ordinary person; this is sometimes called the 'great events theory'. Another perspective is that people choose to become leaders and learn leadership skills. The best-supported theory around leadership skill development is known as the 'authentic, full-range transformational leadership theory'.

Perhaps the answer lies somewhere in between traits, situations and skills. And we must not forget the fundamental importance of values in energizing a leader. Values give the leader the purpose, the fuel and the standards a leader needs to tackle the world's most difficult problems and bring the impossible to reality. To lead with meaning is to lead by example, driven by a burning purpose. Gandhi took Thoreau's theory of 'civil non-violent disobedience' and translated it into reality. He brought together a nation and along the way taught the world to listen to people without weapons but with the power of the moral force within. Gandhi's leadership meant freedom for 60 per cent of humanity who were then under the colonial thrall.

I believe that leaders are important for three primary reasons. First, leaders manage through times of change. They determine the direction a group of people will take, and move them from their current status to an exciting future. Second, leaders make things happen. They shape the culture by role-modelling their deeply held values. They respect uncertainty and use tools appropriately to get the job done. Third, leaders are revolutionaries. They face reality and mobilize resources to make the impossible a reality. And importantly, they inspire others to do the same.

At Infosys, and in the rest of the world, leadership is about getting ordinary people to achieve extraordinary goals—an exceptionally difficult task. Sustaining the accomplishments of a leader requires a wide number of other leaders to avoid the 'Walt Disney scenario'. After Disney died, his company spent a decade wondering what he would have done in a given situation. An organization dominated by a single charismatic leader cannot sustain itself. In the end, it's a team of excellent, passionate, visionary leaders with a wide range of viewpoints that produces better decisions and sustains the leadership legacy. That is what we have practiced at Infosys, and what I hope others will take away from this book.

NOTES ON CONTRIBUTORS

Author Biographies

MATT BARNEY, PHD is the Vice President and Director for the Infosys Leadership Institute. Dr Barney is the seniormost Infosys leader responsible for the selection, development, research and succession of senior and high-potential leaders worldwide. Previously, he has held similar roles at Intel, AT&T, Lucent Technologies, Motorola and Merck. He has published and presented papers and books in areas including Lean Six Sigma, leadership development, psychometrics, human capital, risk management and simulations. He holds a BS in psychology from the University of Wisconsin, Madison and an MA and PhD in industrial–organizational psychology from the University of Tulsa. He is a Motorola Master Black Belt and a certified Risk Manager by the Institute for Professional Education. In 2007, he was awarded the distinction of 'Future Leader' by *Human Capital* magazine.

PRADEEP CHAKRAVARTHY is Principal, Leadership Development for the Infosys Leadership Institute. He has a Bachelors degree in political science from MCC, a Masters in international relations from Jawaharlal Nehru University, Delhi and a Masters in industrial relations and personnel management from the London School of Economics. He joined ILI in June 2005. Pradeep is a columnist for the *Hindu Business Line*, and a heritage enthusiast.

S. GOPALAKRISHNAN (KRIS) is Chief Executive Officer and Managing Director of Infosys. Kris is one of the founders of Infosys. His initial responsibilities included the management of design, development, implementation and support of information systems for clients in the consumer products industry in the US. Between 1987 and 1994, he headed the technical operations of KSA–Infosys (a joint venture between Infosys and KSA at Atlanta, USA) as Vice President (Technical). In 1994, he returned to India and was appointed Deputy Managing Director of Infosys. In June 2007, Kris was appointed the CEO and Managing Director of Infosys; he had previously served as the Chief Operating Officer (April 2002), and as the President and Joint Managing Director (August 2006). His responsibilities included customer services, technology, investments and acquisitions. Kris is recognized as a global thought leader. He was selected in Thinkers 50, an elite list of global business thinkers compiled by Des Dearlove and Stuart Crainer in association with the IE Business School, Madrid and the London Business School's Management Innovation Lab. He is the Chairman of the Confederation of Indian Industry (CII) Southern Regional Council and is on the Board of Governors at Indian Institute of Management, Bangalore. He is also the Chairman of Indian Institute of Information Technology and Management (IIITM), Kerala, and Vice Chairman of the Information Technology Education Standards Board (BITES) set up by the Karnataka government and a member of ACM, IEEE and IEEE Computer Society. Kris holds Masters degrees in physics and computer science from the Indian Institute of Technology, Madras.

ASHOK KACKER has over forty years' experience as a business manager and in the field of leadership development. He has worked in leading organizations like Citibank, BHEL, the Comcraft group and the Kalyani group. Ashok's initial areas of work were in finance and international marketing; later he headed two public limited companies and contributed to positioning these companies as significant players in their respective international markets. Ashok's foray into leadership development started as an entrepreneur when he took on the franchise of the US-based MNC, Leadership Management International. His work brought in measurable business results for his clients. His work in developing this practice earned him the World Sales Manager's Award in 2003; he was the first Indian to receive this international recognition. Ashok has been associated with ILI since 2005 and has performed many roles spanning nearly all areas of ILI's work. He currently works as an advisor to ILI.

JEFF KAVANAUGH is a Partner at Infosys Consulting and leads the Product Innovation Consulting practice. He has over twenty years of experience working with clients in product innovation, development, life cycle and strategy. Prior to Infosys Consulting, Jeff has held executive roles in consulting and industry. He is a regular contributor to trade publications and a speaker at industry events.

SATYENDRA KUMAR is Senior Vice President and Group Head–Quality at Infosys Technologies. He drives quality and productivity improvement initiatives, satisfaction measurements and mobilizations for improvements, and Business Process Management (BPM) in the company. With over thirty-two years of experience in leadership positions in the field of quality management, he now plays a significant role in the creation of various innovative frameworks, models and approaches to improve quality within the organization. Kumar started his career in 1977 at an Indian firm which was involved in programming for defence-related electronics. He joined Infosys as Vice President in 2000 and was appointed as Head of Quality and Productivity in 2001. He was pivotal in transforming the outlook of the nascent Quality function from audit orientation to a process improvement and partnership orientation and has overseen the growth of the function from forty to 600+ employees. Kumar has been instrumental in conceptualizing and driving multiple large initiatives like PM Lead, Esteem, Transceed, Infosys Scaling of Outstanding Performance (ISOP) and IPM Plus. He has also led large productivity improvement programmes like the Tools and Reuse initiative which was a first-of-its-kind initiative in the industry. Under his leadership, Quality was awarded the Best Department Award at the Infosys Awards for Excellence for two years in a row in 2007 and 2008. Kumar was also instrumental in helping the company obtain a bouquet of IS certifications starting with ISO 9000.

RAJESWARI MURALI is a former Lead Principal, Leadership Development for the Infosys Leadership Institute and in 2010 became a Practice Leader for Hewitt Associates. She has global experience in both the US and India, in a wide variety of roles and companies including Xerox. She holds an MBA from University of Delhi and a BA in economics from Lady Shri Ram College.

N.R. NARAYANA MURTHY is the Founder-Chairman of Infosys and its Chief Mentor. He founded Infosys in 1981. Under his leadership, Infosys was listed on NASDAQ in 1999. Narayana Murthy articulated, designed and implemented the Global Delivery Model which has become the foundation for the huge success in IT services outsourcing from India. He has led key corporate governance initiatives in India and is an IT advisor to several Asian countries. He serves on the boards of HSBC, Ford Foundation and the UN Foundation and served as a member of the Unilever board between 2007 and 2010. He also serves on the boards of Cornell University, Wharton School, Singapore Management University, Indian School of Business, Hyderabad, International Institute of Information Technology, Bangalore and INSEAD. The *Economist* ranked Narayana Murthy among the ten most admired global business leaders in 2005. He topped the *Economic Times* list of India's most powerful CEOs for three consecutive years from 2004 to 2006. He has been awarded the Padma Vibhushan by the Government of India, the Legion d'honneur by the Government of France, and the CBE by the British government. He is the first Indian winner of Ernst and Young's World Entrepreneur of the Year award and the Max Schmidheiny Liberty prize, and has appeared in the rankings of businessmen and innovators published by *India Today*, *Business Standard*, *Forbes*, *BusinessWeek*, *Time*, CNN, *Fortune* and *Financial Times*. He is a Fellow of the Indian National Academy of Engineering and a foreign member of the US National Academy of Engineering. His best-selling book *A Better India: A Better World* was published by Penguin in 2009.

T.V. MOHANDAS PAI is a member of the Board at Infosys Technologies and the Director and Head of Finacle, Platforms, Administration, Human Resources, Infosys Leadership Institute, Education and Research, and the Chairman of Infosys's Business Process Outsourcing subsidiary. He joined Infosys in 1994 and has served as a member of the Board since May 2000. He served as Chief Financial Officer from 1994 to 2006. As the CFO, Mohan played a strategic role in transforming Infosys into one of the world's most respected and widely known software services companies. He formulated the country's first publicly articulated financial policy for the company and played a key role in branding the company among the investor community and enhancing transparency and disclosure levels. The Infosys Annual Report, under his supervision, won the Best Presented Annual Accounts Award from the Institute of Chartered Accountants of India for ten years in succession as well as from the South Asia Federation of Accountants in 2000. Mohan was an integral part of the Infosys team that enabled the first listing of an India-registered company on NASDAQ and the first sponsored secondary offering of American Depositary Shares by an Indian company. He was voted 'CFO of the Year' in 2001 by IMA India (formerly EIU India) and American Express; he won the 'Best CFO in India' award from *Finance Asia* in 2002, and 'Best Chief Financial Officer in India' in the Best Managed Companies poll conducted by *AsiaMoney* in 2004. Mohan has been active in working with regulators to improve the business ecosystem. He was a member of the Kelkar Committee, constituted by the Ministry of Finance, Government of India for reforming direct taxes, the Non-Resident Taxation Committee and the High-Powered Committee on e-Commerce and Taxation. He is currently a member of the SEBI Accounting Standards Sub-committee and the Empowered Committee for setting up the Tax Information Network of the Government of India. He also works with the union and state governments in the fields of education, Information Technology and business. Mohan is a Trustee of the

International Accounting Standards Committee Foundation, the body that oversees the International Accounting Standards Board.

SIDDHARTH PATNAIK, PHD is Associate Principal, Assessment at the Infosys Leadership Institute. He holds a doctorate from XLRI, Jamshedpur in organizational behaviour, a Masters in sociology and a Bachelors in law. After a brief stint in academics teaching human resource management and organizational behaviour, he joined Infosys Leadership Institute in 2006.

GAURAV RASTOGI is Vice President and Business Practice Head of the Learning Services business that he helped conceptualize and start within Infosys. Gaurav has an MBA from the Indian Institute of Management, Ahmedabad and a BE from the University of Delhi. His career so far has taken him through equity research, executive search, sales, sales transformation and business unit leadership. At Infosys since 2000, Gaurav has been part of Infosys's sales and leadership team in various capacities. He ran Infosys's sales transformation programme from 2003 to 2008, putting in place the institutional framework that would continue Infosys's sales success in the market. He continues to be the internal sponsor for another long-running transformational programme aimed at creating client-trusted advisors within Infosys. Gaurav is based at Infosys's US headquarters in Fremont, California; he is an active blogger and author, and is working on his own book about the offshore services industry.

CHITRA SARMMA is Principal, Leadership Development at the Infosys Leadership Institute. With a career spanning seventeen years, she has held key positions in human resource development in corporations and consultancies, leading HR and OD initiatives in both technology and non-technology firms. She has worked in areas such as HRD strategy formulation and implementation, leadership competency development, organization turnaround, team enhancement and performance coaching. With strengths in conceptualization, design and delivery, she has also worked very effectively with a great variety of technologies of transformation.

AARTI SHYAMSUNDER, PHD is Associate Principal, Assessment at the Infosys Leadership Institute. Originally from Mumbai, Aarti has split her professional life working in the United States and India. She obtained her PhD in industrial–organizational psychology from the University of Akron, Ohio and worked in Portland, Oregon in the area of employee selection, designing, validating and implementing technology-enabled staffing assessments for large, distributed organizations. In 2009 she took the opportunity to move back to her home country to work for Infosys. In her current role, she is involved in the measurement of leadership potential, creation of developmental road maps, evaluation of programme effectiveness as well as research. The transition back to India has been eventful, eye-opening and fulfilling in many ways for her and she looks forward to learning a lot more working in a high-impact organization during one of the most exciting times to be in corporate India.

SREEKUMAR T.S. is Principal, Leadership Development with the Infosys Leadership Institute. He holds a BTech in mechanical engineering from Kerala University. He joined Infosys in 1998. Sreekumar has played lead roles in design, consulting and project/programme management for many Fortune 500 clients across Japan, North America and Europe. He has developed an interest in soft skill development and believes in an inside-out approach to individual transformation. He has actively participated in many self-development workshops and has completed executive education programmes at Stanford and UCLA. He is working on his doctorate in management and yoga.

Leader Biographies

SANGAMESH BAGALI is the Head of Client Solutions–Retail, Consumer Packaged Goods (CPG) and Logistics for Infosys Technologies. In his role, he anchors proposal pursuits for new prospects and existing clients. He has managed select client relationships in the retail, CPG and logistics sectors, being responsible for account growth and business development and managing the respective Infosys teams. Sangamesh has thirteen years of experience working with retail companies and specializes in the grocery business. His areas of interest include Demand Planning and Forecasting, Perpetual Inventory Management and Shelf Merchandising.

RAMESH CHOGULE is the Delivery Manager for the SAP Life Sciences practice in the Enterprise Solutions unit at Infosys. Ramesh has over thirteen years of experience in ERP and Supply Chain Management, most of it in the Life Sciences domain.

GOPAL DEVANAHALLI is Vice President and Independent Business Unit Head, Communications, Media and Entertainment, Infosys BPO. Gopal is also responsible for Infosys BPO's mergers and acquisitions (M&A) activities. He has over eighteen years of professional experience; he has been with Infosys since 1999 and with Infosys BPO since August 2007. He is also the Co-Chairman of the Bangalore chapter of the International Association of Outsourcing Professionals (IAOP). Gopal has a postgraduate diploma in management from the Indian Institute of Management, Calcutta, and an

MSc (Tech.) in computer science from Birla Institute of Technology and Science, Pilani.

SUBHASH DHAR is Senior Vice President and Head of the Communications, Media and Entertainment business unit at Infosys. He is also a member of the Executive Council, responsible for sales and marketing for the firm, and serves on the board of Infosys Australia. Subhash joined Infosys in 1997 as a member of its e-Business practice and has since served in several capacities. In 2007, he was chosen by the World Economic Forum as one of the twenty-five Young Global Leaders from India. Subhash holds a degree in computer science from the Birla Institute of Technology, Mesra, Ranchi, and an MBA from the Indian Institute of Management, Bangalore.

GIRISH A.R. is Associate Vice President and Head–Consumer Retail Labs for Infosys. Girish is a management graduate from Indian Institute of Management, Bangalore and a mechanical engineer from UVCE, Bangalore. He has fifteen years of experience working for Infosys. His experience includes software development, technology and business consulting and IP development and commercialization. He is a five-time winner of the Infosys Excellence Award for Innovation and Business Solutions.

NANDITA GURJAR is the Senior Vice President and Group Head, Human Resources, Infosys Technologies. Nandita was appointed as the Human Resources Head in December 2007. With over 122,000 employees, she is focussed on making Infosys the preferred choice of global talent. Earlier, Nandita established and headed the Human Resources department at Infosys BPO. She was instrumental in scaling up the HR department as the business grew to US$ 250 million with 16,000 employees, five centres in India and six global centres. Nandita joined Infosys in 1999 and founded the Learning and Development unit to implement learning and training effectiveness and set benchmarks for growth and development. The HR practices she has instituted have been recognized by international forums such as American Society for Training and Development and Workforce Optima, among others. Nandita holds a degree in literature from Nizam College, Hyderabad, and a Masters degree in psychology from Osmania University.

CHANDRASHEKAR KAKAL is a member of the Executive Council and Senior Vice President and Global Head of the Enterprise Solutions group at Infosys. He is also a member of the Board of Infosys Consulting Inc. Kakal holds a mechanical engineering degree from Bangalore University and an MBA in international business from Asian Institute of Technology, Bangkok. He also holds a graduate diploma in materials management from Indian Institute of

Materials Management. Kakal joined Infosys in 1999 and has served in several capacities. He was one of the first to focus on package implementation and related services in Enterprise Solutions. He established Infosys, Hyderabad in 2000 and was its head for four years. Under his leadership, Hyderabad was recognized as the best managed centre at Infosys. As part of the founders of the Enterprise Solutions group, Kakal started the Oracle ERP practice. Later, he incubated the CRM and Microsoft Dynamics practices. He also restructured the group to offer end-to-end solutions in Supply Chain, Human Capital Management and Enterprise Application Integration. Under his leadership, the Enterprise Solutions group has grown to be the largest and best managed unit at Infosys, winning internal awards for excellence and being recognized for leadership by analysts for SAP and Oracle ERP services.

NANDAN KALUSKAR is Practice Engagement Manager with the Product Engineering division of Infosys based in New Jersey. Nandan is a 1993 graduate in electronics and telecommunications engineering from Mumbai University and since then has worked for Siemens, HCL Perot Systems and now Infosys across the world. At Infosys since 2004, Nandan led programmes in process design, large programme management and product development and has played the key architect role in laying a framework for MSA and contractual compliances across the organization. Nandan attributes his entrepreneurial skills to his upbringing and the mentorship he received from his spiritual guru (also a successful entrepreneur) early in his life. At the age of twenty-one, he formed a trust to build a temple and hospital in rural India along with his guru and some likeminded people.

K. MURALI KRISHNA is Vice President and Head of Global IT at Infosys Technologies. Murali has twenty-five years of experience, all at Infosys. Before taking on his current role in 2007, he was heading the Systems Integration Business unit which is the global practice working across geographies delivering technology-driven differentiators.

MICHEL LANGLOIS is Senior Vice President of Junos Software at Juniper Networks, a leading telecom network equipment provider, and has been a client of Infosys for several years. He grew through the ranks at Cisco Systems as an engineer, rising through management to lead as SVP their central engineering group (over 5,000 employees), which included IOS software, generally regarded as the 'operating system of the Internet'. He is now leader of Juniper's Junos software, which has been integral to that company's rapid growth rate (second fastest company to $1 billion in annual revenues and currently nearly $4 billion). He is the only non-Infosys leader featured in this book.

SRIDHAR MARRI is Vice President and Head–Communication Design Group at Infosys Technologies. He is the author of Infosys's tagline 'Powered by Intellect, Driven by Values'. Sridhar has more than twenty years of multi-disciplinary experience in journalism, user experience design, design education and management. He currently leads one of India's largest user experience design teams and has been involved in several cross-functional initiatives at Infosys. He conceptualized and had been instrumental in launching India's first corporate television channel, InfyTV, for Infosys employees distributed across the globe. Under Sridhar's leadership, Infosys became the first Indian company to win the coveted World's Ten Best-Designed Intranets Award by Nielsen Norman Group in 2007. Sridhar is an alumnus of National Institute of Design, Ahmedabad and Indian Institute of Management, Calcutta.

SRIKANTAN ('TAN') MOORTHY is Senior Vice President and Group Head for Education and Research (E&R) for Infosys. He has worked in the IT industry for over twenty-five years. An engineer from Bangalore University by training, Tan spent twelve years in the US working in strategy formulation, operations management and talent development. During his tenure at Infosys, Tan managed client delivery for a large business unit managing projects worth over $200 million with a team of more than 4,000 people. As head of Education and Research at Infosys, Tan's primary responsibility is talent development through competency building. Over 15,000 new engineers go through the famous six-month training programme run by E&R every year. Tan is also a part of the ACM (Association for Computing Machinery) professional development committee.

MANOJ NARAYAN is Senior Engagement Manager in the Solutions and Consulting group focussed on developing Validation and QA solutions at Infosys. He has over eleven years of IT experience spanning complex solution consulting, programme management and delivery in functional and automated testing solutions. He has managed Testing Centre of Excellence programmes and Automation Competency Centres for major financial institutions in North America.

ANAND NATARAJ is a Vice President heading Infrastructure Management Services (IMS) at Infosys. Before taking over IMS, he was with the CME unit of Infosys. Anand has been in Infosys for six years. He has built and groomed a global team which has created a market dominating position for Infosys in the Communication Service Provider (CSP) segment. Anand has worked very closely with various people from IMS in the past and contributed strongly in winning the largest deal for IMS and Infosys till date. The IMS share in this deal was more than $200 million over five years and this was closed without any RFP due to excellent relationships with the executive suite at a leading telecom cable service provider in USA. Anand also heads the Mid-Atlantic Geo Cluster in the US where he has been focusing on building a small company culture and has organized multiple activities to enhance employee engagement spanning community meetings, sports and culture, brand building in local universities, training and communication rollouts. Anand is the recipient of multiple awards of excellence; he holds a Bachelors degree in engineering from Bangalore University and an MBA from Indian Institute of Management, Bangalore.

VALMEEKA ('VAL') NATHAN is Vice President and Head of the Product Lifecycle and Engineering Solutions (PLES) business unit at Infosys. With over twenty-five years of experience, he plays a significant role in bringing about market leadership, revenue growth and profitability to stakeholders in engineering and PLM business solutions across the value chain from multiple global industry verticals across Asia Pacific, Japan, Europe and the US. Val joined Infosys in 2005 as Head of Product Lifecycle and Engineering Solutions. He was designated as Vice President in 2006 and recognized by the Infosys Board for transformational business achievements within two years. Val played an instrumental role in tripling operating profits, ensuring 35 per cent year-on-year growth. He has been recognized as a champion for business excellence and has been selected for the role of Senior Examiner for ISOP 2009. He won the Tara Innovation and Originality Award for Innovation Design in 1988. He holds a Bachelors degree in mechanical engineering from Birla Institute of Technology and Science, Pilani.

RISHI RAJ PAUL has held several positions in his ten-year tenure at Infosys, including business development, consulting, project management, programme management and implementation. In each, he has excelled in understanding the business environment in which Infosys operates and the relationships and networks needed to be successful. In his current role as Global Alliance Manager, Rishi is responsible for Oracle Solutions, Alliances, Innovation Centre and joint business development with Oracle.

N.R.A. PRASAD (PRASAD NANJANAGUDU) is Associate Vice President and Global Engagement Manager for the Aerospace and Defence businesses of Infosys in Europe. He comes with over twenty-four years' experience in the aerospace industry and consulting in Information Technology/Engineering Services. A Bangalore university topper in engineering with a Masters from Indian Institute of Technology, Madras, Prasad began his career at Hindustan Aeronautics as a management trainee. Subsequently he moved to the IT industry and held senior positions at TCS managing large programmes at

Bajaj and Philips in India and at EDS and GE in USA. He had a short stint at a Silicon Valley start-up before moving to Infosys in 2001.

U.B. PRAVIN RAO is Senior Vice President and Head of Retail, Consumer Products Group and Logistics Practice in Infosys. In his role, he is responsible for providing services to Retail, CPG and Logistics clients in North America and Europe. The group contributes to over 12 per cent of Infosys revenues. Pravin also heads Infrastructure Management Services (IMS) in Infosys. In this role, he is responsible for providing Infrastructure Management Services to clients globally. The group contributes to over 4 per cent of Infosys revenues. He also serves as a Director on the board of Infosys Australia. Pravin joined Infosys in 1986; prior to his current role, he was Delivery Head for the Europe practice. In his twenty-plus years at Infosys, he has worked on engagements with clients primarily in retail and financial services. He holds a Bachelors degree in engineering.

RAJESWAR RAO is Associate Vice President and Head–Independent Validation Services (IVS) at Infosys. He has twenty-two years of overall IT experience and over ten at Infosys. He currently leads the practice in IVS providing Validation Services to the entire BFS-US clients and core banking implementations worldwide. He has actively participated in several change management programmes.

MRITUNJAY (MUNJAY) SINGH is Associate Vice President at the Banking and Capital Markets (BCM) unit of Infosys with over eighteen years of professional experience in various capacities. He is an electronics engineer from Institute of Technology, Banaras Hindu University. Prior to joining Infosys, he worked for nine years in different companies like Tata Steel, Kanbay and Quinnox in India and USA.

B.G. SRINIVAS is a member of Infosys's Executive Council and Senior Vice President heading the Manufacturing, Product Engineering and Product Lifecycle and Engineering Solutions business units. He also serves as a Director on the Boards of Infosys BPO, Infosys Consulting and Infosys Sweden. BG was previously the head of European operations for Infosys. He also set up the Enterprise Solutions practice in Infosys. Before joining Infosys in 1999, BG worked with ABB Ltd for fourteen years in various roles including Head–Manufacturing. He holds a BE in mechanical engineering from Bangalore University.

V. SRIRAM heads the Japan Business Unit for Infosys. He started working for Infosys thirteen years ago, and has enjoyed living and working in Japan for that period. An engineer by training, he started his career in technical support. Looking for new horizons, he got a Masters in business management from Indian Institute of Management, Ahmedabad and tried his hand at new product launches and business development before finally joining Infosys. From that start (when Infosys was a $26 million company employing just a thousand people), his relationship and networking leadership journey has traversed several obstacles and learning points to becoming a strong leader in this area.

K. SURYAPRAKASH (SURY) is Vice President and Head of Information Systems at Infosys. Sury has over twenty years of experience, all at Infosys. Prior to his present role Sury was the Delivery Head for the Manufacturing practice. He has been involved in a number of Greenfield ventures including setting up the Infosys China operations.

ANAND SWAMINATHAN is a Vice President in Hi-Tech Manufacturing, and has been with Infosys for more than eleven years, most of which he has spent in the US. His journey towards becoming a strong relationship and networking leader has been a little unconventional. From a finance background, he jumped into manufacturing redesign and organizational change management, only to get interested in the IT sector, especially in transformational programmes. Subsequently, at Infosys, he grew to become a leader in client services specializing in cultivating strategic and large client relationships.

MANISH TANDON is Vice President and Head–Independent Validation and Testing Solutions, Infosys Technologies. Manish is responsible for formulating and executing the business strategy for the Independent Validation and Testing Solutions practice at Infosys. He mentors the unit specifically in meeting business goals and targets. In addition, he manages critical relationships with client executives, industry analysts and deal consultants, and anchors the training and development of key personnel. Manish has about nineteen years of industry experience, including three years of entrepreneurial experience. He joined Infosys in 1996 and has performed multiple roles in project management, sales and client relationship management. Prior to his current role, Manish was the Vice President and Head of Client Services for the Retail, CPG and Logistics practice. Here, he was a part of the unit's management committee and responsible for strategy formulation, strategy execution and managing more than forty client relationships in the US. In particular, Manish built the company's CPG practice and grew it by nearly $80 million in two years. In his thirteen-year career with Infosys, his contributions have been recognized internally in the areas of sales and account management, customer satisfaction and people development. Manish received his Bachelors degree in engineering from the Indian Institute of Technology, Kanpur and his Masters degree in business administration from the Indian Institute of Management, Bangalore.

ASHOK VEMURI is a member of the Executive Council at Infosys and Head–Americas and Global Head–Banking and Capital Markets (BCM). He is also a member of the Boards of Infosys Consulting, Infosys China and Infosys Public Services. As a member of the Executive Council, Ashok plays a significant role in defining the strategic direction for the company with specific responsibility for business operations in the Americas. Ashok was selected as Young Global Leader by the World Economic Forum in 2009. As a perspicacious practitioner and keen observer of global sourcing, he has been widely quoted in leading publications. Ashok is also recognized for his thought leadership and is a frequent speaker at conferences and symposiums organized by American Bankers Association, Asia Society and Waters. *Business Today*, a leading business magazine, selected Ashok as a member of the League of Extraordinary Managers and one of the top twenty-five hottest young talents in India Inc. Ashok has a Bachelors degree in physics from St. Stephen's College, Delhi and a Masters in business management from the Indian Institute of Management, Ahmedabad.

YOGANAND T.D. is Regional Manager, Information Technology Service, Support and Operations with the Computer and Communications division of Infosys in Mysore, India. He worked at IBM Global Services and Toyota Kirloskar Motors before joining Infosys in 2000. He holds a Bachelors in electrical and electronics engineering from SJCE, Mysore.